THE GREAT WAR

THE GREAT WAR

Field Marshal von Hindenburg

Edited and Introduced by Charles Messenger

FRONTLINE BOOKS, LONDON

A Greenhill Book

First published in Great Britain in 2006 by
Greenhill Books, Lionel Leventhal Limited
www.greenhillbooks.com

This paperback edition published in 2013 by Frontline Books

an imprint of Pen & Sword Books Ltd,
47 Church Street, Barnsley, S. Yorkshire, S70 2AS
www.frontline-books.com
Copyright © Lionel Leventhal Limited, 2006
Introduction © Charles Messenger, 2006

The right of Marshal von Hindenburg to be identified as the author
of this work has been asserted by him in accordance with the
Copyright, Designs and Patents Act 1988.

ISBN: 978-1-84832-724-5

CIP data records for this title are available from the British Library

For more information on our books, please visit
www.frontline-books.com, email info@frontline-books.com
or write to us at the above address.

Printed and bound by CPI Group (UK) Ltd, Croydon, CR0 4YY

Contents

PART III
From Our Transfer to Main Headquarters to
the Collapse of Russia

Contents

Contents

PART IV
The Fight for a Decision in the West

Contents

PART V
Beyond Our Powers

Maps

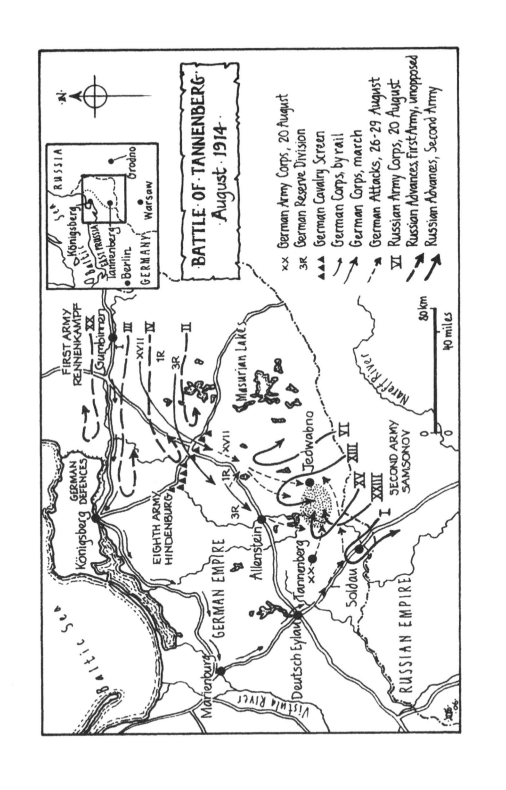

BATTLE · OF · TANNENBERG ·
August · 1914 ·

xx   German Army Corps, 20 August
3R   German Reserve Division
▲▲▲   German Cavalry Screen
      German Corps, by rail
      German Corps, march
      German Attacks, 26-29 August
XI   Russian Army Corps, 20 August
      Russian Advances, First Army, unopposed
      Russian Advances, Second Army

80 km
40 miles

FIRST ARMY
RENNENKAMPF

Gumbinnen

Masurian Lakes

Narew River

GERMAN
DEFENCES

Königsberg

EIGHTH ARMY
HINDENBURG

GERMAN EMPIRE

Allenstein

Deutsch Eylau

Tannenberg

Marienburg

Vistula River

Baltic Sea

Jedwabno

Soldau

SECOND ARMY
SAMSONOV

RUSSIAN EMPIRE

RUSSIA
Grodno
Königsberg
Baltic
EAST PRUSSIA
Tannenberg
Berlin
GERMANY
Warsaw

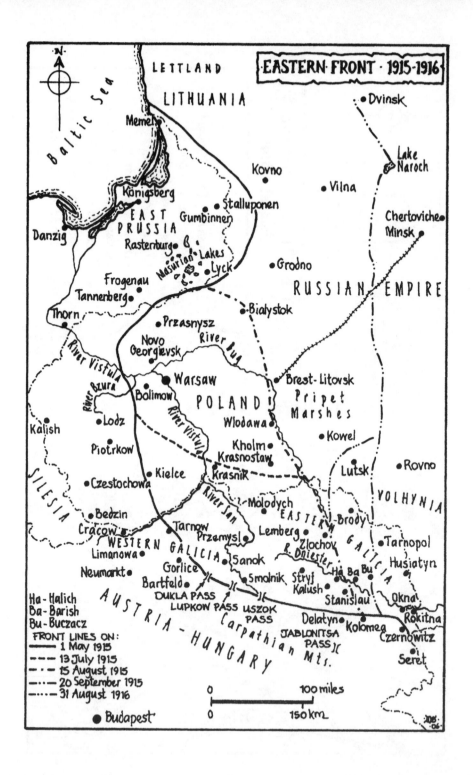

THE·WAR·FRONTS·1916-1918

BRITAIN

North Sea

London

NORWAY

SWEDEN

Gulf of Bothnia

Archangel

JUTLAND

DENMARK

Baltic Sea

Petrograd

HOLLAND

BELGIUM

WESTERN FRONT

Verdun

FRANCE

SWITZ.

Berlin

GERMANY

Tannenberg

Riga

THE ITALIAN FRONT

Caporetto

AUSTRIA-HUNGARY

Przemysl

Lodz

Lemberg

THE EASTERN FRONT

RUSSIAN

EMPIRE

Rome

ITALY

Adriatic Sea

THE SERBIAN FRONT

Belgrade

THE RUMANIAN FRONT

·N·

BULGARIA

THE SALONICA FRONT

Salonica

Black Sea

Caspian Sea

THE GALLIPOLI FRONT

Aegean

Constantinople

OTTOMAN EMPIRE

Trebizond

Sarikamis

Baku

THE CAUCASUS FRONT

THE PERSIAN FRONT

Mediterranean Sea

CYRENAICA

Bir Hakeim

THE SENUSSI FRONT

THE PALESTINE FRONT

Damascus

Jerusalem

Gaza

Baghdad

Hamadan

Cairo

Suez

Akaba

Kut

Basra

EGYPT

THE ARAB FRONT

THE MESOPOTAMIAN FRONT

Persian Gulf

Red Sea

0   500 km

0   300 miles

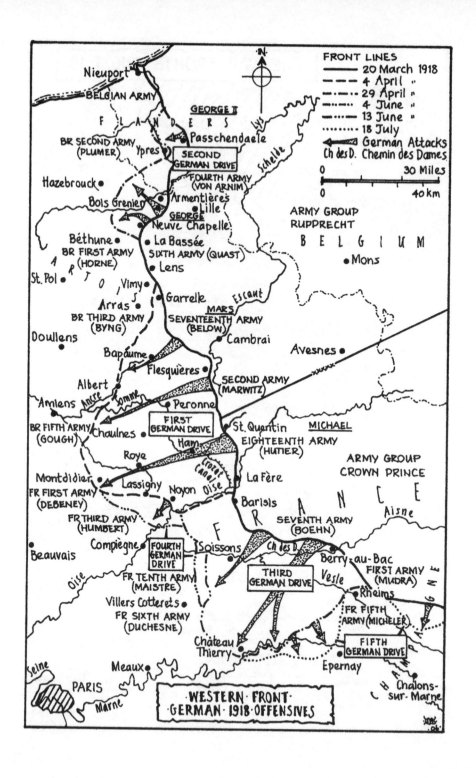

FRONT LINES
—————— 20 March 1918
– – – – 4 April "
–·–·–·– 29 April "
–··–··– 4 June "
–···–···– 13 June "
············ 18 July "
⟵ German Attacks
Ch des D. Chemin des Dames

0 —————————— 30 Miles
0 —————————— 40 km

Nieuport
BELGIAN ARMY
F L A N D E R S
GEORGE II
BR SECOND ARMY (PLUMER)
Ypres
Passchendaele
SECOND GERMAN DRIVE
Hazebrouck
FOURTH ARMY (VON ARNIM)
Bois Grenier
Armentlères
Lille
GEORGE
Neuve Chapelle
Béthune
La Bassée
BR FIRST ARMY (HORNE)
SIXTH ARMY (QUAST)
St. Pol
A R T O I S
Lens
Vimy
Arras
Garrelle
BR THIRD ARMY (BYNG)
MARS
SEVENTEENTH ARMY (BELOW)
Doullens
Cambrai
Bapaume
Flesquières
SECOND ARMY (MARWITZ)
Albert
Amiens Ancre Somme
Peronne
FIRST GERMAN DRIVE
BR FIFTH ARMY (GOUGH)
Chaulnes
St. Quentin
MICHAEL
Ham
EIGHTEENTH ARMY (HUTIER)
Roye
Montdidier
Lassigny
Noyon
Oise
La Fère
FR FIRST ARMY (DEBENEY)
Barisis
FR THIRD ARMY (HUMBERT)
F R A N C E
Compiègne
FOURTH GERMAN DRIVE
Soissons
Ch des D.
Berry-au-Bac
Beauvais
FR TENTH ARMY (MAISTRE)
THIRD GERMAN DRIVE
Vesle
FIRST ARMY (MUDRA)
Rheims
Villers Cotterets
FR SIXTH ARMY (DUCHESNE)
FR FIFTH ARMY (MICHELER)
FIFTH GERMAN DRIVE
Château Thierry
Epernay
Seine
Meaux
Marne
PARIS
Chalons-sur-Marne

BELGIUM
Mons
ARMY GROUP RUPPRECHT
Escaut
Avesnes
ARMY GROUP CROWN PRINCE
Aisne
SEVENTH ARMY (BOEHN)

WESTERN FRONT
GERMAN 1918 OFFENSIVES

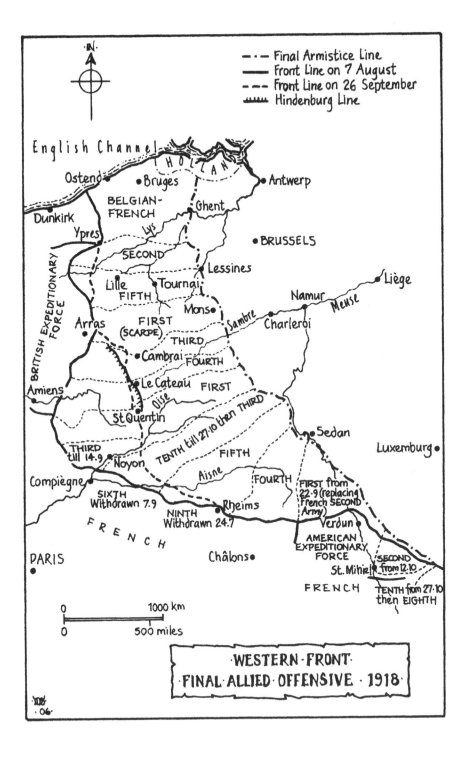

Legend:
- — · — Final Armistice Line
- ——— Front Line on 7 August
- – – – Front Line on 26 September
- ⊔⊔⊔⊔ Hindenburg Line

N

English Channel

HOLLAND

Ostend • Bruges • Antwerp

Dunkirk

BELGIAN-FRENCH

Ghent

Ypres

Lys

SECOND

Lille

FIFTH

Tournai

Lessines

• BRUSSELS

• Liège

Namur

Meuse

Mons

Sambre

Charleroi

Arras

FIRST (SCARPE)

THIRD

Cambrai

FOURTH

BRITISH EXPEDITIONARY FORCE

Amiens

Le Cateau

FIRST

Oise

St Quentin

Sedan

Luxemburg •

THIRD till 14.9

Noyon

TENTH till 27.10 then THIRD

FIFTH

FIRST from 22.9 (replacing French SECOND Army)

Compiègne

Aisne

FOURTH

SIXTH Withdrawn 7.9

Rheims

NINTH Withdrawn 24.7

Verdun

F R E N C H

AMERICAN EXPEDITIONARY FORCE

PARIS

Châlons •

St. Mihiel

SECOND from 12.10

F R E N C H

TENTH from 27.10 then EIGHTH

0 ————— 1000 km
0 ————— 500 miles

· WESTERN · FRONT ·
· FINAL · ALLIED · OFFENSIVE · 1918 ·

JOB · 06 ·

Introduction

Paul Ludwig Hans Anton von Beneckendorff und von Hindenburg was not only one of the dominant figures of the Great War but also of 20th-century Germany. He wrote his biography in the immediate aftermath of the German defeat in 1918. It has been long out of print and hence not easily accessible. It is therefore not before time that it should be republished since it provides a unique insight in the conduct of Germany strategy during 1914–18. However, to make it more digestible to a 21st-century readership this edition has been abridged and the original title, *Out of My Life*, changed.

Von Hindenburg was the epitome of the old-style Prussian officer, a character which was only finally laid to rest in 1945. Created by Frederick the Great, this class was almost feudal in nature, receiving a privileged position in society in return for absolute loyalty to the monarch. Privilege, however, did not mean wealth. Rather, frugality was the watchword of the Prussian officer corps. Son of a middle piece officer, von Hindenburg took the traditional route through cadet school to a commission in the Guards. This placed him close to the royal family, which had its advantages. He was also lucky in the timing of his commission in that it enabled him to see action and distinguish himself in both the war against Austria and the 1870 conflict with France. The climax of this early period of his life was undoubtedly being witness to the unification of Germany under the King of Prussia in the Hall of Mirrors at Versailles in January 1871.

Any ambitious German officer prior to 1914 needed to graduate from the War Academy and don the crimson striped trousers of the Great General Staff, the brain of the German Army and the first professional military staff body in the world. Von Hindenburg successfully achieved this and found himself working harder than ever before. Often he was 'double hatted', holding down two staff positions simultaneously – a not unusual occurrence. It must have been a relief to him, after eight years of this demanding existence, to be given a regimental command. But his long stint on the staff had given him a good grounding in strategy, operations and tactics, as well as an understanding of civil–military relationships. Thereafter, he rose steadily through the ranks, finally becoming a corps commander, the highest peacetime German field command, in 1905, a position he held for six years before voluntarily retiring.

Von Hindenburg had reached the age of 64 when he hung up his sword. In normal times he could expect no further use for his services, but the Europe of 1911 was one of growing tension. Two armed camps – the Triple Entente (France, Russia, Britain) and the Triple Alliance (Germany, Austria-Hungary, Italy) – glowered at each other. In eastern Europe, notably in the Balkans, nationalism was becoming ever more strident. There was colonial rivalry in Africa and the Dreadnought race between Britain and Germany. Von Hindenburg followed events closely and the outbreak of war seems to have come as no surprise. With it came hopes that he might he recalled to duty.

The call came quicker than perhaps he expected. The story of his meeting on Hanover railway station with Erich Ludendorff, fresh from distinguishing himself with his brigade in front of Liege a few days earlier, has been told many times. It was the first time that the two men had come across one another, the one a Prussian aristocrat and the other a Pomeranian commoner, but half an hour's conversation on how to deal with the growing crisis in East Prussia made it appear that they had known one another all their lives. Ludendorff's powerful intellect and nervous energy acted as the perfect foil for his commander's phlegmatism and powers of leadership. They became one of the most formidable partnerships in military history and a perfect example of the ideal commander/chief-of-staff relationship. In German eyes, as von Hindenburg states, the division of their powers was never 'clearly demarcated' and that it was personality which provided the key to a successful partnership. In truth, they had a similar mindset through their training at the War Academy and it was widely acknowledged under the German system that the chief of staff was often the originator of plans.

The spectacular results of Hindenburg's first campaign against the Russians made him a national hero, but it was to be the beginning of a frustration that would grow as the war progressed. Both he and Ludendorff were well aware that Germany's greatest fear was waging a two front war. The von Schlieffen plan with which the country went to war was designed to achieve a quick knock-out blow against France before turning on the slower mobilising Russians. The attack in the West failed to achieve its objective and Hindenburg and Ludendorff were convinced that a decision must therefore be sought in the east. The problem was Germany's main ally, Austria-Hungary. Its army was an imperfect instrument compared with that of the Germans, not least because it was made up of ten races, many speaking different languages, and some of these had an ethnic affinity to the Russians and could not be deployed against them.

Erich von Falkenhayn, who had assumed as Chief of Staff of the German Army in the Field in mid-September 1914, was an avowed Westerner and unwilling to transfer the necessary number of divisions from France and Flanders to enable von Hindenburg to strike a decisive blow, although during 1915 he and his Austrian allies did score some significant victories. In his book, von Hindenburg is careful not to attack von Falkenhayn directly, although he expresses consternation when, just prior to being appointed commander of the German armies in the East, Ludendorff was temporarily whisked away from him. Another frustration was that Italy's entry into the war on the Allied side in May 1915 proved a diversion to Austrian attention on the war against Russia. The year 1916 was to prove even more difficult. While von Hindenburg agreed with the concept of the attack on Verdun, he condemned its continuation after the offensive was clearly failing. This, and the opening of the Somme, meant that the chances of achieving significant success on the Eastern Front were severely reduced. Indeed, the Russians launched an offensive of their own, mainly against the Austrians, who lost a considerable amount of ground. Taken alongside a prolonged and costly mountain campaign against the Italians, it knocked much of the stuffing out of the Austro-Hungarian Army.

Others, too, criticised von Falkenhayn for the bankruptcy of his strategy at Verdun. His cause was not helped when he confidently asserted that Rumania would not declare war on the Central Powers until autumn 1916, only to have the rug pulled from under his feet when that country entered the conflict in late August. The Kaiser immediately summoned von Hindenburg to ask him his advice on this new development. Von Falkenhayn felt he was being sidelined and promptly resigned, allowing the von Hindenburg–Ludendorff partnership to take control of Germany's destiny.

Von Hindenburg now found himself having to juggle manpower to meet the demands of a number of fronts. The immediate problem was Rumania. Although its army was not well trained, the real danger was that its Russian neighbour would become involved and that the Austrian southern flank would come under serious threat. However, since Rumania's entry had been expected for some time, plans had been made to deal with it. Furthermore, the Russian support did not materialise. Consequently, Rumania had been overrun before the end of the year. But there were clamours for German troops elsewhere. The Austrians wanted them to bolster their forces in Galicia and to help break the deadlock in the Italian Alps. Bulgaria, engaged in a campaign against French, British, and Greek troops in Salonica, also wanted a German stiffening. There was also Turkey, fighting the Russians in Armenia – and British and Dominion troops in Mesopotamia and Palestine – and beginning to tire. The continuing pressure on the Somme and at Verdun meant that he could spare little from the Western Front for other theatres. Conversely, the more the Germans were able to tie down Allied troops away from this theatre, the better their prospects in the West.

The year 1917 was dominated in German eyes by the US entry into the war. Von Hindenburg was convinced by late January 1917 that, in spite of President Wilson's assertion that America was 'too proud to fight', the country would join the Allies. In this respect, von Hindenburg was a strong supporter of the renewed unrestricted submarine warfare campaign since he believed that this could prevent US forces from being deployed to Europe, a vain hope as it turned out. Rightly assuming that the Allies would renew their attacks on the Western Front, he and Ludendorff turned once more to the Eastern Front, recognising that Russia was beginning to crumble from within. Victory against Russia was all but achieved by the end of the year, enabling von Hindenburg to switch troops to the West, but not as many as he would have liked. Russian prevarications during the peace negotiations at Brest-Litovsk and a sally into the Ukraine to secure additional food sources tied down significant forces.

In the West, von Hindenburg was forced to give ground early in 1917 to conserve manpower, but his troops were able to hold the British attack at Arras and that by the French at Chemin des Dames in the spring. While he recognised that French losses significantly reduced their capacity for offensive action, it is noteworthy that, even after the war, von Hindenburg did not realise how close the French Army came to breaking point on account of the mutinies which erupted. The British summer offensive in Flanders resulted in another battle of attrition. The Germans adopted new more fluid defensive tactics, which undoubtedly contributed to the British failure to break through, but it is interesting that von Hindenburg draws attention to the problems of ensuring that the troops fully understood what was behind them. He admits that the attack at Cambrai came as a surprise and acknowledges, for the first time in the book, the potential of the tank. He attributes the British failure to exploit their initial success to rigidity of thought. Indeed, he thinks little of his opponents; only British obstinacy and the French artillery gain his respect.

1918 was 'make or break' as far as the Germans were concerned. Not only was it a question of propping up ever more tired and debilitated allies, but there was the realisation that ever more US troops were arriving in France and that they would inevitably tip the manpower balance decisively in favour of the Allies. Consequently, the Germans had to attack in the West. Von Hindenburg stresses that the decision to strike at the British sector was not made for political reasons, but because the ground was more favourable for achieving a breakthrough. While the first few days of the March 1918 offensive saw dazzling German successes, there was a penalty to be paid for traversing the old Somme battlefields – the paucity of communications, which made resupply difficult. Abandoned British supply dumps did help, but they also diverted attention away from maintaining momentum, as did the growing tiredness of the attackers. Von Hindenburg observes that by this time the troops did not have the same discipline as earlier. Another factor was the arrival of French reinforcements to stem the tide. Hence this attack was closed down and another mounted in Flanders. A successful attack here would not only deny the Channel ports to the BEF but would also enable long-range guns to bombard southern England. Again, the area of attack threw up difficulties for the supply system and the French came once more to the rescue.

Von Hindenburg and Ludendorff remained convinced that seizure of the Channel ports was the key to restoring Germany's fortunes, but now decided that this could only be achieved if the French were kept away; hence the three German summer offensives in the French sector. The key, according to von Hindenburg, was the town of Rheims, which he saw as being as important a communication centre as Amiens was in the context of the March offensive. If this could be captured it would not only ease the resupply situation, but should keep the French sufficiently tied down for the Flanders attack to be renewed. The Germans failed, however. Yet, a renewal on the Lys offensive was still on the cards on July 17, when Ludendorff visited Crown Prince Rupprecht's army in Flanders to discuss the plans for it. But the following day saw a French counter-attack into the German salient across the Marne. Such was its success that the Germans were forced back north of the Marne. It was the end of German offensive action in the West.

The key turning point came on August 8 1918, when the British attacked at Amiens, exposing, as von Hindenburg points out, the weaknesses now apparent in the German defences. It was clear that Germany could no longer win, but von Hindenburg advised the Kaiser that the time to seek peace had not yet arrived, pointing out that a considerable amount of hostile territory still remained in German hands and that they should wait until the military situation improved. Ludendorff, suffering increasingly from strain, believed that the war should be ended, although von Hindenburg does not mention this nor their subsequent differences of opinion. As the Allies responded to Foch's call of 'Tout le monde à la bataille!' with a succession of attacks on the Western Front, Germany's allies began to crumble. First to fold was Bulgaria in the face of an Allied offensive in Salonika. The Turks were decisively defeated by Allenby in Palestine, while a further offensive in northern Italy caused a rapidly disintegrating Austria-Hungary to make peace overtures.

In Germany itself there was also growing unrest, with the scent of revolution wafting over the country. A new government favouring a negotiated peace was formed under Prince Max of Baden. Ludendorff, who had received medical treatment for his condition and was now in a more optimistic frame of mind, believed that the situation could be restored provided sufficient reinforcements were made available. The government, now negotiating with President Wilson on the basis of his Fourteen Points, took little notice. Von Hindenburg, convinced that Wilson was demanding unconditional surrender, also felt that the Army must fight on, even if the government was lukewarm in its support. Declaring that the Army was being betrayed by the government, Ludendorff tendered his resignation, but von Hindenburg felt it his duty to remain at his post. His last act was to bid farewell to his 'All Highest War Lord', who was now forced to abdicate.

While Ludendorff retired to Sweden to write his memoirs, von Hindenburg remained in charge of the Army until the signing of the Treaty of Versailles, when he resigned. Ludendorff came under the spell of Hitler and took part in the abortive 1923 Munich Putsch and was then persuaded to stand as the Nazi candidate in the 1925 presidential election. He came bottom of the poll and retired into obscurity, dying in 1937. Von Hindenburg was also persuaded to stand for president and, as the national unity candidate, won in 1925. He remained head of the German state until his death in 1934, unable to prevent Hitler's rise to power.

The Great War shows its author as a man of simple beliefs. He gave the Kaiser almost godlike status and remained faithful to the creed of the Prussian officer – Honour, Duty, Loyalty – throughout his long life. He was modest, yet popular, and his door seems to have been open to everyone. During the years up until 1914 he clearly lived a contented life and fulfilled much of his ambition. He stood up well to the war years, better than his

intellectually more able and highly strung partner. But writing in the immediate aftermath of defeat and subsequent civil war, there is a growing bitterness in his book, especially when it comes to the year 1918. In von
Hindenburg's eyes the German soldier proved himself superior to all his foes
throughout the war. If the government had fully supported him by a total
mobilisation, both military and industrial, of the country, an honourable
peace could have been achieved rather than the humiliating terms which
the Allies were eventually able to dictate. In other words, the German Army
was ultimately stabbed in the back. It was the very same message that helped
to bring the Nazis to power.

Note on the Abridgement
I have cut the original text by approximately one third. Much of it repre-
sents von Hindenburg's philosophising, some of which is little more than a
rant. Other passages are paeans of praise for the Kaiser and the House of
Hohenzollern. There are also a number of asides, whose omission does not
detract from the story. In addition, he has a tendency towards repetition, an
indication that the book was written in a hurry. I have left proper names,
both of people and places, with their original spelling. Very occasionally I
have run two sentences together, adding a connecting word. Otherwise, the
original translation remains as it was in the 1920 English edition.

CHARLES MESSENGER, 2006

Foreword

The memoirs that follow owe their inception not to any personal inclination to authorship, but to the many requests and suggestions that have been made to me.

It is not my intention to write an historical work, but rather to interpret the impressions under which my life has been spent, and to define the principles on which I have considered it my duty to think and act. Nothing was farther from my mind than to write an apology or a controversial treatise, much less an essay in self-glorification. My thoughts, my actions, my mistakes have been but human. Throughout my life and conduct my criterion has been, not the approval of the world, but my inward convictions, duty and conscience.

The following pages of reminiscences, written in the most tragic days of our Fatherland, have not come into being under the bitter burden of despair. My gaze is steadfastly directed forward and outward.

I gratefully dedicate my book to all those who fought with me at home and in the field for the existence and greatness of the Empire.

September, 1919.

Part I

Days of Peace and War
before 1914

Chapter One

My Youth

The son of a soldier, I was born in Posen in 1847. My father was then a lieutenant in the 18th Infantry Regiment. My mother was the daughter of Surgeon-General Schwichart, who was also then living in Posen.

The simple, not to say hard, life of a Prussian country gentleman in modest circumstances, a life which is virtually made up of work and the fulfilment of duty, naturally set its stamp on our whole stock. My father too was heart and soul in his profession. Yet he always found time to devote himself, hand in hand with my mother, to the training of his children — for I had two younger brothers as well as a sister. Both my parents strove to give us a healthy body and a strong will ready to cope with the duties that would lie in our path through life. But they also endeavoured, by suggestion and the development of the tenderer sides of human feeling, to give us the best thing that parents can ever give — a confident belief in our Lord God and a boundless love for our Fatherland and — what they regarded as the prop and pillar of that Fatherland — our Prussian Royal House.

The soldier's nomadic lot took my parents from Posen to Cologne, Graudenz, Pinne in the Province of Posen, Glogau and Kottbus. Then my father left the service and went to Neudeck.

At Pinne my father, in accordance with the custom then obtaining, commanded a company of Landwehr as supernumerary captain. His service duties did not make very heavy demands on his time, so that just at the very period when my young mind began to stir he was able to devote special attention to us children. He soon taught me geography and French, while the schoolmaster Kobelt, of whom even now I preserve grateful memories, instructed me in reading, writing and arithmetic. To this epoch I trace my passion for geography, which my father knew how to arouse by his very intuitive and suggestive methods of teaching.

It was while I was at Glogau that I entered the Cadet Corps. It can certainly be said that in those days life in the Prussian Cadet Corps was consciously and intentionally rough. The training was based, after true concern for education, on a sound development of the body and the will. Energy and resolution were valued just as highly as knowledge.

Our high spirits did not suffer from the hard schooling of our cadet life. I venture to doubt whether the boyish love of larking, which no doubt at times reached the stage of frantic uproar, showed to more advantage in any other school than among us cadets. We found our teachers understanding, lenient judges.

At first I myself was anything but what is known in ordinary life as a model pupil. In the early days I had to get over a certain physical weakness which had been the legacy of previous illnesses. When, thanks to the sound method of training, I had gradually got stronger, I had at first little inclination to devote myself particularly to study. It was only slowly that my ambitions in that direction were aroused, ambitions which grew with success, and finally brought me, through no merit of mine, the calling of the specially gifted pupil.

In my first year as cadet, the summer of 1859, we had a visit at Wahlstatt from the then Prince Frederick William, later the Emperor Frederick, and his wife. It was on this occasion that we saw for the first time almost all the members of our Royal House. Never before had we raised our legs so high in the goose-step, never had we done such break-neck feats in the gymnastic display which followed as on that day. It was a long time before we stopped talking about the goodness and affability of the princely pair.

In October of the same year the birthday of King Frederick William IV was celebrated for the last time. It was thus under that sorely tried monarch that I put on the Prussian uniform which will be the garb of honour to me as long as my life lasts. I had the honour in the year 1865 to be attached as page to Queen Elizabeth, the widow of the late King. The watch which Her Majesty gave me at that time has accompanied me faithfully through three wars.

At Easter, 1863, I was transferred to the special class, and therefore sent to Berlin. The Cadet School in that city was in the new Friedrichstrasse, not far from the Alexanderplatz. For the first time I got to know the Prussian capital, and was at last able to have a glimpse of my all-gracious sovereign, King William I, at the spring reviews when we paraded on Unter den Linden and had a march past in the Opernplatz, as well as the autumn reviews on the Tempelhofer Feld.

The opening of the year 1864 brought a rousing, if serious atmosphere into our lives at the Cadet School, The war with Denmark broke out, and in the spring many of our comrades left us to join the ranks of the fighting troops. Unfortunately for me I was too young to be in the number of that highly envied band. I need not try to describe the glowing words with which our departing comrades were accompanied. We never troubled our heads about the political causes of the war. But all the same we had a proud feeling that a refreshing breeze had at last stirred the feeble and unstable structure of the German union, and that the mere fact was worth more than all the speeches and diplomatic documents put together.

I left the Cadet Corps in the spring of 1865. My own personal experiences and inclinations throughout my life have made me grateful and devoted to that military educational establishment.

Chapter Two

In Battle for the Greatness of
Prussia and Germany

On April 7, 1865, I became a second-lieutenant in the 3rd Regiment of Foot Guards. The regiment belonged to those troops which had been reorganised when the number of active units was greatly increased in 1859–60. When I joined it the young regiment had already won its laurels in the campaign of 1864. The historic fame of any military body is a bond of unity between all its members, a kind of cement which holds it together even in the worst of times. It gives place to an indestructible something which retains its power even when, as in the last great war, the regiment has practically to be reconstituted time after time. The old spirit very soon permeates the newcomers.

In my regiment, which had been formed out of the 1st Regiment of Foot Guards, I found the good old Potsdam spirit, that spirit which corresponded to the best traditions of the Prussian Army at that time. The Prussian Corps of Officers in those days was not blessed with worldly goods – a very good thing. Its wealth consisted of its frugality. The consciousness of a special personal relation to the King – 'feudal loyalty', as a German historian has put it – permeated the life of the officer and compensated for many a material privation.

At the time I joined the regiment, which was then stationed at Danzig, the political events of the following months were already casting their shadows before. It was true that mobilisation had not yet been ordered, but the decree for the increase of establishments had already been issued and was in course of execution.

In face of the approaching decisive conflict between Prussia and Austria our political and military ideas travelled over the tracks of Frederick the Great. It was in that train of thought that when we were in Potsdam, to which the regiment was transferred immediately our mobilisation was complete, we took our Grenadiers to the tomb of that immortal sovereign. Even the Order of the Day which was issued to our army before the invasion of Bohemia was inspired by thoughts of him, for its closing words ran: 'Soldiers, trust to your own strength, and remember that your task is to defeat the same foe which our greatest King once overthrew with his small army.'

From the political point of view we realised the necessity of settling the question of Prussian or Austrian supremacy, because within the framework of the Union, as then constituted, there was no room for two great Powers to develop side by side. One of the two had to give way, and as agreement could not be reached by political methods the guns had to speak. But beyond that train of ideas there was no question of any national hostility against Austria.

In this war we trod in the footsteps of Frederick the Great – in actual fact as well as in a metaphorical sense. The Guard Corps, for example, in invading Bohemia from Silesia by way of Branau was taking a route that had often been taken before. And the course of our first action, that at Soor, led us on June 28 into the same region and in the same direction – from Eipel on Burkersdorf – against the enemy as that in which, on September 30, 1747, Prussia's Guard had moved forward in the centre of the great King's army which was advancing in the rigid line of that time during the Battle of Soor.

Our 2nd Battalion, of which I was commanding the first skirmishing section (formed out of the third rank in accordance with the regulations of those days), had no opportunity that day of appearing in the front line, as we formed part of the reserve, which had already been separated from the rest before the battle, as the tactical methods of those days decreed. But all the same, we had found an opportunity of exchanging shots with Austrian infantry in a wood north-west of Burkersdorf. We had made some prisoners, and later on we drove off and captured the transport of about two squadrons of enemy Uhlans who were resting, all unsuspecting, in a glen.

Straight from the excitement of battle, I was familiarised on the very next day with what I may call the reverse side of the medal. I was assigned the sad duty of taking sixty grenadiers to search the battlefield and bury the dead – an unpleasant task, which was all the more difficult because the corn was still standing. By dint of enormous exertions and at times passing other units by running in the ditches by the roadside, I and my men caught up my battalion about midday. The battalion had already joined the main body of the division and was on the march to the south. I came up just in time to witness the storming of the Elbe crossing at Königinhof by our advance guard.

On June 30 I was brought face to face with the sober realities of war's more petty side. I was sent with a small escort to take about thirty wagons, full of prisoners, by night to Tartenau, get a load of food supplies for the empty wagons, and bring them all back to Königinhof. It was not before July 2 that I was able to join my company again. It was high time, for the very next day summoned us to the battlefield of Königgrätz.

The following night I went out on a patrol with my platoon in the direction of the fortress of Josephstadt, and on the morning of July 3 we were in our outpost camp, wet and cold and apparently unsuspecting, by the southern outskirts of Königinhof. Soon the alarm was given, and shortly after we received the command to get our coffee quickly and be ready to march. Careful listeners could hear the sound of guns in the south-west. Opinions as to the reasons for the alarm being given were divided. The generally accepted view was that the 1st Army, under Prince Frederick Charles, which had invaded Bohemia from Lausitz – we formed part of the 2nd Army commanded by the Crown Prince – must have come into contact with a concentrated Austrian corps somewhere.

The order to advance which now arrived was greeted with joy. In torrents of rain and bathed in perspiration, though the weather was cold, our long columns dragged themselves forward along the bottomless roads. A holy ardour possessed me, and reached the pitch of fear lest we should arrive too late.

My anxiety soon proved to be unnecessary. After we had ascended from the valley of the Elbe we could hear the sound of guns ever more clearly. Further, about eleven o'clock we saw a group of the higher Staff on horseback standing on an eminence by the roadside and gazing south through their glasses. They were the Headquarters Staff of the 2nd Army, under the supreme command of our Crown Prince, subsequently the Emperor Frederick.

Our advance took us at first straight across country; then we deployed, and before long the first shells began to arrive from the heights by Horonowes. The Austrian artillery justified its old excellent reputation. One of the first shells wounded my company commander, another killed my wing NCO just behind me, while shortly after another fell into the middle of the column and put twenty-five men out of action. When, however, the firing ceased and the heights fell into our hands without fighting, because they were only an advanced position lightly held by the enemy for the purpose of surprise and gaining time, there was quite a feeling of disappointment among us. It did not last for long, for we soon had a view over a large part of a mighty battlefield. Somewhat to our right heavy clouds of smoke were rising into the dull sky from the positions of our 1st and the enemy's army on the Bistritz. The flashes of the guns and the glow of burning villages gave the picture a peculiarly dramatic colouring. The mist, which had become much thicker, the high corn, and the formation of the ground apparently hid our movements from the enemy. The fire of the enemy batteries which soon opened on us from the south, without being able to stop us, was therefore remarkably innocuous. And so we pressed on as fast as the formation of the country, the heavy, slippery ground, and the corn, rape and beet would allow. Our attack, organised according to all the rules of war then in vogue, soon lost cohesion. Individual companies, indeed individual sections, began to look for opponents for themselves. But everyone pressed on. The only co-ordinating impulse was the resolution to get to close quarters with the enemy.

Between Chlum and Nedelist our half battalion – a very favourite battle formation in those days – advancing through the mist and high-standing corn, surprised some enemy infantry coming from the south. The latter were soon forced to retire by the superior fire of our needle-guns. Following them with my skirmishing section in extended order, I suddenly came across an Austrian battery, which raced past us with extraordinary daring, unlimbered and loosed off case-shot at us. A bullet which pierced my helmet grazed my head, and for a short time I lost consciousness. When I recovered we went for that battery. We captured five guns, while three got away. I felt a proud man and gave a sigh of relief when, bleeding from a slight wound in the head, I stood by my captured gun.

But I had little time to rest on my laurels. Enemy jäger, easily recognisable by the feathers in their caps, sprang up from among the wheat. I beat them off and followed them up to a sunken road.

When I reached the sunken road to which I have referred I took a good look round. The enemy jäger had vanished in the rain and mist. The villages in the neighbourhood – Westar was immediately in front, Rosberitz on my right, and Sweti on my left – were obviously still in possession of the enemy. Fighting was already going on for Rosberitz. I was quite alone with my section. Nothing was to be seen of our people behind me. The detachments in close order had not followed me southwards, and appeared to have veered to the right. I decided to bring my isolation on that far-flung battlefield to an end by following the sunken road to Rosberitz. Before I reached my goal several more Austrian squadrons shot past us, not noticing me and my handful of men. They crossed the sunken road at a level place just ahead of me, and shortly after, as the sound of lively rifle fire showed me, came into contact with some infantry north of Rosberitz, whom I could not see from where I was. Soon a number of riderless horses swept back past us, and before long the whole lot came pelting by again in wild confusion. I sent a few shots after them, as the white cloaks of the riders made an excellent target in the poor light.

When I reached Rosberitz I found the situation there very critical. Sections and companies of different regiments of our division were dashing themselves furiously against very superior forces of the enemy. At first there were no reinforcements behind our weak detachments. The bulk of the division had been drawn away to the village of Chlum, situated on a height, and was violently engaged there. My half battalion, which I had been lucky enough to rejoin at the eastern outskirts of Rosberitz, was therefore the first reinforcement.

I really cannot say which was the more surprised, the Austrians or ourselves. However, the enemy masses concentrated and closed in on us from three sides in order to recover complete possession of the village. Fearful as was the effect of the fire from our needle-guns, as each wave collapsed a fresh one came to take its place. Murderous hand-to-hand fighting took place in the streets between the thatched cottages on fire. All idea of fighting in regular units was lost. Everyone shot and stabbed at random to the best of his ability. Before long we were in serious danger of being cut off. Austrian bugles were being blown in a side street which came out behind us, and we could hear the roll of the enemy's drums, which made a more hollow sound than ours. We were hard pressed in front as well, and there was nothing for it but to retire. We were saved by a burning roof which had fallen into the street and formed a barrier of flame and thick smoke. We escaped under its protection to the shelter of a height just north-east of the village.

We were furiously disappointed, and refused to withdraw any further. As the most senior officer present, Major Count Waldersee of the 1st Regiment of Foot Guards ordered the two standards we had to be planted in the ground. The men flocked to them, and the units were reorganised. Reinforcements were already coming up from the rear, and so, with drums beating, we all stormed forward once more against the enemy, who had contented himself with recovering possession of the village. However, he soon evacuated it in order to conform to the general retreat of his army.

In the evening of the battle we proceeded to Westar, and remained there until we left the battlefield for good. The doctor wanted to send me to hospital on account of my head wound, but as I expected there would be another battle behind the Elbe I contented myself with poultices and a light bandage, and for the rest of the march had to wear a cap instead of my helmet.

When we crossed the Elbe by a temporary bridge at Pardubitz on the evening of July 6 the Crown Prince was waiting there for the regiment, and gave us his thanks for our behaviour in the battle. We thanked him with loud cheers and continued our march, proud of the praise lavished upon us by the Commander-in-Chief of our army, who was also the heir to the Prussian throne, and prepared to follow him to further battlefields.

However, the rest of the campaign brought us nothing but marches, certainly no events worth mentioning. The armistice which followed on July 22 found us in lower Austria about 30 miles from Vienna. When we began our homeward march soon after, we were accompanied by an unwelcome guest, cholera. We only got rid of it by degrees, and then not before it had exacted a large toll of victims from our ranks.

Continuing our march home, we crossed the frontiers of Bohemia and Saxony on September 2, and on the 8th the frontier of the Mark of Brandenburg at the Grosenhain–Elster road. A triumphal arch greeted us. We marched through it on our homeward way to the strains of 'Heil dir im Siegerkranz'. I need not try to describe our feelings!

On September 20 we made our triumphal entry into Berlin. The grand review followed on what is now the Königsplatz, but was then a sandy parade-ground. The site of the present General Staff building was occupied by a timber yard, which was connected with the town by a lane bordered with willows. Starting from the parade-ground, the troops marched under the Brandenburger Tor, up the Linden to the Opernplatz. Here took place the march past His Majesty the King. Blücher, Scharnhorst and Gneisenau looked down from their pedestals. They might well be pleased with us!

My battalion had assembled in the Floraplatz in order to take its place in the column. It was here that my Commanding Officer handed me the Order of the Red Eagle, 4th Class, with swords, and told me to put it on at once, as the new decorations were to be worn for the triumphal march. As I looked about me, apparently in some embarrassment, an old lady stepped out of the crowd of spectators and fastened the decoration to my breast with a pin. So whenever I have crossed the Floraplatz in later years, whether walking or riding, I have always gratefully remembered the kind Berlin lady who once gave the eighteen-year-old lieutenant his first order there.

After the war Hanover was assigned to the 3rd Guards Regiment as peace station. The intention was to pay the former capital a special compliment. We were not pleased to be sent there, but when the hour of parting struck, twelve years later, as the regiment was transferred to Berlin, there was not a man in its ranks who did not regret leaving it. I myself had to leave the beautiful town as early as 1873, but I had then grown so fond of it that I took up residence there after my retirement from the service later on.

In the summer of 1867 His Majesty the King visited Hanover for the first time. When he arrived I was in the guard of honour which was drawn up before the palace in George's Park, and my War Lord made me happy by asking me on what occasion I had won the Order of Swords. In later years, after I had also won the Iron Cross in 1870–1, my Kaiser and King has often asked me the same question when I have been reporting for transfer or promotion. I always thought of this first occasion with the same joy and pride as possessed me then.

When the war of 1870 broke out I took the field as adjutant of the 1st Battalion. My Commanding Officer, Major von Seegenberg, had gone through the campaigns of 1864 and 1866 as a company commander in the regiment. He was a war-hardened old Prussian soldier of irresistible energy and tireless concern for the welfare of his troops. The relations between us were good on both sides.

The opening of the campaign brought my regiment, as indeed the whole Guard Corps, bitter disappointment, inasmuch as we marched for weeks and yet did not come into contact with the enemy. It was not until after we had crossed the Moselle above Pont à Mousson and nearly reached the Meuse that the events west of Metz on August 17 summoned us to that neighbourhood. We turned north, and after an extraordinarily tiring march reached the battlefield of Vionville in the evening of that day. Relics of the fearful struggle of our 3rd and 10th Corps on the day before met our eyes at every turn. Of the military situation as a whole we knew next to nothing. Thus it was in an almost complete mental fog that on August 18 we marched from our camp at Hannonville, west of Mars la Tour, and reached Doncourt about mid-day. Although this was a relatively short march, it required an enormous effort owing to the fact that it was carried out in close mass formation, and that we unfortunately crossed the Saxon (12th) Corps. Besides, the heat was terrific, the dust awful, and we had been unable to get enough water since the previous day.

We halted at Doncourt, and began to think of cooking a meal. Rumours ran round that Bazaine had marched west and so got away. The enthusiasm of the previous day had somewhat waned. Suddenly a tremendous cannonade started in the east. The 9th Corps had got into touch with the enemy. The 'stand to' cheered us all up. Our nerves began to brace themselves up again and our hearts to beat faster and stronger. We resumed our march to the north. The impression that we were on the eve of a great battle grew stronger from minute to minute. We went on, and quite close to Batilly received orders to unfurl our colours. This was done to the accompaniment of a threefold 'hurrah'. What a moving moment that was! Almost simultaneously some Guard batteries galloped past us, going east towards the enemy's positions. The main features of the battle became more distinct. From the heights of Amanweiler right to St Privat thick, heavy clouds of smoke were rising. Enemy infantry and artillery were posted there in several successive lines. For the time being their fire was directed with extreme fury against our 9th Army Corps. Its left wing was apparently commanded by the enemy. We could not make out more.

To avoid a frontal attack against the enemy's lines we took a gulley which ran parallel to the enemy's front for about three miles, and turned north to Ste Marie aux Chênes. This village had been attacked and captured by the advance guard of our division and part of the 12th Corps, which was marching on Auboué on our left. After the capture of Ste Marie our brigade deployed immediately south of the village and on a front facing it. We rested. Truly a peculiar kind of rest! Stray bullets, from enemy riflemen pushed forward from St Privat, fell here and there among our formations in close order. Several men were wounded.

I turned the situation over in my mind. Away to the east, almost on the right flank of our present front, lay St Privat, crowning a gentle sloping hill and connected with Ste Marie aux Chênes, about a mile and a quarter away, by a dead-straight road bordered with poplars. The country north of this road was for the most part concealed by the trees, but gave the same impression of lack of cover as that south of the road. On the height itself an almost unearthly silence reigned. Our eyes strove involuntarily to pierce the secrets we suspected there. Apparently it was not thought necessary on our side to try and pierce the veil by reconnaissance. So we remained quietly where we were.

About half-past five in the afternoon our brigade received orders to attack. We were to press forward in a northerly direction on the east side of Ste Marie, and when we had crossed the road, wheel to attack St Privat. The thought that these skilful movements could be taken in the right flank from St Privat sprang to one's mind at once.

Just before our brigade rose up, the whole neighbourhood of St Privat sprang to life and shrouded itself in the smoke of lines of French infantry. What had happened was that the 4th Guards Brigade, which was not in our division, was already pressing on south of the road. For the time being the whole force of the enemy's fire was turned against it. These troops would have been reduced to pulp in a very short time if we, the 1st Guards Brigade, had not immediately attacked north of the road, and thereby taken the burden off them. Indeed, it seemed almost impossible to get forward at all.

My Commanding Officer rode forward with me to reconnoitre the country ahead and give the battalion its route direction within the orbit of the brigade. A hurricane of continuous fire now swept over us from every quarter. Yet we had to try and execute the movement which had been begun. We managed at length to cross the road. Once across, the compact columns formed a front against the enemy lines, and in open order stormed forward towards St Privat. Every man tried his hardest to get to close quarters with the enemy in order to use his rifle, which was inferior to the *chassepot*. The sight was as terrible as impressive. The ground behind the mass surging forward, as if against a hailstorm, was strewn with dead and wounded, and yet the brave troops pressed on without stopping. They were gradually deprived of their officers and NCOs, who had to be replaced by the best of the fusiliers and grenadiers. As I was riding forward I saw the general of the Guard Corps, Prince Augustus of Würtemberg, on horseback at the outskirts of Ste Marie. He was following the terrible crisis in which his splendid regiment was involved and looked like being destroyed. It is said that just opposite him Marshal Canrobert was standing at the entrance to St Privat.

To get his battalion out of the vortex of the masses north-east of Ste Marie and give it the necessary room to fight, my Commanding Officer did not make it form a front against St Privat, but at first made it follow a fold of the ground, and continue the original movement to the north. We had thus a certain amount of cover, but we made so great a detour that after wheeling we formed the left wing of the brigade. In these circumstances we managed, with increasing losses, to get half-way to Ste Marie Roncourt.

Before we could prepare to envelop St Privat we had to see what the situation was at Roncourt, which the Saxons from Aboué did not yet seem to have reached. I rode forward, found the village unoccupied either by friend or foe, but noticed that there was French infantry in the quarries east of the village. I was successful in getting two companies of my battalion into Roncourt in time. Soon after the enemy made a counter-attack from the quarry, but was beaten off. It was now possible for the two other companies, no longer anxious about their flanks and rear, to turn against the northern exit from St Privat to relieve – at least to some extent – the fearful frontal attack of the rest of the brigade. Later, after Roncourt had been occupied by parts of the 12th Corps, the two companies we had used there were brought up.

On the enemy's side it was an unceasing storm of rifle-fire from several lines of infantry, fire which strove to make all life impossible on the broad, exposed field of attack. On our side it was a line – a line with innumerable gaps – formed by remnants of units which did not merely cling to the ground, however, but strove time after time to close with the enemy in spasmodic rushes. I held my breath as I watched the scene in utter anguish lest an enemy counter-attack should hurl our men back. But except for an attempt to break out with cavalry north of St Privat, an attempt which did not survive the first charge, the French did not leave their positions.

There was now a pause in the infantry action. Both sides were exhausted and lay facing one another, firing but seldom. The halt in the hostilities on the battlefield was so marked that I rode along the firing line from the left wing almost to the centre of the brigade without feeling I was running any risk. Now, however, our artillery which had been brought up began its work of preparation, and before long fresh forces, the 2nd Guards Brigade from Ste Marie, made their appearance among the fast vanishing remnants of the 4th and 1st, while Saxon reinforcements approached from the north-west. The pressure on the tortured infantry was relieved. There, where death and ruin seemed the only prospect, a fresh battle spirit seemed to stir, a new will to victory was born, which reached its heroic climax in a fierce charge at the enemy. It was an indescribably moving moment when our foremost lines rose for the final assault just as the sun was going down. No orders urged them on. Spiritual enthusiasm, a stern resolve to conquer and the holy lust of battle drove them forward. This irresistible impetus carried everything away with it. The bulwark of the foe was stormed as darkness descended. A fierce exultation seized all our men.

The softer sides of human emotion came to the surface when, late in the evening, I counted the remnants of our battalion and on the next morning visited the yet smaller fragments of the other units of my regiment. At such times we think not only of the victory that has been won, but of the price which has been paid for it. The 3rd Guards Regiment had suffered losses of 36 officers and 1,060 non-commissioned officers and men, of which 17 officers and 306 men were killed. All the Guards infantry regiments had similar losses to show.

On August 19 we buried our dead, and in the afternoon of the 20th we marched away to the west. On the way our divisional commander, Lieutenant-General von Pape, gave us his thanks for our victory, but laid special emphasis on the fact that we had only done our bounden duty. He concluded with these words, 'In short, what applies to us is the old soldier's hymn: "Whether thousands to left, Or thousands to right, Of all friends bereft, A soldier must fight."' Our reply was a thunderous cheer for His Majesty the King.

After the battle the commander of my battalion, as the only unwounded Staff officer, took over the command of the regiment. I remained his adjutant in his new post.

The course of the operations which came to such a memorable conclusion at Sedan brought little of note in my way. We were present at the prelude, the Battle of Beaumont, on August 30, but being in the reserve were only spectators. On September 1 also, I followed the course of the battle mainly in the rôle of a looker-on. The Guard Corps formed the north-eastern section of the iron ring which closed in on MacMahon's army during that day. In particular the 1st Guards Brigade was held in readiness behind the heights east of the Givonne valley from the morning to the afternoon. I used this period of inactivity to visit the long line of Guard batteries posted at the edge of the heights. They were firing across the valley at the French lying on the wooded heights on the far side. From this point we had a comprehensive view of the whole region from the Forest of Ardennes to the valley of the Meuse. I felt as if I could almost touch the heights of Illy and the French positions west of the Givonne stream, including the Bois de la Garonne. The catastrophe to the French Army thus developed practically before my eyes. I was able to observe how the German ring of fire gradually closed in on the unhappy enemy and watch the French making heroic efforts, though these were doomed to failure from the start, to break through our encircling lines by thrusts at different points.

In the morning of September 2 we had a visit from the Crown Prince, who brought us the first news of the capture of Napoleon and his army, and in the afternoon it was followed by that of our King and military leaders. It is impossible to form any conception of the unexampled enthusiasm with which the monarch was received. The men simply could not be kept in the ranks. They swarmed round their dearly-loved master, and kissed his hands and feet. His Majesty saw his Guards for the first time in the campaign. With tears streaming down his face he thanked us for all we had done at St Privat. This was indeed a rich reward for those fateful hours! Bismarck was also in the King's suite. In Olympian calm he was riding at the end of the cavalcade, but he was recognised and received a special cheer, which he accepted with a smile.

In the morning of September 3 my regiment received an order to advance on Sedan and drive any French who happened to be outside the fortress within its walls. The idea of this was to prevent the large bodies of our enemy who were roving round the outskirts from being tempted to pick up the enormous numbers of rifles that were lying about, and make the attempt, however hopeless, to cut their way through. I rode on ahead through the Bois de la Garonne to the heights immediately above the town. There I discovered that the 'Red-Trousers', which added such a picturesque touch to the landscape, were merely harmless searchers for cloaks and coats which they wanted to take with them into captivity.

The intervention of my regiment was therefore unnecessary; a few patrols from other troops which were encamped nearby were all that was required. When I rode back with this news to my regiment, which was coming up behind, I saw a cloud of dust in the woods on the road going north. A French military doctor who was standing in front of Quérimont Farm (which had been converted into a hospital), and accompanied me part of the way, told me that in that cloud of dust was the Emperor Napoleon, who was on his way to Belgium with a guard of Black Hussars. If I had reached that road a few minutes earlier I should have been an eye-witness of the historic spectacle.

In the evening of that day we left the battlefield and returned to our quarters. Then, after a day's rest, we resumed our march on Paris.

On September 19, from the plateau of Gonesse, five miles north-east of St Denis, we had our first glimpse of the French capital. The gilded domes of the Invalides and other churches sparkled in the morning sunlight. I am sure that when the Crusaders gazed for the first time on Jerusalem their feelings were the same as ours when we saw Paris lying at our feet. We started off at three o'clock in the morning, while it was still dark, and spent the entire day – a beautiful autumn day – lying in the stubble fields ready to intervene if we or the neighbouring divisions met with difficulty in placing and occupying our outpost line. It was not until late in the afternoon that we got back to billets. We remained for some time in quarters at Gonesse, a place which enjoys some historical note from the fact that in 1815 Blücher and Wellington, who had reached Paris, met here to discuss the future course of the operations.

Instead of a complete and speedy victory, we were to be faced with many months of thoroughly exhausting and thankless investment operations, which were but seldom interrupted on our front by any noteworthy sortie. Their monotony was first broken about Christmas, when the bombardment of the forts made things a little more lively in a military sense.

The middle of January brought me a special event. I was sent, with a sergeant, as representative of my regiment to the proclamation of the Emperor at Versailles.

It was a peculiar collection of carriages which made its entrance into Versailles as the sun was setting. There were representatives of every type of vehicle which could be scraped up from the châteaux, villas and farms round Paris. The greatest sensation was made by a potato-wagon the driver of which was celebrating the day by displaying a huge Prussian flag – there was no German flag as yet – to right and left of his seat. I soon found myself in a good billet in the Avenue de Paris kept by a cheerful old lady, and in the evening we all assembled for an excellent supper – a luxury we had not known for ages – in the Hôtel des Reservoirs.

The ceremony of the 18th is familiar enough. I have countless impressions of it. It goes without saying that the personality of my all-gracious King and master had the most inspiring and yet the most touching effect upon me. His calm and simple, yet commanding presence gave the ceremony a greater sanctity than all external pomp. The affectionate enthusiasm for the illustrious sovereign was fully shared by all present, no matter to what German tribe they belonged. Indeed our South German brothers gave the most vociferous expression to their joy at the foundation of the 'German Empire'. For historic reasons we Prussians were somewhat more reserved, for we had learned to know our own value at a time when Germany was but a geographical expression.

January 19 began with an inspection of the old French royal palace with its proud collection of pictures immortalising the glories of France. We also visited the great park. Then the sudden thunder of cannon from the town burst upon us. The garrison of Versailles had already received the alarm and was on the march. What had happened was that the French had made their great sortie from Mont Valérien. We watched the battle for a considerable time in the capacity of idle spectators. In the afternoon we started out on our homeward journey, and late that night I reached the headquarters of my regiment at Villers le Roi, five miles north of St Denis, thankful that I had been privileged to witness the great historic event and do honour to him who was now my Emperor.

The fruitless sortie from Mont Valérien was France's last great effort. It was followed on the 26th by the capitulation of Paris and on the 28th by the general armistice. Immediately after the surrender of the forts our brigade was pushed forward into the western bend of the Seine between Mont Valérien and St Denis. We found good, well-furnished billets just on the bank of the river, opposite Paris and close to the Pont de Neuilly.

There I had an opportunity to make at least a nodding acquaintance with Paris. In the morning of March 2 I went for a ride in the company of an orderly officer of the Guard Hussars, across the Pont de Neuilly, to the Arc de Triomphe. I could not keep away from it any more than my friend Bernhardi, then lieutenant of Hussars and the first man to enter Paris, had been able to the day before. Then I rode down the Champs Elysées, through the Place de la Concorde and the Tuileries to the Louvre, and finally returned home along the Seine and through the Bois de Boulogne. Throughout my ride I let the historical monuments of the past of a great enemy produce their full effect upon me. The few inhabitants who showed themselves adopted an attitude of aloofness.

It was before Paris too that we celebrated His Majesty's birthday on March 22. It was a lovely, warm spring day, and we had a field service in the open air, a salute of guns from the forts, and banquets for both officers and men. The cheerful prospect of a speedy return home, our duty loyally done, doubled our enthusiasm. But we were not to leave France quite so soon as we hoped, for at first we had to remain on the northern front of Paris in and around St Denis, and were thus witnesses of the struggle between the French Government and the Commune.

Even during the siege we had been able to follow the first developments of the new revolutionary movement. We knew of the insubordination displayed by certain circles of political extremists towards the Governor of Paris. When the armistice was concluded the revolutionary movement began to show its head even more openly. Bismarck had said to the French plenipotentiaries: 'You came by revolution and a second revolution will sweep you away.' It looked as if he were going to be right.

Speaking generally, our interest in this Revolution was small at first. It was only from the beginning of March, when the Commune began to get the upper hand and the development of events seemed to point to an open conflict between Paris and Versailles, that we paid more attention. And now while German corps isolated the capital of France on the north and east, in a certain sense as the allies of the Government troops, the latter began their long and weary attack on Paris from the south and west. Events outside the walls of the fortress could best be followed from the heights above the Seine at Sannois, four miles north-west of Paris. Certain commercially-minded Frenchmen had established telescopes there which they allowed, on payment, any German soldier to use who wished to see the drama of a civil war. I myself made no use of these facilities, but contented myself with getting a peep at what was going on in Paris from a top window in the Cerf d'Or Hotel at St Denis (when I reported for the daily orders there), or when I went out riding on the island in the Seine by St Denis. Tremendous fires from the end of April revealed the track of the fighting in the centre of the town. I remember that on May 23, in particular, I had the impression that the whole of the inner quarters of Paris were threatened with destruction.

At long last I saw the end of the Commune one day from my top window in St Denis. Outside the main walls of Paris Government troops surrounded Montmartre, and from its northern declivity, then unbuilt on, stormed the commanding height which was the last bulwark of the insurgents.

We turned our backs on the French capital at the beginning of June, and after three days in the train reached our happy, victorious Fatherland.

Chapter Three

Work in Peacetime

Peace training was again resumed in all quarters. For the next few years I was still employed on regimental duty. I then followed my own inclination for a higher military training, sat for the *Kriegsakademie*, and was duly accepted in 1873.

The first year did not quite come up to my expectations. Instead of studying military history and the lessons of recent battles we were mostly regaled on the history of the art of war and the tactics of earlier days. These were secondary matters. In addition we were compelled to take mathematics, which only a few of us would require later in the form of trigonometry in the Survey Department. It was only with the last two years and his posting to other arms that the ambitious young officer could be completely satisfied.

When my time at the *Kriegsakademie* came to an end I first returned to my regiment at Hanover for six months, and then in the spring of 1877 was attached to the General Staff. In April, 1878, my transfer to the General Staff followed, and I was promoted to the rank of captain. A few weeks later I was posted to the Headquarters Staff of the 2nd Army Corps at Stettin. My military career outside regimental duty begins at this point, for subsequently I was only twice employed with troops until I was appointed to the command of a division.

The General Staff was certainly one of the most remarkable structures within the framework of our German Army. Side by side with the distinctly hierarchical form of the commands it constituted a special element which had its foundation in the great intellectual prestige of the Chief of Staff of the Army, Field-Marshal Count von Moltke. The peace training of the General Staff officer offered a guarantee that in case of war all the commanders in the field should be controlled from a single source, and all their plans governed by a common aim. The influence of the General Staff on those commanders was not regulated by any binding order. It depended far more on the military and personal qualities of the individual officer. The first requirement of the General Staff officer was that he should keep his own personality and actions entirely in the background. He had to work out of sight, and therefore be more than he seemed to be.

As I was the youngest Staff Officer at Corps Headquarters I was naturally mainly occupied with smaller matters. That was very disappointing for me at first, but then I subsequently acquired a love for the work, because I recognised its importance for the execution of the larger plans and the welfare of the troops. It was only in the annual General Staff rides that I had a chance of interesting myself in higher matters, in my capacity as the handy-man of the Corps Commander.

I must not omit from my story the fact that I had been married at Stettin. My wife, too, is a soldier's child, being the daughter of General von Sperling, who was Chief of Staff of the 6th Corps in 1866 and Chief of Staff of the 1st Army in 1870–1. He had died after the war with France.

I found in my wife a loving mate who shared with me loyally and untiringly my joys and sorrows, my cares and labours. She presented me with a son and two daughters. The son did his duty in the Great War as an officer on the General Staff. Both daughters are married, and their husbands likewise fought in the Great War.

In 1881 I was transferred to the 1st Division at Königsberg. This change gave me greater independence, brought me into closer contact with the troops, and took me back to my native province. After three years on the Staff of the 1st Division I was transferred to the command of a company in the 58th Infantry Regiment, stationed at Fraustadt in Posen.

In this return to regimental duty I was taking charge of a company which was recruited almost exclusively from Poles. I thus learned to know the very great difficulties which the ignorance of officers and men of each other's tongue placed in the way of a good understanding between them. I myself did not know Polish except for a few expressions which I had picked up in childhood. It was thus very difficult for me to have any influence on the company, and it was made even more difficult by the fact that the men were distributed in thirty-three civilian billets, even including the windmills on the outskirts of the town. Taking it all round, however, my experiences with Polish recruits were not unfortunate. The men were industrious, willing and – what I must particularly emphasize – devoted so long as I bore in mind their difficulties in learning their work, and also did all I could for their welfare.

In the summer of 1885 I was transferred to the Great General Staff. A few weeks later I was a major. I was in the department of Colonel Count von Schlieffen, subsequently General and Chief of the General Staff of the Army, but I was also placed at the disposal of the department of Colonel Vogel von Falkenstein, who was subsequently Corps Commander of the 8th Army Corps, and then Director of the Corps of Engineers and Pioneers. In this latter department I co-operated for more than a year in the first working-out of the Field Service Regulations, a fundamental code of instruction issued by His Majesty's command. I thus came into touch with the most distinguished departmental heads of that time.

In the spring of 1886 His Royal Highness, Prince William of Prussia, took part in the manœuvres at Zossen, which lasted several days. These were intended to provide a practical test of the soundness of the new regulations before they were actually introduced. It was the first time I had the honour of meeting him who later was to be my Kaiser, King and Master, William II. In the following winter the Prince attended a war game of the Great General Staff. On this occasion I was the commander of the 'Russian Army'.

It was in these years that Field-Marshal Count von Moltke handed over all direct business with the departments of the Great General Staff to his assistant, General Count Waldersee. But in spite of the change his spirit and prestige still governed everything. No special guarantee was required that Count Moltke should at all times be held in infinite honour, or that any of us could forget his wonderful influence.

Our first Emperor – a great Emperor – had left us three years before. I took part in the vigil in the Cathedral, and was permitted to render the last services there to my Imperial and Royal master, whom I so dearly loved. His son, the Emperor Frederick, Germany's pride and hope, was permitted to reign for but a short time. He died of an incurable disease a few months after his father. The Great General Staff was then away on a General Staff ride in East Prussia. We therefore took the oath to His Majesty the Emperor and King, William II, in Gumbinnen. I thus pledged my fealty to my present War Lord in the same spot at which twenty-six years later I was to translate it into action.

Fate was kind to me in that I found a very great variety of employment within the General Staff. Even while I was attached to the Great General Staff I was assigned the duty of teaching tactics at the *Kriegsakademie*. I derived great pleasure from this work, and continued it for five years. It is true that the demands on me were very great, as in addition to this I had to do other work simultaneously, both in the Great General Staff and subsequently as the first General Staff Officer with the Headquarters Staff of the

3rd Army Corps. In these circumstances the day of twenty-four hours often seemed too short. It was quite usual for me to work the whole night through.

My transfer to the War Ministry in 1889 brought me a totally different sphere of work. I there took over a section of the Common War Department. This change is attributable to the circumstance that my former divisional general, General von Verdy, had become War Minister, and summoned me to the Ministry when he remodelled it. I was therefore director of a section when I was still a major.

Although at the start this change did not correspond to my wishes and inclinations, I subsequently attached a very high value to the experience I gained by my occupation with affairs and a sphere of work which had hitherto been unknown to me. I had plenty of opportunity of becoming acquainted with formality and red tape (which are scarcely altogether avoidable) and the bureaucratic attitude of the minor officials. But I also came to realise the strong sense of duty with which everyone was imbued, though working at the highest pressure.

The most stimulating part of my work was the issue of Field Engineering regulations, and the initiation of the use of heavy artillery in an ordinary action. Both stood the test of the Great War.

But although I came to realise that my employment at the War Ministry had been extremely valuable to me, I was none the less very glad to be freed from the bureaucratic yoke when I was appointed to the command of the 91st Infantry Regiment at Oldenburg in 1893.

The position of commander of a regiment is the finest in the army. The commander sets the stamp of his personality on the regiment, and it is the regiment which carries on tradition in the army. The training of his officers, not only in service, but also in social matters, and the control and supervision of the training of the troops are his most important tasks. I endeavoured to cultivate a sense of chivalry among my officers, and efficiency and firm discipline in my battalions. I also fostered the love of work and independence side by side with a high ideal of service. The fact that infantry, artillery and cavalry were all comprised in the garrison gave me an opportunity for frequent exercises with combined arms.

On my appointment, in 1896, as Chief of Staff to the 8th Army Corps at Coblenz I came for the first time into close contact with our Rhine Provinces. The high spirits and friendly attitude of the Rhinelanders were particularly pleasant to me. To tell the truth, I had to get used to their habit of sliding over the serious questions of life, as also to their temperament, which is more sentimental than that of the North Germans.

As the result of my employment for nearly four years as Chief of Staff of an Army Corps I was so advanced in seniority that there was now no question of my appointment to the command of an infantry brigade. At the conclusion of that period I was therefore appointed to the command of the 28th Division at Karlsruhe in 1900. In the division all three arms were united for the first time under one command. The duties of a divisional commander are therefore more varied, and demand a sphere of activity which is principally concerned with the great business of war.

With a feeling of deep gratitude I left Karlsruhe in January, 1905, when the confidence of my All-Highest War Lord summoned me to the command of the 4th Army Corps. In assuming my new duties I took over a position of unlimited responsibility, a position which is usually held longer than other military posts and on which the holder, like the commander of a regiment, sets the stamp of his personality. I myself pursued the principles that had previously guided me, and I think I may claim some success. The affection of my subordinates, to which I had always attached high importance as one of the mainsprings of efficiency, was, at any rate, expressed in the most moving way when I left this splendid post after eight and a quarter years.

My military career had carried me much farther than I had ever dared to hope. There was no prospect of war, and as I recognised that it was my duty to make way for younger men, I applied in the year 1911 to be allowed to retire. It was anything but easy for me to put an end to a relationship that had lasted for years, a relationship that was very dear to me, and more especially to part from my 4th Corps, for which I had a great affection. But it had to be! I never suspected that within a few years I should gird on the sword again and, like my men, be permitted to serve my Army Corps, my Emperor and Empire, my King and Fatherland once again.

Part II

The Campaign in the East

Chapter Four

The Struggle for East Prussia

I
The Outbreak of War and My Recall

The unruffled course of my life after the year 1911 gave me a chance to devote my spare time to following political events in the world. What I thus saw was not indeed of a nature likely to fill me with satisfaction. I was not in the least anxious, but I could not get rid of a certain oppressive feeling. I was in a sense forced to the conclusion that we were venturing into the distant ocean of world politics before our foundations in Europe itself had been sufficiently secured. Whether the political storm-clouds hung over Morocco or gathered over the Balkans, I shared with the majority of my countrymen a vague feeling that our German foundations were being undermined. In recent years we had unquestionably been in the presence of one of those chauvinistic waves which seemed to recur at regular intervals in France. Their origin was known. They found their support in Russia or England – or both – quite indifferent to who or what was the open or secret, known or unknown driving force there.

I have never ignored the special difficulties with which German foreign policy has been faced. The dangers involved in our geographical situation, our economic necessities, and last, but not least, our frontier provinces with their mixed nationalities, stared us in the face. The policy of our enemies which succeeded in reconciling all their jealousies against us did not, in my opinion, require a high degree of skill. In the long run it was mainly responsible for the war. We neglected to make preparations to meet that danger. From the point of view of procuring allies our policy seemed to be inspired more by a code of honour than a proper regard for the needs of our people and our world situation.

To me as a soldier, the contrast between Austria-Hungary's political claims and her domestic and military resources was particularly striking. To meet the huge armaments with which Russia had restored her position after the war in Eastern Asia we Germans had certainly increased our defences, but we had not required the same measures of our Austro-Hungarian allies. It may have been a simple matter for the statesmen of the Danube Monarchy to meet all our suggestions for the increase of Austro-Hungarian armaments with a recital of their domestic difficulties, but how was it that we found no means of presenting Austria-Hungary with a definite alternative in this matter? We already knew of the enormous numerical superiority of our prospective enemies. Ought we to have permitted our allies to make no use of a large part of their national resources available for the common defence? What advantage was it for us to have Austria-Hungary as a bulwark far to the south-east, when this bulwark was cracked at points innumerable and did not dispose of enough defenders to man its walls?

From the earliest times it seemed to me doubtful to rely on any effective help from Italy. It was an uncertain quantity; questionable even if the Italian statesmen favoured the idea. We had had an excellent opportunity of realising the weaknesses of the Italian Army in the war in Tripoli. Since that war the situation of Italy had improved but little, thanks to the shaky condition of its finances. In any case, it was not ready to strike.

It was along such lines that my thoughts and anxieties moved in those years. I had already had two personal experiences of war, on both occasions under strong and resolute political leadership combined with clear and straightforward military objectives.

And now the war was upon us! The hopelessness of our prospects of compromising with France on the basis of the *status quo*, soothing England's commercial jealousy and fear of rivalry and satisfying Russia's greed without breaking faith with our Austrian Ally, had long created a feeling of tension in Germany, compared with which the outbreak of war was felt almost as a release from a perpetual burden we had carried all our lives. The soldier within me sprang to life again and dominated everything else. Would my Emperor and King need me? Exactly a year had passed without my receiving any official intimation of this kind. Enough younger men seemed available. I put myself in the hands of Fate and waited in longing expectation.

2
To the Front

THE news from the various theatres of war realised our hopes and wishes. Liége had fallen, the action at Mülhausen had come to a victorious conclusion, and our right wing and centre were passing through Belgium. The first news of the victory in Lorraine was just reaching the country, rejoicing all hearts. In the East, too, the trumpets of victory were sounding. Nowhere had anything happened which seemed to justify any anxiety.

At three o'clock in the afternoon of August 22 I received an inquiry from the Headquarters of His Majesty the Emperor as to whether I was prepared for immediate employment.

My answer ran: 'I am ready.'

Even before this telegram could have reached Main Headquarters I received another. It was to the effect that my willingness to accept a post in the field was assumed as a matter of course, and informed me that General Ludendorff was to be assigned to me. Further telegrams from Main Headquarters explained that I was to leave for the East immediately to take command of an army.

About three o'clock in the morning I went to the station, imperfectly equipped, as time had been short, and waited expectantly in the well-lit hall. It was only when the short special train steamed in that I wrenched my thoughts away from the hearth and home which I had had to leave so suddenly. General Ludendorff stepped briskly from the train and reported as my Chief of Staff of the 8th Army.

Before that moment the general had been a stranger to me, and I had not yet heard of his feats at Liége. He first explained the situation on the Eastern Front to me as communicated to him on August 22 at Main Headquarters (Coblenz) by Colonel-General von Moltke, Chief of the General Staff. It appeared that the operations of the 8th Army in East Prussia had taken the following course: At the opening of hostilities the army had left the 20th Army Corps, strengthened by fortress garrisons and other Landwehr formations in a position covering the southern frontier of East and West Prussia from the Vistula to the Lötzen Lakes. The main body of the army (1st and 17th Army Corps, 1st Reserve Corps, 3rd Reserve Division, the garrison of Königsberg, and the 1st Cavalry Division) had been concentrated on the Eastern frontier of East Prussia, and had there attacked the Russian Niemen Army, which was advancing under General Rennenkampf. There had been an action at Stallupönen on August 17, and another at Gumbinnen on the 19th and 20th. During the battle at Gumbinnen news had been received of the approach of the Russian Narew Army, under General Samsonoff, towards the German frontier between Soldau and Willenberg. The Commander of our 8th Army had therefore reason to expect that the Russians would have crossed that stretch of the frontier by the 20th. In view of this threat to their communications from the south, the Headquarters Staff broke off the action at Gumbinnen and reported to Main Headquarters that they were not in a position to hold the country east of the Vistula any longer.

General von Moltke had not approved of that decision. It was his opinion that an attempt must be made to destroy the Narew Army before we could think of abandoning East Prussia, so important from the military, economic and political point of view. The conflict between the views of Main Headquarters and those of the Army Headquarters Staff had necessitated a change in the command of the 8th Army.

At the moment the situation of this army appeared to be as follows: It had successfully shaken off the enemy. The 1st Army Corps and the 3rd Reserve Division were moving west by rail, while the 1st Reserve Corps and the 17th Army Corps were marching for the line of the Vistula. The 20th Army Corps was still in its positions on the frontier.

Before long I and my new Chief of Staff were at one in our view of the situation. Even while at Coblenz General Ludendorff had been able to issue such preliminary orders as brooked no delay, orders intended to secure the continuance of operations east of the Vistula. The most important of these was that the 1st Army Corps should not be brought too far west, but directed on Deutsch-Eylau, that is towards the enemy and behind the right wing of the 20th Corps. Everything else must and could be left for decision when we reached Army Headquarters at Marienburg. Our conference had taken scarcely more than half an hour. We then went to bed.

As I knew from my own experience, the relations between the Chief of Staff and his General, who has the responsibility, are not theoretically laid down in the German Army. The way in which they work together and the degree to which their powers are complementary are much more a matter of personality. The boundaries of their respective powers are therefore not clearly demarcated. If the relations between the General and his Chief of Staff are what they ought to be, these boundaries are easily adjusted by soldierly and personal tact and the qualities of mind on both sides.

I myself have often characterised my relations with General Ludendorff as those of a happy marriage. I realised that one of my principal tasks was, as far as possible, to give free scope to the intellectual powers, the almost superhuman capacity for work and untiring resolution of my Chief of Staff, and if necessary clear the way for him, the way in which our common desires and our common goal pointed – victory for our colours, the welfare of our Fatherland and a peace worthy of the sacrifices our nation had made.

The harmony of our military and political convictions formed the basis for our joint views as to the proper use of our resources. Differences of opinion were easily reconciled, without our relations being disturbed by a feeling of forced submission on either side. The hard work of my Chief of Staff translated our thoughts and plans into action at our Army Headquarters and, later, at Main Headquarters when the responsibilities of that post were entrusted to us. His influence inspired everyone, and no one could escape it without running the risk of finding himself off the common path. How otherwise could the enormous task have been done and full effect given to the driving force?

3
Tannenberg

Early in the afternoon of August 23 we reached our Headquarters at Marienburg. We thus entered the region east of the Vistula which was to form the immediate theatre of our operations. At this moment the situation at the front had undergone the following development:

The 20th Corps had been withdrawn from its positions on the frontier by Neidenburg to Gilgenburg and east of it. In touch with this corps on the west the garrisons of the fortresses of Thorn and Graudenz were along the frontier as far as the Vistula. The 3rd Division had arrived at Allenstein as a reinforcement for the 20th Army Corps. After considerable delay the entrainment of the 1st Army Corps for Deutsch-Eylau had begun. The 17th Corps and the 1st Reserve Corps had reached the neighbourhood of Gerdauen on foot. The 1st Cavalry Division was south of Insterburg facing Rennenkampf's army. The garrison of Königsberg had passed through Insterburg in its retreat to the west. With a few exceptions there were no noteworthy bodies of infantry of Rennenkampf's Niemen Army on the west side of the Angerapp. Of the two Russian cavalry corps one was reported close to Angerburg, the other west of Darkehmen. Of Samsonoff's Narew Army apparently one division had reached the neighbourhood of Ortelsburg, while Johannisburg was said to be in the enemy's possession. For the rest the main body of this army seemed to be still concentrating on the frontier with its western wing at Mlawa.

In the pocket-book of a dead Russian officer a note had been found which revealed the intention of the enemy Command. It told us that

Rennenkampf's Army was to pass the Masurian Lakes on the north and advance against the Insterburg–Angerburg line. It was to attack the German forces presumed to be behind the Angerapp while the Narew Army was to cross the Lötzen–Ortelsburg line to take the Germans in flank.

The Russians were thus planning a concentric attack against the 8th Army, but Samsonoff's Army now already extended farther west than was originally intended.

What indeed could we do to meet this dangerous enemy scheme? It was dangerous less on account of the audacity of the conception than by reason of the strength in which it was to be carried out – at any rate strength from the point of view of numbers. During the months of August and September Russia brought up no fewer than 800,000 men and 1,700 guns against East Prussia, for the defence of which we had only 210,000 German soldiers and 600 guns at our disposal.

Our counter-measures were simple. In the first place we opposed a thin centre to Samsonoff's solid mass. I say thin, not weak. For it was composed of men with hearts and wills of steel. Behind them were their homes, wives and children, parents and relatives and everything they had. It was the 20th Corps, brave East and West Prussians. This thin centre might bend under the enemy's pressure but it would not break. While this centre was engaged two important groups on its wings were to carry out the decisive attack.

The troops of the 1st Corps, reinforced by Landwehr – likewise sons of the threatened region – were brought for the battle from the right, the north-west, the troops of the 17th Corps and the 1st Reserve Corps, with a Landwehr brigade, from the left, the north and north-east. These men of the 17th Corps and 1st Reserve Corps as well as the Landwehr and Landsturm also had behind them everything which made life worth living.

We had not merely to win a victory over Samsonoff. We had to annihilate him. Only thus could we get a free hand to deal with the second enemy, Rennenkampf, who was even then plundering and burning East Prussia. It was thus a case for complete measures. Everything must be thrown in which could prove of the slightest use in manœuvre warfare and could at all be spared. The fortresses of Graudenz and Thorn disgorged yet more Landwehr fit for the field. Moreover, our Landwehr came from the trenches between the Masurian Lakes, which were covering our new operations in the east, and handed over the defence there to a smaller and diminishing number of Landsturm. Once we had won the battle in the field we should no longer need the fortresses of Thorn and Graudenz, and should be freed from anxieties as regards the defiles between the lakes.

Our cavalry division and the Königsberg garrison with two Landwehr brigades were to remain facing Rennenkampf, who might fall upon us like an avalanche from the north-east at any time. But at the moment we could not yet say whether these forces would really be sufficient. They formed but a light veil which would easily be torn if Rennenkampf's main columns moved or his innumerable cavalry squadrons advanced, as we had to fear. But perhaps they would not move. In that case the veil would be enough to cover our weakness. We had to take risks on our flanks and rear if we were to be strong at the decisive point. We hoped we might succeed in deceiving Rennenkampf. Perhaps he would deceive himself. The strong fortress of Königsberg with its garrison and our cavalry might assume the proportions of a mighty force in the imagination of the enemy.

But even supposing Rennenkampf cradled himself in illusions to our advantage, would not his High Command urge him forward in forced marches to the south-west – in our rear? Would not Samsonoff's cry for help bring him in hot haste to the battlefield? Caution with regard to Rennenkampf was therefore necessary, though we could not carry it to the extent of leaving strong forces behind, or we should find ourselves weaker on the battlefield than we ought to be.

Such was our plan and such our line of reasoning before and for the battle. We compressed these ideas and intentions into a short report which we sent from Marienburg to Main Headquarters on August 23:

'Concentration of the army for an enveloping attack in the region of the 20th Corps planned for August 26.'

On the evening of the 23rd I took a short walk on the western bank of the Nogat. From there the red walls of the proud castle of the Teutonic Knights, the greatest brick monument of Baltic Gothic, made a truly wonderful picture in the evening light. Thoughts of a noble chivalry of the past mingled involuntarily with conjecture as to the veiled future. The sight of the refugees flying past me from my home province deepened the sense of responsibility that possessed me. It was a melancholy reminder that war not only affects the fighting man, but proves a thousandfold scourge to humanity by the destruction of the very essentials of existence.

On August 24 I motored with my small Staff to the Headquarters of the 20th Corps, and thus entered the village which was to give its name to the battle so soon to blaze up.

Tannenberg! A word pregnant with painful recollections for German chivalry, a Slav cry of triumph, a name that is fresh in our memories after more than five hundred years of history. Before this day I had never seen the battlefield which proved so fateful to German culture in the East. A simple monument there bore silent witness to the deeds and deaths of heroes. On one of the following days we stood near this monument while Samsonoff's Russian Army was going to its doom of sheer annihilation.

Among the Staff at the Corps Headquarters I found the confidence and resolution which were essential for the success of our plan. Moreover, they had a favourable opinion of the *morale* of the troops at this spot, which was at first the crucial point for us.

The day brought us no decisive information either about Rennenkampf's operations or Samsonoff's movements. Apparently it only confirmed the fact that Rennenkampf was moving forward very slowly. We could not see the reason for this. Of the Narew Army, we knew that its main columns were pressing forward against the 20th Corps. Under its pressure this corps refused its left wing. There was nothing doubtful about this measure. Quite the contrary. The enemy, following up, would all the more effectively expose his right flank to our left enveloping column which was marching on Bischofsburg. On the other hand the hostile movement which was apparently in progress against our western wing and Lautenburg attracted our attention, as it caused us some anxiety. We had the impression that the Russians were thinking of enveloping us in turn at this point and coming in on the flank of our right column as it executed the enveloping movement we projected.

August 25 gave us a rather clearer picture of Rennenkampf's movements. His columns were marching from the Angerapp, and therefore on Königsberg. Had the original Russian plan been abandoned? Or had the Russian leaders been deceived by our movements and suspected that our main force was in and around the fortress? In any case we must now have not the slightest hesitation in leaving but a thin screen against Rennenkampf's mighty force. On this day Samsonoff, obviously feeling his way, was directing his main columns towards our 20th Corps. The corps on the Russian right wing was undoubtedly marching on Bischofsburg, and therefore towards our 17th Corps and 1st Reserve Corps, which had reached the district north of this village on this day. Apparently further large Russian forces were concentrating at Mlawa.

This day marked the conclusion of the stage of expectation and preparation. We brought our 1st Corps round to the right wing of the 20th Corps. The general attack could begin.

August 26 was the first day of the murderous combat which raged from Lautenburg to north of Bischofsburg. The drama on which the curtain was rising, and whose stage stretched for more than sixty miles, began not with a continuous battle line but in detached groups; not in one self-contained act, but in a series of scenes.

General von François was leading his brave East Prussians on the right wing. They pushed forward against Usdau with a view to storming the key to this part of the southern battle front next day. General von Scholtz's magnificent corps gradually shook off the chains of defence and addressed themselves to the business of attack. Fierce was the fighting round Bischofsburg that this day witnessed. By the evening magnificent work had been done on our side at this point. In a series of powerful blows the wing corps of Samsonoff's right had been defeated and forced to retreat on Ortelsburg by the troops of Mackensen and Below (10th Corps and 1st Reserve Corps), as well as Landwehr. But we could not yet realize how far-reaching our victory had been. The Staff expected to have to meet a renewed and stout resistance south of this day's battlefield on the following day. Yet was their confidence high.

It was now apparent that danger was threatening from the side of Rennenkampf. It was reported that one of his corps was on the march through Angerburg. Would it not find its way to the rear of our left enveloping force? Moreover, disquieting news came to us from the flank and rear of our western wing. Strong forces of Russian cavalry were in movement away there in the south. We could not find out whether they were being followed up by infantry. The crisis of the battle now approached. One question forced itself upon us. How would the situation develop if these mighty movements and the enemy's superiority in numbers delayed the decision for days? Is it surprising that misgivings filled many a heart, that firm resolution began to yield to vacillation, and that doubts crept in where a clear vision had hitherto prevailed? Would it not be wiser to strengthen our line facing Rennenkampf again and be content with half-measures against Samsonoff? Was it not better to abandon the idea of destroying the Narew Army in order to ensure ourselves against destruction?

We overcame the inward crisis, adhered to our original intention, and turned in full strength to effect its realisation by attack. So the order was issued for our right wing to advance straight on Neidenburg, and the left enveloping wing 'to take up its position at 4 A.M. and intervene with the greatest energy'.

August 27 showed that the victory of the 1st Reserve Corps and 17th Corps at Bischofsburg on the previous day had had far-reaching results. The enemy had not only retired, but was actually fleeing from the battlefield. Moreover, we learned that it was only in the imagination of an airman that Rennenkampf was marching in our rear. The cold truth was that he was slowly pressing on to Königsberg. Did he, or would he, not see that Samsonoff's right flank was already threatened with utter ruin and that the danger to his left wing also was increasing from hour to hour? For it was on this day that François and Scholtz stormed the enemy's lines at and north of Usdau and defeated our southern opponent.

Now, when the enemy's centre pushed forward farther towards Allenstein–Hohenstein, it was no longer victory but destruction that lured it on. For us the situation was clear. On the evening of this day we gave orders for the complete encirclement of the enemy's central mass, his 13th and 15th Corps.

The bloody struggle continued to rage on August 28. On the 29th a large part of the Russian Army saw itself faced with total annihilation at Hohenstein. Ortelsburg was reached from the north, Willenberg, through Neidenburg, from the west. The ring round thousands and thousands of Russians began to close. Even in this desperate situation there was plenty of Russian heroism in the cause of the Tsar, heroism which saved the honour of arms but could no longer save the battle.

Meanwhile Rennenkampf was continuing to march quietly on Königsberg. Samsonoff was lost at the very moment when his comrade was to give proof of other and better military qualities. For we were already in a position to draw troops from the battle front to cover the work of destruction in which we were engaged in the great cauldron, Neidenburg–Willenberg–Passenheim, and in which Samsonoff sought for death in his despair. Swelling columns of prisoners poured out of this cauldron. These were the growing proofs of the greatness of our victory. By a freak of fortune it was in Osterode, one of the villages which we made our Headquarters during the battle, that I received one of the two captured Russian Corps Commanders, in the same inn at which I had been quartered during a General Staff ride in 1881 when I was a young Staff officer. The other reported to me next day at a school which we had converted into an office.

As the battle proceeded we were able to observe what splendid raw material, generally speaking, the Tsar had at his disposal. I had the impression that it doubtless contained many qualities worth training. As in 1866 and 1870, I noticed on this occasion how quickly the German officer and soldier, with their fine feeling and professional tact, forgot the former foe in the helpless captive. The lust of battle in our men quickly ebbed away and changed to deep sympathy and human feeling. It was only against the Cossacks that our men could not contain their rage. They were considered the authors of all the bestial brutalities under which the people and country of East Prussia had suffered so cruelly. The Cossack apparently suffered from a bad conscience, for whenever he saw himself likely to be taken prisoner he did his best to remove the broad stripe on his trousers which distinguished his branch of the service.

On August 30 the enemy concentrated fresh troops in the south and east and attempted to break our encircling ring from without. From Myszaniec – that is, from the direction of Ostrolenka – he brought up new and strong columns to Neidenburg and Ortelsburg against our troops, which had already completely enveloped the Russian centre and were therefore presenting their rear to the new foe. There was danger ahead; all the more so because airmen reported that enemy columns twenty-three miles long – therefore very strong – were pressing forward from Mlawa. Yet we refused to let go of our quarry. Samsonoff's main force had to be surrounded and annihilated; François and Mackensen sent their reserves – weak reserves, it is true – to meet the new enemy. Against their resistance the attempt to mitigate the catastrophe to Samsonoff came to nought. While despair seized on those within the deadly ring, faint-heartedness paralysed the energies of those who might have brought their release.

Rennenkampf appears to have intended to attack the line of the Deime, east of Königsberg and between Labiau and Tapiau, this day. From the region of Landsberg and Bartenstein his masses of cavalry were approaching the battlefield of Tannenberg. However, we had already concentrated strong forces, weary but flushed with victory, for defence in the neighbourhood of Allenstein.

On August 31 I was able to send the following report to my Emperor and King:

'I beg most humbly to report to Your Majesty that the ring round the larger part of the Russian Army was closed yesterday. The 13th, 15th and 18th Army Corps have been destroyed. We have already taken more than 60,000 prisoners, among them the Corps Commanders of the 13th and 15th Corps. The guns are still in the forests and are now being brought in. The booty is immense though it cannot yet be assessed in detail. The Corps outside our ring, the 1st and 6th, have also suffered severely and are now retreating in hot haste through Mlawa and Myszaniec.'

4
The Battle of the Masurian Lakes

The sound of battle on the field of Tannenberg had hardly died down before we had begun to make our preparations for the attack on Rennenkampf's

Russian Army. On August 31 we received the following telegraphic instructions from Main Headquarters:

11th Corps, Guard Reserve Corps and 8th Cavalry Division are placed at your disposal. Their transport has begun. The first task of the 8th Army is to clear East Prussia of Rennenkampf's army.

It is desired that with such troops as you can spare you should follow up the enemy you have just beaten in the direction of Warsaw, bearing in mind the Russian movements from Warsaw on Silesia.

When the situation in East Prussia has been restored you are to contemplate employing the 8th Army in the direction of Warsaw.

These orders were exactly what the situation required. They gave us a clear objective and left the ways and means to us. We considered we had reason to believe that what was left of Samsonoff's quondam army was a remnant which had already withdrawn to the shelter of the Narew or was on its way there. We had to count on its being reinforced. But that could not be for a considerable time. For the moment it appeared that all that was required was that this remnant should be watched by weak troops along the line of our southern frontier. Everything else must be assembled for the new battle. Even the arrival of the reinforcements from the West did not, in our opinion, enable us to employ forces in striking south over the line of the Narew.

It was quite clear what the word 'Warsaw' meant in the second part of the order. In accordance with the plan of joint operations the armies of Austria-Hungary were to take the offensive from Galicia in the direction of Lublin, exercising their main pressure on the eastern portion of Russian Poland, while German forces in East Prussia were to hold out a hand to their allies across the Narew. It was a largely conceived, fine plan, but in the existing situation it produced grave embarrassments. It did not take account of the fact that Austria-Hungary had sent a large army to the Serbian frontier, that 800,000 Russians had been sent against East Prussia, least of all that it had been betrayed with all its details to the Russian General Staff in peace time.

The Austro-Hungarian Army, after making a hazardous attack on superior Russian forces, was now involved in critical frontal battles, while at the moment we were not in a position to render any direct assistance, though we were holding up large hostile forces. Our Allies had to try and hold on until we had beaten Rennenkampf too. Only then could we come to their help, if not in full strength at least with our main forces.

As is known, Rennenkampf was then on the Deime – Allenburg – Gerdauen – Angerburg line. We did not know what the enemy had by way of secrets in the region south-east of the Masurian Lakes. The district of Grajevo was suspicious in any case. A good deal of movement was on foot there. Even more suspicious was the whole area behind the Niemen Army. In that quarter there was a continuous movement of trains and marching columns. Apparently that movement was to the west and south-west. Rennenkampf had doubtless received reinforcements. The Russian reserve divisions from the interior were now ready to take the field. Perhaps all that had hitherto been available were single corps which the Russian High Command believed they no longer needed against the Austrians in Poland. Would these units be sent to Rennenkampf or brought up near him, either to give him direct support or to strike at us from some unsuspected quarter?

We had therefore to be at once cautious and bold. It was this dual require-ment which gave their peculiar character to the movements we now initi-ated. We first established our front on a broad arc from Willenburg to the outskirts of Königsberg. This took us until September 5, broadly speaking. Then our line moved forward. Four corps (the 20th, 11th, 1st Reserve and Guard Reserve) and the troops from Königsberg advanced against the enemy's front on the Angerburg–Deime line. Two corps (the 1st and 17th) were to push through the lake region. The 3rd Reserve Division, as the right echelon of our enveloping wing, had to follow south of the Masurian Lakes, while the 1st and 8th Cavalry Divisions had to be held in readiness behind the main columns, to range at large as soon as the lake defiles were forced. Such were the forces against Rennenkampf's flank. So the scheme differed from the movements which had led to the victory of Tannenberg. This grouping of our columns was imposed upon us by the necessity of securing ourselves against Rennenkampf's strong reserves. In this way fourteen infantry divisions were told off to attack the front, in spite of the fact that its breadth was more than ninety-five miles.

On the 6th and 7th we were approaching the Russian lines and began to see rather more clearly. There were strong Russian columns near Insterburg and Wehlau, perhaps even stronger ones north of Nordenburg. They made no movement at first, and in no way interfered with us as we deployed for battle before their lines.

The two corps on our right (1st and 17th) began to force their way through the chain of lakes on September 7, while at Bialla the 3rd Reserve Division shattered half of the Russian 20th Corps in a brilliant action. We were entering upon the crisis of our new operations. The next few days would show whether Rennenkampf intended to attempt a counter-attack and whether his resolution to do so was as great as his resources. To add to his already formidable superiority three more reserve divisions appeared to have reached the battlefield. Was the Russian commander still waiting for more? Russia had more than three million fighting men on her western front, while the Austro-Hungarian armies and ourselves had scarcely a third of that number.

The battle blazed up along the whole front on September 8. Our frontal attack made no progress, but things went better on our right wing. In that quarter two corps had broken through the enemy's lake defences and were turning north and north-east. Our objective was now the enemy's line of communications. Our cavalry appeared to have an open road in that direction.

On the 9th the battle raged further. On the front from Angerburg to the Kurisches Haff it had no appreciable result, but our bold thrust east of the lakes made headway, although the two cavalry divisions were not able to break down the unexpected resistance they encountered with the speed we could have wished. The 3rd Reserve Division defeated an enemy several times its own strength at Lyck, and thus freed us once and for all from danger in the south.

How were things going in the north? Our airmen believed they could now clearly identify two enemy corps at and west of Insterburg, as well as see another marching on Tilsit. What would be the fate of our corps, strung out fighting on a long front if a Russian avalanche of more than a hundred battalions, led by resolute wills, descended upon them? Yet it is easy to understand what our wishes and words were on the evening of this September 9: 'Rennenkampf, come what may, do not abandon this front of yours we cannot force. Win your laurels with the attack of your centre.' We had now full confidence that by resolutely pressing home our attack on the wing we could snatch back such laurels from the Russian leader. Unfortunately the Russian commander knew what we were thinking. He had not sufficient determination to meet our plans with force, and lowered his arms.

In the night of September 9–10 our patrols entered the enemy's trenches near Gerdauen and found them empty. 'The enemy is retreating.' The report seemed to us incredible. The 1st Reserve Corps immediately pressed forward against Insterburg from Gerdauen. We urged caution. It was only about midday of the 10th that we were compelled to accept the improbable and unpalatable fact. The enemy had actually begun a general retreat, even though he offered a stout resistance here and there, and indeed threw heavy columns against us in disconnected attacks. It was now our business to draw the corps and cavalry divisions on our right wing sharply north-east, and set them at the enemy's communications with Insterburg and Kovno.

On we pressed! If ever impatience was comprehensible it was comprehensible now. Rennenkampf was retiring steadily. He, too, seemed to be impatient. Yet our impatience was in striving for victory, while his brought him confusion and dissolution.

Some of the corps of the Niemen Army were marching back into Russia in three columns very close together.

The movement was effected but slowly, as it had to be covered by strong rearguards which kept back the Germans who were following up hard. September 11, in particular, was a day of bloody fighting from Goldap right to the Pregel.

In the evening of that day it was quite clear to us that only a few days more remained for us to carry out the pursuit. The development of the general situation in the Eastern theatre was having its effect. We suspected, rather than gathered from the definite reports which reached us, that the operations of our allies in Poland and Galicia had failed! In any case, it was no good thinking of our thrust across the Niemen in Rennenkampf's rear. But if our operation at the last moment was not to prove a failure within the framework of the whole allied plan, the enemy's army must at least reach the protection of the Niemen sector so weakened and shaken that the bulk of our troops could be released for that co-operation with the Austro-Hungarian Army which had become urgently necessary.

On September 18 the 3rd Reserve Division reached Suvalki on Russian soil. Rennenkampf's southern wing escaped envelopment by our 1st Corps south of Stallupönen by the skin of its teeth. Brilliant were the feats of several of our units engaged in the pursuit. They marched and fought and marched again until the men were dropping down from fatigue. On the other hand, it was on this day that we were able to withdraw the Guard Reserve Corps from the battle-front and hold it ready for further operations.

On September 10 our troops reached Eydtkuhnen, firing in the back of the Russian horde fleeing before them. Our artillery blew great gaps in the tightly packed masses, but the herding instinct filled them up again. Unfortunately we did not reach the great main road from Wirballen to Wylkowyszki this day. The enemy knew that this would spell annihilation to many of his columns which nothing now could stop. He therefore scraped together everything he had in the way of battle-worthy units, and threw them against our exhausted troops south of the road. We had only one day more for the pursuit. By the next Rennenkampf's forces would have taken refuge in that region of forest and marsh which lies west of the Olita–Kovno–Wileny sector of the Niemen. We should not be able to follow them there.

On September 15 the fighting was over. After a pursuit of more than sixty miles, a distance we had covered within four days, the battle of the Masurian

Lakes had ended on Russian soil. When the fighting concluded, the bulk of our units were fit for fresh employment elsewhere.

I have no room here to speak of the brilliant exploit performed during these days by Von der Goltz's Landwehr Division and other Landwehr formations in their battles with enemy forces many times their own strength in the region of our southern frontier, and while covering our right flank almost as far as the Vistula. By the time these actions were concluded, my command of the 8th Army had come to an end. At that point our troops had pressed forward to Ciechanov, Prassnysz and Augustovo.

Chapter Five

The Campaign in Poland

I
I Leave the Eighth Army

At the beginning of September we had heard from the Headquarters of the Austro-Hungarian Army that their armies in the neighbourhood of Lemberg were in serious peril and that a halt had been called to the further advance of the Austro-Hungarian 1st and 4th Armies.

Since that time we had followed events in that quarter with great anxiety and received further and worse reports. The following telegrams throw the best light on the sequence of events:

From us to Main Headquarters on September 10, 1914.

> It seems to me questionable whether Rennenkampf can be decisively beaten as the Russians have begun to retreat early this morning. As regards plans for the future there is a question of concentrating an army in Silesia. Could we rely on further reinforcement from the west? We can dispense with two corps from this front.

This was sent on September 10, the very day on which Rennenkampf had begun that retirement to the east which had so much surprised us.

Telegram from Main Headquarters to us on September 13:

> Release two corps as soon as possible and prepare them for transport to Cracow. . . .

Cracow? That sounded odd! We thought so, and said even more on the subject. In our perplexity we wired as follows to Main Headquarters on September 13:

71

Pursuit ended this morning. Victory appears complete. Offensive against the Narew in a decisive direction is possible in about ten days. On the other hand Austria, anxious about Rumania, asks direct support by the concentration of the army at Cracow and in Upper Silesia. For that, four army corps and one cavalry division are available. Railway transport alone would take about twenty days. Further long marches to the Austrian left wing. Help would come too late there. Immediate decision required. In any case the army must retain its independence there.

This was on the day on which Rennenkampf was beginning to vanish into the marshes of the Niemen with the loss of not merely a few feathers, but a whole wing, and grievously stricken as well.

On September 14 Main Headquarters replied to us as follows:

In the present situation of the Austrians an operation over the Narew is no longer considered hopeful. Direct support of the Austrians is required on political grounds.

It is a question of operations from Silesia. . . .

The independence of the army will be retained even in case of joint operations with the Austrians.

So that was it!

On September 15 I had to part from General Ludendorff. He had been appointed Chief of Staff of the newly formed 9th Army. On September 17, however, His Majesty gave orders that I was to take over the command of this army while retaining my control of the 8th Army which had been left behind to protect East Prussia, but was now reduced by the loss of the 11th, 17th and 20th Corps, as well as the 1st Cavalry Division, which had been given up for the 9th Army. The separation from my Chief of Staff was therefore truly a short one and in the early morning hours of September 18 I left the Headquarters of the 8th Army at Insterburg for a two days' journey by car across Poland to the Silesian capital, Breslau.

2
The Advance

We had come to the conclusion that our best course was to concentrate our army in the region of Kreuznach in Central Silesia. From there we thought we should have more room to manoeuvre against the northern flank of the Russian Army group in Poland, the exact position of which had not been established at the moment.

We therefore concentrated our troops (11th, 17th, 20th, Guard Reserve Corps, Woyrsch's Landwehr Corps, the 35th Reserve Division and the 8th Cavalry Division) north of Cracow in that closest touch with the left wing of the Austro-Hungarian Army which Main Headquarters had ordered. Our own Headquarters were fixed for a time at Beuthen, in Upper Silesia. The Austro-Hungarian Command were sending from Cracow a weak army of only four infantry divisions and one cavalry division north of the Vistula. They did not think they could spare anything more from the south side of the river, for they themselves were bent on a decisive attack in that quarter. This plan of our Allies was certainly bold and did credit to its authors. The only question was whether there was any prospect that, in spite of all the reinforcement it had received, the greatly weakened army could carry it into execution. My doubts were tempered by the hope that as soon as the Russians had noticed the presence of German troops in Poland they would throw their full weight against us and thereby facilitate the victory of our Allies.

The picture of the situation which we drew for ourselves when the movements began was somewhat vague. All we knew for certain was that the Russians had only been following the retiring Austro-Hungarian armies over the San very slowly of late. Further, there were signs that north of the Vistula there were six or seven Russian cavalry divisions and an unknown number of brigades of frontier guards. A Russian army seemed to be in process of formation at Ivangorod. Apparently some of the troops of this army had been drawn from the armies which had previously faced us in East Prussia while others had come fresh from Asiatic Russia. Further, we had received reports that a great entrenched position west of Warsaw and fronting west was in course of construction. We were therefore marching into a situation which was quite obscure, and must be prepared for surprises.

We entered Russian Poland and immediately realised the full meaning of what a French general, in his description of the Napoleonic campaign of 1806 in which he had taken part, called a special feature of military operations in this region – mud! And it really *was* mud in every form, not only mud in the natural sense, but mud in the so-called human habitations and even on the inhabitants themselves. Our movements were thus rendered extraordinarily difficult by the state of the roads. The enemy obtained an inkling of what we were doing and took counter-measures. He withdrew half a dozen corps from his front against the Austrians with the obvious intention of throwing them across the Vistula south of Ivangorod for a frontal attack upon us.

On October 6 we crossed the line Opatow–Radom and reached the Vistula. We here drove back such portions of the enemy's forces as were west

of the river. At this point it was apparent that our northern flank was threatened from the Warsaw–Ivangorod line. In these circumstances it was impossible, for the time being, to continue our operation across the Vistula south
of Ivangorod in an easterly direction. We must first deal with the enemy in
the north. Everything else depended on the issue of the considerable actions
which were to be expected in that quarter. A curious strategic situation was
thus developing. While hostile corps from Galicia were making for Warsaw
on the far side of the Vistula our own corps were moving in the same
northerly direction but on this side of the river. To hold up our movement
to the left the enemy threw large forces across the Vistula at and below
Ivangorod. In a series of severe actions these were thrown back on their
crossing-places, but we were not in a position to clear the western bank
entirely of the enemy. Two days' march south of Warsaw our left wing came
into touch with a superior enemy force and threw it back against the fortress.
About one day's march from the *enceinte* our attack came to a standstill.

On the battlefield south of Warsaw our most important capture was a
Russian Army order which fell into our hands and gave us a clear picture of
the enemy's strength and intentions. From the confluence of the San to
Warsaw it appeared that we had four Russian armies to cope with, that is
about sixty divisions, against eighteen of ours. From Warsaw alone fourteen
enemy divisions were being employed against five on our side. That meant
224 Russian battalions to 60 German. The enemy's superiority was
increased by the fact that as a result of the previous fighting in East Prussia
and France, as well as the long and exhausting marches of more than two
hundred miles over indescribable roads, our troops had been reduced to
scarcely half establishment, and in some cases even to a quarter of their original strength. And these weakened units of ours were to meet fresh arrivals
at full strength – the Siberian Corps, the élite of the Tsar's Empire!

The enemy's intention was to hold us fast along the Vistula while a
decisive attack from Warsaw was to spell our ruin. We accordingly decided,
while maintaining our hold of the Vistula upstream from Ivangorod, to
bring up from that quarter to our left wing all the troops we could possibly
release, and hurl them at the enemy south of Warsaw in the hope of
defeating him before his fresh masses could put in an appearance.

We asked Austria-Hungary to send everything she could spare in the way
of troops in hot haste left of the Vistula against Warsaw. The Austrian High
Command showed that they fully realised the situation, but at the same time
raised doubts which were hardly in keeping with the emergency. Austria-
Hungary, to whose help we had rushed, was quite prepared to support us
but only by the tedious method – which involved a loss of time – of taking

over from the troops we had left on the line of the Vistula. This would certainly enable us to avoid the mingling of Austro-Hungarian and German units, but it put the whole operation in danger of miscarriage. Counter-proposals from our side led to no result, so we yielded to the wishes of Austria-Hungary in the matter.

3
The Retreat

What we had feared actually materialised. Fresh masses of troops poured forth from Warsaw and crossed the Vistula below it. Our far-flung battle-line was firmly held in front while superior enemy forces, reaching out farther and farther west, threatened to roll up our left flank. The situation could and should not be allowed to remain thus. Our whole joint plan of operations was in danger of not only floundering in the marshes – but of failing altogether. Indeed, it could be said that it had failed already, since the victory we hoped for in Galicia, south of the upper Vistula, had not materialised, although the enemy had brought great masses from there to meet the 9th Army and had therefore weakened himself against our allies. In any case we had to take the unwelcome decision, a decision which was received very unwillingly by the troops at first, to break away clear of the threatened envelopment and find a way out of our perils by other paths. In the night of October 18–19 the battlefield of Warsaw was abandoned to the enemy. With a view to continuing the operation even now, we brought the troops fighting under Mackensen before Warsaw back to the Rawa–Lowicz line, i.e. about forty miles west of the fortress. We hoped that the enemy would hurl himself against this position, which faced east. With the troops which had been relieved by the Austrians before Ivangorod in the south we would then attempt a decisive blow at the main body of the Russian Army group in the bend of the Vistula. A condition precedent to the execution of this plan was that Mackensen's troops should withstand the onslaught of the Russian hordes and that the Austrian defence of the line of the Vistula should be so strong that the thrust we intended would be safe from any Russian flank movement from the east. In view of the strength of the Vistula line this appeared an easy task for our allies. The Austrian High Command, however, made it much more difficult by their intention, good enough in itself, to attempt a great blow themselves. They decided to leave the crossings of the Vistula at and north of Ivangorod open to the enemy with a view to falling upon the enemy columns as they were in the act of crossing. It was a bold scheme which had often been discussed and executed in war-games and manœuvres in peace, and even in war carried out in brilliant fashion by Field-Marshal Blücher and his Gneisenau at the Katzbach. But it is always a hazardous operation, particularly when the general is not absolutely sure of his troops. We therefore advised against it. But in vain! Superior Russian forces pressed over the Vistula at Ivangorod. The Austrian counter-attack gained no success and was soon paralysed, and finally converted into a retreat.

Of what use was it now to us that the first Russian onslaughts on Mackensen's new front failed? The withdrawal of our Allies had uncovered the right flank of our proposed attack. We had to abandon this operation. I considered that our best course was to continue our retreat and thus break away with a view to being able to employ our army for another blow elsewhere later on. It was in our Headquarters at Radom that the idea took shape within me, at first only in outline, but yet clear enough to serve as a basis for further measures.

I must admit that serious doubts mingled with my resolution. What would the Homeland say when our retreat approached its frontiers? Was it remarkable that terror reigned in Silesia? Its inhabitants would think of how the Russians had laid waste East Prussia, of robbing and looting, the deportation of non-combatants, and other horrors. Fertile Silesia, with its highly developed coal mines and great industrial areas, both as vital to our military operations as daily bread itself! It is not an easy thing in war to stand with your hand on the map and say: 'I am going to evacuate this region!' You must be an economist as well as a soldier. Ordinary human feelings also assert themselves. It is often these last which are the hardest to overcome.

Our retreat in the general direction of Czenstochau began on October 27. The thorough destruction of all roads and railways was to hold back the solid Russian masses until we had got quite clear and found time to initiate fresh operations. The army pressed behind the Widawka and Warta with its left wing in the neighbourhood of Sieradz. Headquarters went to Czenstochau. At first the Russians were hot on our heels, but then the distance between us began to increase.

At this point I cannot help admitting how much the punctual knowledge of the dangers that threatened us was facilitated by the incomprehensible lack of caution, I might almost say *naïveté*, with which the Russians used their wireless. By tapping the enemy wireless we were often enabled not only to learn what the situation was, but also the intentions of the enemy. In spite of this exceptionally favourable circumstance, the situation that was developing made quite heavy enough demands on the nerves of the Command on account of the great numerical superiority of the enemy.

However, I knew that we had our subordinate commanders firmly in hand and had unshakable confidence that the men in the ranks would do everything that was humanly possible. It was this co-operation of all concerned that enabled us to overcome the most dangerous crisis. Yet did it not look as if our final ruin had only been postponed for a time? The enemy certainly thought so and rejoiced. Apparently he considered that we were completely beaten. This seems to have been his view of our plight, for on November 1 his wireless ran: 'Having followed the enemy up for more than 120 versts it is time to hand over the pursuit to the cavalry. The infantry are tired and supply is difficult.' We could therefore take breath and embark on fresh operations.

On this November 1 His Majesty the Emperor appointed me Commander-in-Chief of all the German forces in the East, and at the same time extended my sphere of command over the German eastern frontier provinces. General Ludendorff remained my Chief of Staff. The command of the 9th Army was entrusted to General von Mackensen. We were thus relieved of direct command of the army, but our influence on the whole organisation was all the more far-reaching.

We selected Posen as our Headquarters. Yet even before we took up residence there we had, at Czenstochau on November 3, come to the final decision as to our new operations.

4
Our Counter-attack

The consideration that formed the basis of our new plan was this: In the existing situation, if we tried to deal purely frontally with the attack of the Russian 4th Army, a battle against overwhelming Russian superiority would take the same course as that before Warsaw. It was not thus that Silesia would be saved from a hostile invasion. The problem of saving Silesia could only be solved by an offensive. Such an offensive against the front of a far superior enemy would simply be shattered to pieces. We had to find the way to his exposed, or merely slightly protected flank. The raising of my left hand explained what I meant at the first conference. If we felt for the enemy's northern wing in the region of Lodz we must transfer to Thorn the forces to be employed in the attack. We accordingly planned our new concentration between that fortress and Gnesen. In so doing we were putting a great distance between ourselves and the Austro-Hungarian left wing. Only comparatively weak German forces, including Woyrsch's exhausted Landwehr Corps, were to be left behind in the neighbourhood of Czenstochau. It was a condition precedent to our flanking movement by the left that the Austro-Hungarian High Command should relieve those of our forces moving north in the region of Czenstochau by four infantry divisions from the Carpathian front, which was not threatened at this time.

For our new concentration in the region of Thorn and Gnesen all the Allied forces in the East were distributed among three great groups. The first was formed by the Austro-Hungarian Army on both sides of the upper Vistula, the two others of our 8th and 9th Armies. We were not able to fill the gaps between the three groups with really good fighting troops. We had to put what were practically newly formed units into the sixty-mile gap between the Austrians and our 9th Army. The offensive capacity of these troops was pretty low to start with, and yet we had to spread them out so much along the front of very superior Russian forces that to all intents and purposes they formed but a thin screen. From the point of view of numbers, the Russians had only to walk into Silesia to sweep away their resistance with ease and certainty. Between the 9th Army at Thorn and the 8th on the eastern frontier of East Prussia we had practically nothing but frontier guards reinforced by the garrisons of Thorn and Graudenz. Facing these troops was a strong Russian group of about four army corps north of Warsaw on the northern banks of the Vistula and the Narew. If this Russian group had been sent forward through Mlawa the situation which had developed at the end of August before the Battle of Tannenberg would have been repeated. The line of retreat of the 8th Army therefore appeared to be once more seriously threatened. From the critical situation in Silesia and East Prussia we were to be released by the offensive of the 9th Army in the direction of Lodz against the flank of the Russian main mass which was only weakly protected. It is obvious that if the attack of this army did not get home quickly the enemy masses would concentrate upon it from all sides. The danger of this was all the greater because we were not numerically strong enough, nor were our troops good enough in quality, to pin down the Russian forces in the bend of the Vistula, as well as the enemy corps north of the middle Vistula, by strong holding attacks, or indeed mislead them for any considerable length of time. In spite of all this we intended to make our troops attack everywhere, but it would have been a dangerous error to expect too much from this.

Everything in the way of good storm troops had to be brought up to reinforce the 9th Army. It was to deliver the decisive blow. However great was the threat to the 8th Army, it had to give up two corps to the 9th. Under these circumstances it was no longer possible to continue the defence of the recently freed province on the Russian side of the frontier; our lines had to be withdrawn to the Lake region and the Angerapp. This was not an easy decision. As the result of the measures of which I have spoken the total strength of the 9th Army was brought up to about five and a half corps and five cavalry divisions. Two of the latter had come from the Western Front. In spite of our earnest representations Main Headquarters could not see their way to release further units from that side. At this moment they were still hoping for a favourable issue to the Battle of Ypres. The full extent and meaning of the difficulties of a war on two fronts were revealing themselves once more.

The lack of numbers on our side had again to be made good by speed and energy. I felt quite sure that in this respect the command and the troops would do everything that was humanly possible. By November 10 the 9th Army was ready. On the 11th it was off, with its left wing along the Vistula and its right north of the Warta. It was high time, for news had reached us that the enemy also intended to take the offensive. An enemy wireless betrayed to us that the armies of the north-west front, in other words all the Russian armies from the Baltic to, and including Poland, would start for a deep invasion of Germany on November 14. We took the initiative out of the hands of the Russian Commander-in-Chief, and when he heard of our operation on the 13th he did not dare to venture on his great blow against Silesia, but threw in all the troops he could lay hands on to meet our attack. For the time being Silesia was thus saved, and the immediate purpose of our scheme was achieved. Would we be able to go one better and secure a great decision? The enemy's superiority was enormous at all points. Yet I hoped for great things!

It would exceed the limits of this book if I were now to give a summary, however general, of the military events which are compressed into the designation 'Battle of Lodz'. In its rapid changes from attack to defence, enveloping to being enveloped, breaking through to being broken through, this struggle reveals a most confusing picture on both sides. A picture which in its mounting ferocity exceeded all the battles that had previously been fought on the Eastern Front!

The battles of this Polish campaign, however, did not end with Lodz, but were continuously fed by both sides. More troops came to us from the West, but they were anything but fresh. Most of them were willing enough, but they were half exhausted. Some of them had come from an equally hard, perhaps harder struggle – the Battle of Ypres – than we had just fought. In spite of that, we tried with them to force back the Russian flood we had successfully dammed. And indeed for a long time it looked as if we should succeed. But in the long run, as in the battle of Lodz, it was seen that once more our forces were not sufficient for this contest with the most over-whelming superiority which faced us in every battle. We should have been able to do more if our reinforcements had not come up in driblets. We should have been able to put them in simultaneously. But the colossal block we tried to roll back to the east only moved a short stretch, then lay still, and nothing would shift it. Our energies flagged. But it was not only in battle that they were dissipated, but also in – the marshes!

The approach of winter laid its paralysing hand on the activity of friend and foe alike. The line which had already become rigid in battle was now covered with snow and ice. The question was who would be the first to shake this line from its torpor in the coming months?

Chapter Six

1915

I
The Question of a Decision

The achievements of Germany and the German Army in the year 1914 will only be appreciated in all their heroic greatness when truth and justice have free play once more, when our enemies' attempt to mislead world opinion by propaganda is unmasked, and when Germany's passion for self-criticism to the point of self-mutilation has made way for a quiet, judicial examination. I have no doubt that all this will come in due course.

Yet in spite of all our achievements the mighty work that had been forced upon us was not crowned with success. Up to this point our battles had saved us for the time being, but they had not brought us final victory. The first step to such a consummation was a decision on at least one of our fronts. We had to get out of the military, political and economic ring that had been forged about us, a ring which threatened to squeeze the breath out of our bodies even in a moral sense. The reasons why victory had hitherto escaped us were debatable, and they will remain debatable. The fact remains that our High Command believed themselves compelled prematurely to draw away to the East strong forces from the West, where they were trying to secure a rapid decision. Whether an exaggerated idea of the extent of the successes hitherto obtained in the West had a great effect on that decision must remain uncertain. Whatever the cause, the result was half-measures. One objective was abandoned; the other was never reached.

In many a conversation with officers who had some knowledge of the course of events in the western theatre in August and September, 1914, I have tried to get an unbiased opinion about the transactions which proved so fateful for us in the so-called 'Battle of the Marne'. I do not believe that one single cause can make our great plan of campaign, unquestionably the right one, responsible. A whole series of unfavourable influences was our undoing. To these I must add (1) the watering-down of our fundamental scheme of deploying with a strong right wing; (2) the fact that through mistaken independent action on the part of subordinate commanders, our left wing, which had been made too strong, allowed itself to be firmly held; (3) ignorance of the danger to be apprehended from the strongly fortified, great railway-nexus of Paris; (4) insufficient control of the movements of the armies by the High Command; (5) perhaps also the fact that at the critical moment of the battle certain subordinate commands were not in close enough touch with a situation not in itself unfavourable.

May I, however, here express a decided opinion that the failure of our first operation in the West brought us into a position of great peril, but in no way made the further prosecution of the war hopeless for us. If I had not been firmly convinced of this I should have deemed it my duty, even in the autumn of 1914, to make appropriate representations to higher authority, even to my All-Highest War Lord himself. Our army had displayed qualities so brilliant and so superior to those of all our enemies, that in my opinion if we had concentrated all our resources we could have secured a decision, at any rate at the outset, in one of our theatres of war, in spite of the growing numerical superiority of the enemy.

West or East? That was the great question, and on the answer to it our fate depended. Of course Main Headquarters could not allow me a deciding voice in the solution of this problem. The responsibility for that lay alone and exclusively on their shoulders. I consider, nevertheless, that I have the right and duty to bring forward my views on this subject, and express them frankly and openly.

From the general point of view, the so-called decision in the West was traditional. I might perhaps say national. In the West was the enemy whose chauvinistic agitation against us had not left us in peace even in times of peace. In the West, too, was now that other enemy who every German was convinced was the motive force working for the destruction of Germany. Compared with that, we often found Russia's greed for Constantinople comprehensible. Her longings for East and West Prussia were not taken seriously and it was commonly believed that it would be relatively easy for us to come to an understanding with Russia by the methods of peace.

Even to me the decisive battle in the West, a battle which would have meant final victory, was the *ultima ratio*, but an *ultima ratio* which could only be reached over the body of a Russia stricken to the ground. Should we ever be able to strike Russia to the ground? Fate answered this question in the affirmative but only two years later, when it was too late. For by that time our situation had fundamentally changed. The numbers and resources of our other foes had in the meantime reached giant proportions, and in the circle of their armies Russia's place had been taken by America, with her youthful energies and mighty economic powers!

I believed that in the winter of 1914–15 we could answer the question, whether we could overthrow Russia, in the affirmative. Of course our goal was not to be reached in a single great battle, but only through a series of such and similar battles. The preliminary conditions for this were present, as had already been revealed, in the generalship of the Russian Army commanders, though not of their Commander-in-Chief. Tannenberg had showed it clearly. Lodz would have shown it, perhaps on an even greater scale, if we had not had to take the battles in Poland against too great a numerical superiority upon our shoulders, and so to speak stop half-way to victory for lack of numbers.

I have never underestimated the Russians. In my opinion the idea that Russia was nothing but despotism and slavery, unwieldiness, stupidity and selfishness was quite false. Strong and noble moral qualities were at work there, if only in comparatively restricted circles. Love of country, self-reliance, perseverance and broad views were not entirely unknown in the Russian Army. How otherwise could the huge masses have ever been put in motion, and the nation and troops have been willing to accept such hecatombs of human life? But what the Russian masses lacked were those great human and spiritual qualities which among us are the common property of the nation and the army.

The previous battles with the armies of the Tsar had given our officers and men a feeling of unquestioned superiority over the enemy. This conviction, which was shared by the oldest Landsturm man with the youngest recruit, explains the fact that here in the East we could use formations, the fighting value of which would have prevented their employment on the Western Front except in emergencies. Of course there were limits to the use of such troops, in view of the demands which had to be made on the endurance and strategic mobility of the units in the eastern theatre. The main blow had to be delivered, time and time again, by really effective divisions. If the numbers required to carry through some decisive operation could not be obtained by new formations, it was my opinion that they should be obtained from the Western Front, even if it meant evacuating part of the occupied territory.

These views are not the result of a process of reasoning after the event or *post hoc* criticism. It has been urged against them that the Russians were in a position in case of need to withdraw so far into the so-called 'vast spaces' of their Empire that our strategic impetus must be paralysed the farther we followed them. I think that these views were inspired far too much by memories of 1812, and that they did not take sufficient account of the development and transformation of the political and economic conditions obtaining at the heart of the Tsar's realms. I am thinking more particularly of the railways. Napoleon's campaign drove but a comparatively small wedge into vast Russia, thinly populated, economically primitive and, from the point of view of domestic politics, still asleep. What a different thing a great modern offensive would have been! At bottom it was these views which were the subject of controversy between Main Headquarters, as then constituted, and my Army Headquarters.

2

Battles and Operations in the East

I can only deal in broad outlines with the events of the year 1915 in the East. On our part of the Eastern Front fighting was resumed with the greatest violence. It had never completely died down. With us, however, it did not rage with quite the same fury as in the Carpathians, where the Austro-Hungarian armies in a desperate struggle had to protect the fields of Hungary from the Russian floods. The critical situation had taken even my Chief of Staff there for a time. The real reasons which led to our separation at this moment I have never known. I asked my Emperor to cancel the order. His Majesty graciously approved. After a short time General Ludendorff returned, full of grave experiences and holding even graver views of the condition of affairs among the Austro-Slav units.

The idea of a decision in the East must have been particularly welcome to the Austro-Hungarian General Staff. It must have recommended itself to them not only on military, but also on political grounds. They could not remain blind to the progressive deterioration of the Austro-Hungarian armies. If the war were dragged out for a long time the process would apparently make more headway in the armies of the Danube Monarchy than in that of their opponents. Further, the Austrians were fearful that the threatened loss of Przemysl would not only increase the tension of the situation on their own front, but that under the impression which the fall of this fortress must make on the nation the signs, even then quite distinguishable, of the disintegration of the State and loss of confidence in a favourable termination of the war, would increase and multiply. Moreover, Austria-Hungary was already feeling herself threatened in the rear by the political attitude of Italy. A great and victorious blow in the East could fundamentally change the unhappy situation of the State.

Looking at the situation in that light, I took the side of General Conrad when he suggested to the German High Command a decisive operation in the eastern theatre. Main Headquarters considered that they could not place at my disposal the reinforcements which I considered necessary for such a decision. Of the plans proposed, therefore, only one was allotted to my sphere of command, the great blow which we delivered in East Prussia.

At the beginning of the year four army corps were placed at our disposal and transferred from home and the Western Front. They were detrained in East Prussia. Part went to reinforce the 8th Army and part to form the 10th Army under General von Eichhorn. They deployed and separated with a view to breaking out from both wings of our lightly held entrenched position from Lötzen to Gumbinnen. The 10th Russian Army of General Sievers was to suffer deep envelopment through our two strong wings which were to meet ultimately in the East on Russian soil and thus annihilate to a great extent everything the enemy had not got away.

On February 5 precise battle orders were issued from Insterburg, whither we had gone to direct the operations. From the 7th onwards they set in motion the two groups on the wings, a movement recalling in some respects our celebrated Sedan. And it was indeed a Sedan which finally befell the Russian 10th Army in the region of Augustovo. It was there that our mighty drive came to an end on February 21, and the result was that more than 100,000 Russians were sent to Germany as prisoners. An even larger number of Russians suffered another fate.

In spite of the great tactical success of the Winter Battle in Masuria we failed to exploit it strategically. We had once more managed practically to destroy one of the Russian armies, but fresh enemy forces had immediately come up to take its place, drawn from other fronts to which they had not been pinned down. In such circumstances, with the resources at our disposal in the East, we could not achieve a decisive result. The superiority of the Russians was too great.

The Russian answer to the Winter Battle was an enveloping attack on our lines on the far side of the Old Prussian frontier. Russian blood flowed in streams in the murderous encounters north of the Narew and west of the Niemen, which lasted into the spring. Thank God it was on Russian soil! The Tsar may have had many soldiers, but even *their* number dwindled noticeably as the result of such massed sacrifices. The Russian troops which went to destruction before our lines were missing later on when the great

German and Austro-Hungarian attack farther south made the whole Russian front tremble.

At this time the most violent fighting was in progress not only on the frontiers of Prussia but in the Carpathians also. It was there that the Russians tried throughout the whole winter at any price to force the frontier walls of Hungary. They knew, and were right, that if the Russian flood could sweep into Magyar lands it might decide the war and that the Danube Empire would never survive such a blow.

The fearful and continuous tension of the situation in the Carpathians and its reaction on the political situation imperiously demanded some solution. The German General Staff found one. In the first days of May they broke through the Russian front in Northern Galicia and took the enemy's front on the frontiers of Hungary in flank and rear.

My Headquarters was at first only an indirect participant in the great operation which began at Gorlice. Our first duty, within the framework of this mighty enterprise, was to tie down strong enemy forces. This was done at first by attacks in the great bend of the Vistula west of Warsaw and on the East Prussian frontier in the direction of Kovno, then on a greater scale by a cavalry sweep into Lithuania and Kurland which began on April 27. The advance of three cavalry divisions, supported by the same number of infantry divisions, touched Russia's war zone at a sensitive spot. For the first time the Russians realised that by such an advance their most important railways which connected the Russian armies with the heart of the country could be seriously threatened. They threw in large forces to meet our invasion. The battles on Lithuanian soil dragged out until the summer. We found ourselves compelled to send larger forces there, to retain our hold on the occupied region and keep up our pressure on the enemy in these districts which had hitherto been untouched by war. Thus a new German army gradually came into existence. It was given the name of the 'Niemen Army' from the great river of this region.

I have no space to deal with the movement of our armies which began on May 2 in Northern Galicia and, spreading along to our lines, ended in the autumn months east of Vilna. Like an avalanche which apparently takes its rise in small beginnings, but gradually carries away everything that stands in its destructive path, this movement began and continued on a scale never seen before, and which will never again be repeated. We were tempted to intervene directly when the thrust past Lemberg had succeeded. The armies of Germany and Austria-Hungary wheeled to the north between the Bug and the Vistula. The picture that unrolled before our eyes was this: the Russian front in the southern half is stretched almost to breaking.

Its northern half, held firmly on the north-west, has formed a mighty new flank in the south between the Vistula and the Pripet Marshes. If we now broke through from the north against the rear of the Russian main mass all the Russian armies would be threatened with a catastrophe.

The idea which had led to the Winter Battle presented itself once more, this time perhaps in yet broader outlines. The blow must now be delivered from East Prussia, first and most effectively from the Osowiec–Grodno line. Yet the marshes in that region prohibited our advance at that point. We knew that from the thaw in the previous winter. All that was left us was the choice between a break-through west or east of this line. A thrust right through the enemy defences, I might say into the very heart of the Russian Army, demanded the direction past and east of Grodno. We put that view forward. Main Headquarters did not shut their eyes to its advantages, but considered the western direction shorter and believed that a great success could be won on this side also. They therefore demanded an offensive across the Upper Narew. I thought that it was my duty to withdraw my objections to this plan for the time being, for the sake of the whole operation, and in any case await the result of this attack and the further course of the operation. General Ludendorff, however, inwardly adhered to our first plan; but this difference of opinion had no kind of influence on our future thoughts and actions, and in no way diminished the energy with which, in the middle of July, we translated into action the decisions of Main Headquarters, the responsible authority.

Gallwitz's army surged out against the Narew on both sides of Przasnysz. For this attack I went personally to the battlefield, not with any idea of interfering with the tactics of the Army Headquarters Staff, which I knew to be masterly, but only because I knew what outstanding importance Main Headquarters attached to the success of the break-through they had ordered at this point. I wanted to be on the spot so that in case of need I could intervene immediately if the Army Headquarters' Staff needed any further help for the execution of its difficult task from the armies under my command. I spent two days with this army, and witnessed the storming of Przasnysz, for the possession of which there had previously been violent and continuous fighting, and the battle for the district south of the town.

By July 17 Gallwitz had reached the Narew. Under the pressure of the allied armies, breaking in on every side, the Russians gradually began to give way at all points and to withdraw slowly before the menace of envelopment. Our pursuit began to lose its force in incessant frontal actions. In this way we could not gather the fruits which had been sown time and time again on bloody battlefields. We therefore returned to our earlier idea, and having regard to the course the operations were taking, wished to press forward beyond Kovno and Vilna with a view to forcing the Russian centre against the Pripet Marshes and cutting their communications with the interior of the country. However, the views of Main Headquarters required a straightforward pursuit, a pursuit in which the pursuer gets more exhausted than the pursued.

In this period fell the capture of Novo Georgievsk. In spite of its situation as a strategic bridge-head, this fortress had certainly not seriously interfered with our movements hitherto. But its possession was of importance for us at this time, because it barred the railway to Warsaw from Mlawa. Just before the capitulation on August 18 I met my Emperor outside the fortress, and later on it was in his company that I drove into the town. The barracks and other military buildings, which had been set on fire by Russian troops, were still blazing. Masses of prisoners were standing round. One thing we noticed was that before the surrender the Russians had shot their horses wholesale, obviously as a result of their conviction of the extraordinary importance which these animals had for our operations in the East. Our enemy always took the most enormous pains to destroy everything, especially supplies, which could be of the slightest use to his victorious foe.

To clear the way for a later advance on Vilna we sent our Niemen Army out eastwards as early as the middle of July. In the middle of August Kovno fell under the blows of the 10th Army. The way to Vilna was open, but once again we were not strong enough to proceed with the execution of our great strategic idea. Our forces were employed, as before, in following up frontally. Weeks passed before reinforcements could be brought up. Meanwhile the Russians were continuing their retirement to the east; they surrendered everything, even Warsaw, in the hope of at least being able to save their field armies from destruction.

It was only on September 9 that we started out against Vilna. It was possible that even now great results could be obtained in this direction. A few hundred thousand Russian troops might perhaps be our booty. If ever proud hopes were mingled with anxiety and impatience they were mingled now. Should we be too late? Were we strong enough? Yet on we went past Vilna, then south. Our cavalry soon laid hands on the vital veins of the Russians. If we could only grasp them tightly it would mean death to the main Russian armies. The enemy realised the disaster that was threatening, and did everything to avert it. A murderous conflict began at Vilna. Every hour gained by the Russians meant that many of their units streaming eastwards were saved. The tide turned, and our cavalry division had to withdraw again.

The railway into the heart of the country was open to the Russians once more. We had come too late and were now exhausted!

I do not delude myself into thinking that the opposition between the views of Main Headquarters and our own will have an historical interest. Yet, in judging the plans of our High Command, we must not lose sight of the whole military situation. We ourselves then saw only a part of the whole picture. The question whether we should have made other plans and acted otherwise if we had known the whole political and military situation must be left open.

3
Lötzen

In the spring, when activity on our front gradually began to die down, there was no lack of visitors of all kinds, and this was true of the summer also. German princes, politicians, scientists and professional men, as well as commercial men and administrative officials, came to us, brought by the interest which the province of East Prussia, usually so little visited, had acquired in the course of the war. Artists presented themselves with a view to immortalising General Ludendorff and myself with their brushes and chisels; but this was a distinction with which we would have preferred to dispense, in view of our scanty hours of leisure, although we much appreciated the kindness and skill of the gentlemen in question.

Grand Admiral von Tirpitz was a particular visitor. On a long walk that I took with him he told me all the sorrows which vexed his flamingly patriotic, and in particular, seaman's heart. It was a bitter sorrow to him that the mighty weapon he had forged during the best years of his life should be shut up in its home harbours in time of war. It is true that the chances for a naval offensive on our side were uncommonly difficult; but, on the other hand, they did not improve with long waiting. In my opinion, the very great sensitiveness of the English to the phantom of a German invasion would have justified greater activity on the part of our Fleet, and, indeed, heavy sacrifices. The desire of the Grand Admiral's heart was granted in the spring of 1916. Skagerrak gave brilliant proof of what our Fleet could really do.

Herr von Tirpitz also gave expression to his views about our U-boat operations. It was his opinion that we had begun to use this weapon at the wrong time, and then, frightened at the attitude of the President of the United States, lowered the arm which we had raised with such loud shouts of victory – likewise at the wrong time.

In October, 1915, we transferred our Headquarters to Kovno, in the occupied territory. To the former activities of my Chief of Staff were now added the duties of administering, reorganising and exploiting the country with a view to procuring supplies for the troops, the Homeland, and the local population. The increasing amount of work this involved would alone have been enough to take up the whole time and energies of one man. General Ludendorff regarded it as an appendix to his ordinary work, and devoted himself to it with that ruthless energy which is all his own.

Chapter Seven

The Campaign of 1916 up to the End of August

I

The Russian Attack on the German Eastern Front

In my sphere of command the year 1915 had not made its exit with the loud flourish of trumpets of an absolutely complete triumph. There was something unsatisfactory about the final result of the operations and encounters of this year. The Russian bear had escaped our clutches, bleeding no doubt from more than one wound, but still not stricken to death. In a series of wild onslaughts he had slipped away from us. Would he be able to show that he had enough life-force left to make things difficult for us again? We found an opinion prevalent that the Russian losses in men and material had already been so enormous that we should be safe on our eastern front for a long time to come. After our previous experiences we received this opinion with caution, and indeed time was soon to show that this caution was justified.

We were not to be allowed to pass the winter in peace, for it soon appeared that the Russians were thinking of anything but leaving us alone. Things were stirring in and behind the enemy lines along our whole front and, indeed, far away to the south, although at first there was no means of knowing the intentions of the Russian High Command. I regarded the region of Smorgon, Dvinsk and Riga as special points of danger for our lines. To these led the most effective of the Russian railways. But for a long time there were no open signs of an enemy offensive at the three points I have mentioned.

An unusual amount of activity began to be noticeable in the region of Lake Narocz and Postawy from the middle of February onwards. From the mass of intelligence which reached us, the enemy's preparations for an offensive at that point became more and more obvious. At first I had not believed that the Russians would really select for a great blow a point which lay far from their best railways and, further, gave their masses little room to deploy and the subordinate commanders little chance of manœuvring, thanks to the nature of the ground. Coming events revealed to me the arrival of the improbable.

As the Russian preparations proceeded, not one of us realised their enormous scale. We should never have believed that we should have to deal with the whole of the Russian forces – about 370 battalions – held ready in the region of Lake Narocz with the 70 odd battalions which we had gradually collected there.

The Russian attack began on March 18. After an artillery preparation, the violence of which had not previously been paralleled on the Eastern Front, the enemy columns hurled themselves at our thin lines like an unbroken wave. Yet it was in vain that the Russian batteries and machine-guns drove their own infantry forward against the German lines, and in vain that enemy troops held in reserve mowed down their own first lines when these tried to withdraw and escape destruction from our fire. The Russian corpses were piled up in regular heaps before our front. The strain on the defence was certainly colossal. A thaw had set in and filled the trenches with melted snow, dissolved the breastworks, which had hitherto afforded some cover, into flowing mud, and turned the whole battlefield into a bottomless morass. In the icy water the limbs of the men in the trenches became so swollen that they could hardly move; but there remained enough strength and resolution in these bodies to break the enemy onslaughts time and time again. Once more all the Russian sacrifices were in vain, and from March 25 onwards we could look confidently to our heroes at Lake Narocz.

2
The Russian Offensive Against the Austro–Hungarian Eastern Front

'Verdun'! The name was continually on our lips in the East from the beginning of February in this year. We dare only mention it under our breaths and in secret. We pronounced the word in a tone which suggested both doubt and hesitation. And yet the idea of capturing Verdun was a good one. With Verdun in our hands our position on the Western Front would be materially strengthened. It would once and for all remove the salient at our most sensitive point. Perhaps, too, the capture of the fortress would open up further strategic possibilities in the south and west.

In my opinion, therefore, the importance of this fortress justified an attempt to take it. We had it in our power to break off the attack at any time if it appeared impossible to carry it through, or the sacrifices it exacted seemed to be too high. Moreover, had not the boldest and most improbable actions in attacks on fortresses succeeded brilliantly time after time in this war?

After the end of February the word 'Verdun' was no longer uttered secretly, but loudly and joyfully. The name 'Douaumont', like a beacon of German heroism, lit up the far distances of the East and raised the spirits even of those who were now looking with anxious care towards the development of events at Lake Narocz. I must admit that the attack on Verdun was also a bitter disappointment for us, for the enterprise meant that the idea of a decision here in the East had been finally abandoned.

As time went on Verdun was spoken of in yet another tone. Doubts gradually began to prevail, though they were but seldom expressed. They could be summarised shortly in the following question: Why should we persevere with an offensive which exacted such frightful sacrifices and, as was already obvious, had no prospects of success? Instead of the purely frontal attack on the northern arc of the defence, which was supported by the permanent work of Verdun, would it not be possible to use the configuration of our lines between the Argonne Forest and St Mihiel to cut the salient off altogether?

Another word followed Verdun; the word 'Italy', which was mentioned for the first time after the battle of Lake Narocz had ended. This name, too, was uttered with doubt, a doubt far greater and stronger than in the case of Verdun. Indeed, not so much a doubt as an anxious foreboding. The plan of an Austro-Hungarian attack on Italy was bold, and from that point of view had therefore a military claim to success. But what made the plan seem venturesome was our opinion of the instrument with which it was to be carried out. If the best Austro-Hungarian troops were sent against Italy what was left against Russia? Moreover, Russia had not been so badly beaten as was suspected at the end of 1915. At Lake Narocz the immense determination of the Russian masses had again revealed itself in a fury and impetus compared with which the Austro-Hungarian units, many of them largely composed of Slav elements, had shown themselves even less effective than before.

In spite of reports of victories in Italy, our anxiety increased from day to day. It was justified only too soon by the events which now occurred south of the Pripet. On June 4 the Austro-Hungarian front in Wolhynia and the Bukovina absolutely collapsed before the first Russian onslaught. The worst crisis that the Eastern Front had ever known, worse even than those of the year 1914, now began, for this time there was no victorious German Army standing by ready to save. In the West the battle of Verdun was raging, and there were signs of the coming storm on the Somme.

Hitherto, on the German front the Russians had remained in their positions, but in the same strength as before. They had therefore obtained their first victory south of the Pripet with relatively weak forces, and not by the immense masses they usually employed. Brussiloff's plan must certainly be regarded as at the outset a reconnaissance, a reconnaissance on an immense front and carried out with great determination, but still only a reconnaissance, and not a blow with some definite objective. His task was to test the strength of the enemy's lines on a front of nearly 300 miles between the Pripet and Rumania.

However, the Austro-Hungarian wall revealed but few solid stones. It collapsed under the taps of Brussiloff's hammer, and through the gaps poured the Russian masses, which now began to be drawn from our front also. Where should we be able to bring them to a standstill? At first only one strong pillar remained standing in the midst of this conflagration. It was the Southern Army, under its splendid commander, General Count Bothmer. Germans, Austrians and Hungarians – all held together by good discipline.

Everything that could be spared from our part of the great Eastern Front was now sent south, and disappeared on the battlefields of Galicia.

Meanwhile the situation on the Western Front had also become worse. The French and English, in very superior numbers, had hurled themselves at our relatively weak line on both sides of the Somme and pressed the defence back. Indeed, for a moment we were faced with the menace of a complete collapse!

My All-Highest War Lord summoned me and my Chief of Staff twice to his Headquarters at Pless to confer with him over the serious situation on the Eastern Front. It was on the second occasion, at the end of July, that the decision was taken to reorganise the system of command on the Eastern Front. The German General Staff, in return for the offer of a rescuing hand to Austro-Hungary – in spite of the claims of Verdun and the Somme – had demanded a guarantee for a stricter organisation of the command on the Eastern Front. They were right! My sphere of command was accordingly extended to the region of Brody, east of Lemberg. Large Austro-Hungarian forces were placed under my command.

We visited the Headquarters Staffs of the armies newly assigned to us as soon as possible, and found among the Austro-Hungarian authorities perfect cordiality and ruthless criticism of their own weaknesses. I am bound to say that this knowledge was not always accompanied by the resolution to repair the damage that had been done; and yet, if ever an army needed one controlling and resolute will and one single impulse, it was this army, with its mixture of nationalities.

The extension of my sphere of command compelled me to transfer my Headquarters to the south, to Brest-Litovsk. It was there that, on the morning of August 28, I received a command from His Majesty the Emperor to go to his Headquarters as soon as possible. The only reason the Chief of the Military Cabinet gave me was this: 'The position is serious!'

I put down the receiver and thought of Verdun and Italy, Brussiloff and the Austrian Eastern Front; then of the news, 'Rumania has declared war on us.' Strong nerves would be required!

Part III

From Our Transfer to Main Headquarters to the Collapse of Russia

Chapter Eight

My Summons to Main Headquarters

I
Chief of the General Staff of the Field Army

As is known, this was not the first time that my Imperial and Royal master had summoned me to conferences on the military situation and our plans. I therefore expected this time also that His Majesty merely wished to hear my views, personally and orally, about some definite question.

In front of the castle at Pless I found my All-Highest War Lord awaiting the arrival of Her Majesty the Empress, who had come from Berlin and reached Pless shortly after I had. The Emperor immediately greeted me as Chief of the General Staff of the Field Army and General Ludendorff as my First Quartermaster-General. The Imperial Chancellor, too, had appeared from Berlin, and apparently was as much surprised as I myself at the change in the office of Chief of the General Staff, a change which His Majesty announced to him in my presence.

The business of taking over from my predecessor was completed soon after. As we parted General von Falkenhayn gave me his hand with the words: 'God help you and our Fatherland.'

2
The Military Situation at the End of August, 1916

The military situation which gave rise to the change in our High Command was much as follows, judging by my first impressions:

The situation on the Western Front was not without anxiety. Verdun had not fallen into our hands, and the hope of wearing down the French Army in the mighty arc of fire which we had drawn round the northern and north-eastern fronts of the fortress had not been realised. The prospects of a success for our offensive at that point had become more uninviting, but the enterprise had not yet been abandoned. On the Somme the struggle had now been raging nearly two months. There we passed from one crisis to another. Our lines were permanently in a condition of the highest tension.

In the East the Russian offensive in the south-eastern part of the Carpathians was sweeping up to their very crests. After our previous experiences it was doubtful whether this last protecting wall of Hungary could be held against the new attack with the forces now available. Moreover, the situation was extremely critical in the foothills of the north-western Carpathians. It is true that the Russian attacks at this point had died down somewhat, but it was too much to hope that this pause could continue for any considerable length of time.

In view of the collapse on the Galician front, the Austro-Hungarian offensive in the southern Tyrol had had to be abandoned. The Italians, in reply, had themselves passed to the offensive on the Isonzo front. These battles made a very heavy drain on the Austro-Hungarian armies, which were fighting against great superiority and under the most difficult circumstances in a manner worthy of the highest praise.

Lastly, the position in the Balkans at this moment was of importance to the whole situation and the emergencies of the times. The offensive on which, at our suggestion, the Bulgarians had embarked against Sarrail in Macedonia had had to be broken off after gaining preliminary successes. The political objective which was associated with this offensive – to keep Rumania from entering the war – had not been reached.

At the moment the initiative was everywhere in the hands of our enemies. It was to be anticipated that they would put forth their whole strength to keep up their pressure upon us. The prospects of a possibly speedy and victorious conclusion to the war must have inspired our adversaries on all fronts to exert the greatest efforts and endure the heaviest sacrifices. All of them certainly put in their last ounce to give the *coup de grâce* to the Central Powers while Rumania blew a triumphant blast!

The German and Austro-Hungarian armies had few uncommitted and available reserves at the moment. For the time being there was nothing but weak posts, largely Customs and Revenue Police, on the Transylvanian frontier which was immediately threatened. A certain number of exhausted Austro-Hungarian divisions, partly composed of remnants no longer fit to fight, were quartered in the interior of Transylvania. The new formations, which were in course of completion, were not strong enough to be regarded as capable of a serious resistance to a Rumanian invasion of the country. In this respect the situation on the southern bank of the Danube was more favourable to us. A new army, composed of Bulgarian, Turkish and German units, was being concentrated on the Bulgarian side of the Dobrudja frontier and farther up the Danube. It had about seven divisions of very different strengths.

Such were, generally speaking, all the forces we had available for the moment at the most sensitive of all the sensitive spots of our European theatre – the Rumanian frontier. The other troops we needed had to be taken from other battle fronts, from exhausted units which required rest, or obtained by forming new divisions. But it was just in this last respect that our situation was unfavourable, as was that of our Allies. The situation as regards drafts threatened to become critical in view of the perpetual and indeed increasing tension. Further, the consumption of ammunition and material in the long and immense battles on all fronts had become so enormous that the danger that our operations might be paralysed from this cause alone was not excluded.

3
The Political Situation

When the conduct of operations was entrusted to me I regarded the Fatherland's *morale* as serious, though it had not collapsed. There was no doubt that people at home had been bitterly disappointed by the military events of the last few months. Moreover, the privations of daily life had materially increased. The middle classes in particular were suffering very severely from the economic situation, which affected them exceptionally intensely. Food had become very scarce, and the prospects of the harvest were only moderate.

In these circumstances Rumania's declaration of war meant a further burden on the country's resolution. Yet our Fatherland was even now apparently quite prepared to hold out. Of course, it was impossible to say how long and how strongly this resolution would be maintained. In this respect the course of military events in the immediate future would be decisive.

As regards the relations of Germany to her allies, the propagandist declarations of the enemy Press had it that Germany exercised unlimited domination. It was said that we held Austria-Hungary, Bulgaria and Turkey by the throat, so to speak, ready to strangle them if they did not do exactly what we wished. Yet there could not be a greater perversion of the truth than this assertion. I am convinced that nothing showed the weakness of Germany, in comparison with England, more clearly than the difference between the political grip each of them had on their allies.

For instance, if official Italy had ever dared to show an open inclination for peace without British permission, England would have been in a position at any time to compel this ally to continue the policy she had previously pursued simply through fear of starvation. Equally strong and absolutely domineering was England's attitude to France. In this respect, indeed, only Russia was more independent, but here again the political independence of the Tsar's Empire was limited by its economic and financial dependence on England. How much more unfavourable was Germany's position from this point of view! What political, economic or military weapons had we in our hands with which to repress any inclination on the part of any of our Allies to drop out? The moment these States no longer felt themselves chained to us of their own free wills, or by the menace of certain destruction, we had no power to keep them at our side.

Now to our Allies in detail. The domestic circumstances of Austria-Hungary had changed for the worse during the summer of 1916. A few weeks before our arrival in Pless the political leaders there had made no secret to our Government of the fact that the Danube Monarchy could not stand any further burdens in the way of military and political failures. The disappointment at the failure of the offensive against Italy, which had been accompanied by far too many promises, had been very profound. The speedy collapse of the resistance on the frontiers of Galicia and Wolhynia had produced a feeling of uneasy pessimism in the great mass of the Austro-Hungarian people, and this found an echo in the Representative Assembly. Leading circles in Austria-Hungary were undoubtedly under the influence of this mood.

In my opinion there was no reason to doubt the fidelity of Austria-Hungary, but in any case we must make it our business to see that the country was relieved of the pressure upon it at the earliest possible moment.

The domestic situation in Bulgaria was very different – I might say more politically stable – from that of Austria-Hungary. In their war for the political unity of the Bulgarian race the nation was also fighting for the final hegemony of the Balkans. The treaties concluded with the Central Powers and Turkey, in conjunction with her previous military successes, appeared to bring Bulgaria's far-reaching ambitions within range of fulfilment. It is true that the country had entered the new war very exhausted from the last Balkan war. Moreover, nothing like the same universal enthusiasm had marked her entry into the present war as had been displayed in that of 1912. This time it was due far more to cool calculation of her statesmen than to any national impulse. It was no wonder, therefore, that the nation felt satisfied with its present acquisition of the districts in dispute and displayed no strong inclination to embark on fresh enterprises. Taking things all round, I considered that I was justified in hoping that our alliance with Bulgaria would stand any military test.

No less confidence did I feel with regard to Turkey. The Turkish Empire had entered the war without any ambitions for the extension of her political power. Her leading men, particularly Enver Pasha, had clearly recognised that there could be no neutrality for Turkey in the war which had broken out. It could not, in fact, be imagined that in the long run Russia and the Western Powers would continue to heed the moderating influences with regard to the use of the Straits. For Turkey her entry into the war was a question of to be or not to be, far more than for us others. Our enemies were obliging enough to proclaim this far and wide at the very start.

In this war Turkey had hitherto developed powers of resistance which astonished everyone. Her active share in operations surprised friend and foe alike; she tied down strong hostile forces in all the Asiatic theatres. In Germany, Main Headquarters was often reproached later on with dispersion of force for the purpose of strengthening the fighting powers of Turkey. That criticism, however, does not allow for the fact that by thus supporting our ally we enabled her permanently to keep more than a hundred thousand men of the finest enemy troops away from our Central European theatres.

4
The German High Command

The experiences of the spring and summer of 1916 had proved the necessity of a single central and completely responsible authority for our Army and those of our allies. After negotiations with the leading statesmen, a Supreme Command was created. It was conferred on His Majesty the German Emperor. The Chief of the General Staff of the Field Army received the right to issue orders 'in the name of the Supreme Command' and make agreements with the Commanders-in-Chief of the Allied Armies.

Thanks to the friendly spirit and understanding cooperation of the commanders of the Allied Armies, who had otherwise the same status as myself, I was able to confine the use of my new powers to certain particularly important military decisions. The handling of common political and economic questions was not in the province of this Supreme Command.

My principal task was to give our allies the general outlines proposed for joint operations and concentrate their resources and activities with a view to reaching the common goal. It would have been far better for all our interests if our High Command had been able, by suppressing all private interests, and indeed disregarding all considerations which were only secondary as compared with the main decision, to insist on a decisive victory in one of the main theatres of the war. However, in accordance with the unchanging nature of a coalition war, difficulties were often to crop up for our High Command, as they had to bear in mind all kinds of susceptibilities.

As I look back over the past, my impression is confirmed that, from the standpoint of the Supreme Command, the most difficult part of our task was not the great operations, but the attempt to compromise between the conflicting interests of our various allies. One of the greatest obstacles to our plans and decisions was the different quality of the Allied Armies. It was only on taking over the conduct of operations that we gradually came to know what we could expect and demand.

It was during the campaign in Poland that I had first made the acquaintance of the Austro-Hungarian Armies, when they were working in direct co-operation with our troops. Even then they were no longer equal to the demands which we were accustomed to make on our own troops. There is no question that the main cause of the deterioration in the average efficiency of the Austro-Hungarian troops was the extraordinary shock which the Army had suffered in its purely frontal operation at the beginning of the war in Galicia and Poland. It has been urged that the Austro-Hungarian offensive at that time had the result of breaking the onslaught of the Russian masses. On the other hand, it is possible that this result could have been achieved by a less risky method and at far less cost. In any case, the Russian Army recovered from the losses it then suffered, while the Austro-Hungarian Army did not.

The internal framework of the Bulgarian Army was quite different from that of the Austro-Hungarian. It was self-contained from the national point of view. Until the autumn of 1916 the Bulgarian Army had suffered relatively little in the great war. However, in estimating its value we could not forget that quite a short time before it had been engaged in another murderous war in which the flower of the officer corps, and, indeed, the whole of the educated classes of the country, had been destroyed. The reconstruction of the Army was quite as difficult in Bulgaria as in Austria-Hungary. Moreover, the condition of the Balkan countries, virtually still primitive, hindered the introduction and employment of many means that are absolutely necessary both for fighting and transport in modern war. This made itself felt all the more as on the Macedonian front we were faced by first-class French and English troops. For this reason alone it could not be at all surprising that we had to help Bulgaria not only with material, but also with German troops.

The state of affairs in the Turkish Army was otherwise than in the Austro-Hungarian and Bulgarian. Our German Military Mission had scarcely had time to make its presence felt before the war, let alone effect a real improvement in the shaky condition of the Turkish Army, yet they had succeeded in mobilising a large number of Turkish units. Unfortunately, the Army had suffered extraordinarily high losses in the Dardanelles and their first offensive in Armenia. Yet the Turkish Army seemed equal to the task which Main Headquarters first set it – the defence of the Turkish territorial possessions. Indeed, it was to prove possible gradually to employ a considerable number of Turkish units in the European theatre. Our military help to Turkey was practically limited to the delivery of war material and the loan of a large number of officers. In agreement with the Turkish General Staff, the German formations which had been sent to the Asiatic theatres up to the autumn of 1916 were gradually brought back, after the Turks had proved themselves capable of taking over and using the material left behind by these formations.

We sent material even to the Senussi on the north coast of Africa. These we supplied principally with rifles and small arm ammunition, with the help of our U-boats. Though these deliveries were but small, they had an extraordinarily rousing effect on the war spirit among the Mohammedan tribes.

We tried to assist our brothers-in-arms even beyond the north coast of Africa. Thus we took up the idea, which had been mooted by Enver Pasha in 1917, of sending financial help to the tribes of the Yemen which had remained faithful to their Padishah in Constantinople. As the land route thither was closed to us by rebellious nomadic tribes of the Arabian desert, and the coasts of the Red Sea were out of reach owing to the insufficient radius of action of our U-boats, the only way left to us was that of the air. However, much to my regret, we did not possess at that time any airship which could with certainty have overcome the meteorological difficulties of a cruise over the Great Desert. We were, therefore, unable to carry out the plan.

In this connection I may mention, by way of anticipation, that in 1917 I followed with the greatest interest the attempt to send our Protective Force in East Africa arms and medical stores by way of the air. As is well known, the Zeppelin had to return when over the Sudan, as in the meantime the Protective Force had been driven farther south, and transferred the scene of its operations to Portuguese East Africa. I need hardly say with what proud feelings I followed in thought the deeds, the almost superhuman achievements, of this splendid force during the war. They raised a deathless monument to German heroism on African soil.

Looking back on the achievements of our allies, I must admit that in the service of our great common cause they subjected their own powers to the greatest strain that their individual political, economic, military and ethical resources permitted. Of course, none of them attained the ideal, and if it was we who more nearly approached that ideal than the others, it was only due to that mighty inward strength – a strength we did not ourselves realise at first – which we had been acquiring in the course of the last decades.

5
Pless

The Upper Silesian town of Pless had occasionally been selected for headquarters by Main Headquarters at previous periods of the war. The reason for its selection was the fact that it was close to the town of Teschen, in Austrian Silesia, in which the Austrian High Command had its Head-quarters. The advantages that accrued from the possibility of quick personal conferences between the two Headquarters were now the main reason why we stayed there.

It was only natural that the German General Headquarters should form a meeting-place for German and allied princes who wished to have direct discussion with my Imperial Master on political and military questions. The first Sovereign whose personal acquaintance I had the honour of making was the Tsar Ferdinand of Bulgaria. He gave me the impression of a superb diplomatist. His political outlook extended far beyond the frontiers of the Balkans. He was a past-master in the art of explaining the position of his country and keeping it in the foreground when great questions of world-politics were being decided. It was his view that in this war the future of Bulgaria was to be decided by the final elimination of Russian influence and the gathering-in of all men of the Bulgarian race under a single leadership.

It was while we were in residence at Pless that the Emperor Francis Joseph died. Both for the Danube Monarchy and ourselves his death was a loss, the full and impressive import of which was only to be appreciated later. There was no doubt that with his death the ideal bond of union between the various nationalities of the Dual Monarchy was lost. The new Sovereign tried to make good the loss of the moral cement which the Emperor Francis Joseph's death involved, by making concessions to the various nationalities. Even in dealing with elements which were intent on the destruction of the State he believed in the moral effects of political toleration. The method was a total failure. These elements had long made their pact with our common enemies and were far from anxious to break off relations with them.

The impressions I had gained of General Conrad von Hötzendorf as soldier and commander were confirmed in the frequent and active personal intercourse with him which our residence in Pless involved. General Conrad was a gifted personality, a glowing Austrian patriot, and a whole-hearted adherent of our common cause. There was no doubt that it was from the deepest conviction that he proved so obdurate to political influences which strove to break him of that attachment. The general was very broad in his strategic ideas. He knew how to distinguish the central issues of great questions from the desert of secondary matters which had little effect on the decision. He had a peculiarly intimate knowledge of affairs in the Balkans and Italy. Yet on occasion his great plans were based on an over-estimate of what could possibly be expected of the army with which he was entrusted.

I also came to know the military leaders of Turkey and Bulgaria in the course of the autumn and winter at Pless. In his dealings with me, Enver Pasha displayed an unusually firm and free grasp of the elements of strategy in the present war and the methods required. The devotion of this Turk to our common task, great and heavy as it was, was unlimited.

But although Enver Pasha took long views about war, generally speaking he had not received a really thorough military training, or what I might call a General Staff training. This was a drawback which apparently applied to all the Turkish Commanders and their Staffs. In this respect it looked as if it was a question of some natural defect with the Oriental. The Turkish Army appeared to possess only a few officers who were able to master the technical, inside problems of command, a knowledge of which was essential to the execution of well-conceived plans. They seemed not to realise that the General Staff must necessarily look after the details, even in the execution of great operations. The result was that the wealth of Oriental imagination was often quite wasted owing to a lack of a sense of military reality.

Our Bulgarian colleague, General Jekoff, was a very different character from the fertile-minded Turk. He was a man of remarkable powers of observation, not by any means blind to great conceptions, but essentially restricted in his outlook to the sphere of the Balkans.

Chapter Nine

Life at Headquarters

It was impossible to think of a regular routine for our Army Headquarters, with each hour mapped out, during the war of movement in East Prussia and Poland in the autumn of 1914. It was only when our Headquarters was transferred to Posen, in November, 1914, that greater regularity began to be observed in our official and – if such a thing exists in war – unofficial life. Later on our longer stay at Lötzen was particularly favourable for the organisation of a strictly regulated routine.

My appointment as Chief of the General Staff of the Field Army made no material difference to the methods of business we had established and found satisfactory, although in many respects more important and pressing activities took up our time. I usually began the day's business at about nine o'clock – that is, after the morning reports had come in – by visiting General Ludendorff in order to discuss with him any changes in the situation and issue the necessary instructions. As a rule this did not mean a long conference. The military situation was always present to both our minds and we knew each other's thoughts. The decisions were, therefore, usually a matter of a few sentences; indeed, very often a few words were all that was required to establish that mutual understanding which served the general as a basis for his further working-out of the plans.

After this conference I used to go for a walk for about an hour, accompanied by my Adjutant. Occasionally I asked visitors at Headquarters to join me in my morning walk, in the course of which I heard their sorrows as well as their suggestions, and chastened many an anxious soul before he hurled himself upon my First Quartermaster-General to pour out his heart about his wishes, hopes and schemes to that authority whose business it was to go into further details.

After my return to the office I had further conferences with General Ludendorff, and then received the personal reports of my departmental heads in my own office.

Apart altogether from official duties, I had to deal with a mass of personal correspondence. There was quite a large number of people who considered themselves compelled to open their hearts to me in writing about every conceivable occurrence, or acquaint me with their views. It was perfectly impossible for me to read them all myself. I had to employ the services of a special officer for the purpose. Poetry as well as prose figured in this correspondence. Enthusiasm and the reverse were displayed in every possible degree. It was often very difficult to see any connection between the requests made to me and my official position. To take only two of hundreds of examples, it has never been clear to me what I, as Chief of the General Staff, had to do with the removal of refuse in a provincial town – no doubt very necessary in itself, or with the loss of the certificate of baptism of a German lady from Chile. Yet in most cases the writers called on me to help. There is no doubt that written requests of this kind were a proof of a touching, in many cases somewhat naive, confidence in my personal influence. I was only too glad to help, at least with my signature, when time and circumstances permitted. But as a rule I considered it my duty to refrain from intervening personally.

About midday I was regularly summoned to make my report to His Majesty the Emperor. At this conference General Ludendorff described the situation. When more important decisions had to be taken I made the report myself, and requested the Emperor's approval of our plans whenever that was necessary. The Emperor's great trust in us made a special Royal approval unnecessary except in vital questions. For the rest His Majesty usually satisfied himself with hearing our reasons when new operations were proposed. I never remember any differences of opinion which were not composed by my War Lord before the conference was over. The Emperor's wonderful memory for situations was of the greatest help to us at these reports. His Majesty not only made the most careful study of the map, but was in the habit of making sketches himself. The time of our daily report to the Kaiser was frequently also employed in conferences with representatives of the Government.

After the conclusion of the report to the Kaiser my immediate Staff joined me at the luncheon table. The time spent on the meal was cut down to what was absolutely necessary. I attached importance to my officers having time to get a little recreation afterwards or getting away from work in some other way. To my continual personal regret, I could not consent to an extension of the meal-time, even when we had guests with us. Regard for the maintenance of the efficiency of my colleagues had to come before social graces. For the majority of these officers a sixteen-hour day was the rule. Thus we at Main Headquarters were compelled to use our human material to the extreme limit of capacity just as much as the men in the trenches.

The afternoon passed in much the same way as the morning. The longest break for all of us was dinner, which began at eight. After the meal we used to sit round in groups in neighbouring rooms until General Ludendorff gave the signal to break up, at half-past nine punctually. Conversation in our circle was usually very lively. It was perfectly free and absolutely frank, and covered all topics and occurrences that concerned us directly or were of general interest. Nor was there any lack of high spirits. I considered it a duty to my colleagues to encourage this side. It was a pleasure to see that our visitors were obviously surprised by our quiet confidence on the one hand and the spontaneity of our conversation on the other.

After our evening gathering broke up we went back together to the office. The final reports of the day had arrived and the situation on the different fronts been marked on the map. One of the more junior Staff Officers explained it. It depended upon the events in the various theatres whether I had to have a further conference with General Ludendorff or could dispense with his services for the time being. The officers of my immediate Staff now resumed work. Frequently it was at this stage that the last data required for the drawing-up and issue of final orders were given, and it was from now onwards that the innumerable requests, suggestions and proposals of the armies and other services streamed in. The day's work thus never ended before midnight. The reports of the heads of departments to General Ludendorff lasted pretty regularly into the early hours of the next day. There would have to be quite an exceptional lull at the front for my First Quartermaster-General to leave his office before midnight, although he was always back again by eight o'clock next morning.

Our whole life and work and all our thoughts and feelings were shared in common. Even now the memories of this time fill me with grateful satisfaction. Generally speaking, we remained a restricted circle. In view of the official routine, changes of personnel were naturally infrequent. It was occasionally possible to meet the urgent requests of the officers for at least temporary employment at the front. Moreover, occasions arose in which it was necessary to send officers to particularly important parts of our own fronts or those of our Allies. But, generally speaking, the continuity of the very highly-organised and complicated system required that at least the senior officers should remain permanently at their posts at Main Headquarters.

This picture of our life would be incomplete if I said nothing of the visitors who came to us from all parts and at all times. I am not thinking now of our routine dealings with the many professional people who came into official touch with us, but rather of others who were brought to us by many other interests. I gladly opened my door and my heart to them so long as they treated me with the same frankness.

We had a large number of guests, and, in fact, had few days without them. Not only Germany and her Allies, but neutrals also sent us a considerable contingent. Our circle at table often gave me the impression of the most motley mixture of races, and it sometimes happened that a Christian Minister sat down side by side with a Mohammedan believer. People of all social classes and parties received a warm welcome. I was glad to give them my few hours of leisure.

In my circle I pressed the hard and horny hands of artisans and working men, and their frank looks and straightforward words were a real pleasure to me. Representatives of our great industries and men of science introduced us to new discoveries and ideas and waxed enthusiastic over future economic plans. They certainly complained of the narrow-minded bureaucracy at home and the scanty resources put at their disposal for the exploitation of their ideas. On the other hand, bureaucrats grieved over the greed for gold of inventors for what they feared would turn out to be fantasies or mere airy schemes. I well remember the interesting questions of an official very high up in the Treasury service who wanted to know the cost of a shell of every calibre of gun, so that he could calculate the enormous cost of a battle. He spared me the result of his calculations, knowing, no doubt, that I would not limit the consumption of ammunition on that ground.

Count Zeppelin was another of our guests at Pless, and affected us all with the touching simplicity of his manner. Even at that time he considered his airships an antiquated weapon. In his opinion it was the aeroplane which would control the air in future. The Count died soon after his visit, and thus never lived to see the disaster to his Fatherland. Happy man! Two other lords of the air who had gained laurels accepted my invitation – two invincible young heroes: Captain Bölcke and Captain von Richthofen. We liked the merry and modest ways of both of them. Honour to their memories. I had U-boat commanders also among my guests, among them Captain König, the commander of the commercial submarine *Deutschland*.

Thus no class and no clan were kept away from us, and I believe that we really often felt the common pulse of the Army and our Homeland, our allies and ourselves.

Chapter Ten

Military Events to the End of 1916

I
The Rumanian Campaign

Rumania's entry into the war on the side of our enemies was drawing very
nigh when the Austrian Eastern Front collapsed. It is not impossible that the
danger could have been averted even then if effect could have been given
to the German plan of a great counter-attack against the Russian southern
wing which had reached the Carpathians. This operation was not carried
out simply owing to the series of collapses on the Austro-Hungarian front.
The forces to have been used for attack were swallowed up in the defence.

In view of the course the fighting on the Eastern Front was taking in the
middle of August, the German General Staff, in conjunction with General
Jekoff, had adopted the emergency measure of delivering a great blow
against the Entente forces at Salonica with the Bulgarian wing armies. The
idea was a thoroughly sound one both from the military and political point
of view. If the enterprise succeeded, we could expect that Rumania would
be cowed and there would be an end to her hopes – hopes she must even
then have been cherishing – of co-operating with Sarrail. Rumania would
probably be compelled to remain inactive if strong Bulgarian forces were
released for employment elsewhere after a victory over Sarrail. The German
General Staff, indeed, found itself placed to a certain extent in a military
quandary through this very attack of the Bulgarians. As they were compelled to concentrate troops in Northern Bulgaria to exercise a restraining
influence on war fever in Rumania, which was growing stronger every day,
forces which might have been employed for the attack on Sarrail on
the Macedonian front had to be sent to the Danube for political reasons.

The action of Main Headquarters was explained on the one hand by their confidence in the offensive capacity of the Bulgarian Army and on the other by a certain underestimate of the enemy's strength at Salonica. In particular we were absolutely deceived about the value of the newly-formed Serbian units, six infantry divisions, which had made their appearance there.

As regards the Bulgarian attack in Macedonia, the army on the left wing reached the Struma, but, on the other hand, that on the right wing could not get through in the direction of Vodena. This conclusion of the attack in Macedonia faced Main Headquarters with a new and difficult problem. The Rumanian war fever was continually on the increase. It was to be expected that the pause in the Bulgarian operation in Macedonia would rouse the war-like passions of political circles in Bucharest. Should the German General Staff now break off the Bulgarian attack finally with a view to bringing to northern Bulgaria strong Bulgarian forces from the Macedonian front, which had now been materially shortened, or should they venture to transfer to Macedonia the forces they had assembled on the Danube with a view to renewing the attempt to cut the Rumanian Gordian knot with the sword? Rumania's declaration of war solved the problem for Main Headquarters.

Thus had the general situation developed south of the Danube. Not less difficult was the situation north of the Transylvanian Alps. For while Rumania was openly arming, the battles on the German Western Front, as well as those on the Austrian Eastern and South-Western Fronts, were using up all the troops which Main Headquarters seemed to have available as reserves or could possibly still be drawn from parts of the front which were not being attacked. It seemed impossible to release any troops for use against Rumania.

The result was that the Rumanian Declaration of War found us practically defenceless against the new enemy. I have devoted myself expressly to the development of this situation because I wish to make clear how the great crisis arose with which we found ourselves faced on and after that day.

But although the Quadruple Alliance had only made inadequate preparations to meet the Rumanian danger, it goes without saying that their responsible military leaders had come to a decision in good time about the appropriate measures for this eventuality. For this purpose a conference of the Commanders-in-Chief of Germany, Austria-Hungary and Bulgaria had been held at Pless on July 28, 1916. It resulted in the adoption of a plan of campaign in which the following words figured in the decisive Cipher 2:

'If Rumania joins the Entente, the most rapid advance in the greatest possible strength, to keep the war certainly from Bulgarian soil, and as far as possible from Austro-Hungarian, and invade Rumania. For this purpose

'(a) Demonstration of German and Austrian troops from the north, with a view to tying down strong Rumanian forces.

'(b) Rapid advance of Bulgarian troops over the frontier of the Dobrudja against the Danube crossings at Silistria and Tutrakan, with a view to protecting the right flank of the main force.

'(c) Prepare the main force to cross the Danube at Nikopoli, with a view to attack on Bucharest.'

The share of the Turks in a Rumanian campaign was arranged at a conference held with Enver Pasha at Buda-Pesth shortly afterwards. Enver undertook to prepare two Turkish divisions for speedy employment in the Balkan Peninsula.

While my predecessor still held the reins no changes were made in this plan of campaign against Rumania. However, the different Commanders-in-Chief met several times to exchange ideas about it. Moreover, Field-Marshal von Mackensen, who had been appointed to command the troops concentrated south of the Danube, was also heard on the subject. On these occasions two currents of thought were clearly distinguishable. General Conrad favoured the idea of a speedy and relentless advance on Bucharest, while General Jekoff wished to open the campaign in the Dobrudja. When war broke out the forces south of the Danube were still much too weak to carry out simultaneously the double task, i.e. effect a crossing of the Danube and attack Silistria and Tutrakan, which had been set them on this front.

On August 28 my predecessor issued orders to Field-Marshal von Mackensen to attack as soon as possible. The direction and the objective were left to his discretion.

Such was the military situation with regard to Rumania when I took over the conduct of operations on August 29.

In view of our defective preparations, the plan of campaign which had been adopted had lost its original significance. In the first place the enemy had complete freedom of action. Thanks to the state of his preparations and numerical strength, which, unknown to us, had been materially increased by Russian help, it was to be feared that our own forces would be inadequate to limit the Rumanian High Command's freedom of movement to any appreciable degree at the outset. Great objectives and easy victories seemed to beckon to the Rumanians wherever they chose to begin operations – whether across the Alps against Transylvania, or from the Dobrudja against Bulgaria. I was particularly afraid of a Russo-Rumanian offensive towards the south. Bulgarians themselves had expressed doubts whether their soldiers would fight against the Russians. General Jekoff's firm confidence in that respect was by no means universally shared in Bulgaria. No one could doubt that our enemy would rely on Russophile sentiment in at least a large part of the Bulgarian Army. Quite apart from that, it would have been easy for the Rumanians to hold out a hand to Sarrail's army by an attack on the south. What would our position be if the enemy once again succeeded in interrupting our communications with Turkey – the situation which had existed before we embarked on the campaign against Serbia – or, worse still, forcing Bulgaria out of the alliance? Turkey, isolated and simultaneously threatened from Armenia and Thrace, and Austria-Hungary, left with practically no hope, would never have survived a change in the situation so unfavourable to us.

The immediate advance of Mackensen, which my predecessor had ordered, was entirely in keeping with the needs of the hour. On the other hand, there could be no question of a crossing of the Danube with the forces available in northern Bulgaria. It would be enough for our purposes if we robbed the enemy of the initiative in the Dobrudja, and so upset his plan of campaign. But if we were to attain the last object really effectively we must not limit the Field-Marshal's attack to the capture of Tutrakan and Silistria. It would be much better, by exploiting to the full the success in the southern Dobrudja, to try and make the Rumanian High Command anxious about the rear of their main force which was on the Transylvanian frontier. In that we absolutely succeeded. In view of the Field-Marshal's progress to within a menacing distance of the Constanza–Cernavoda line, the Rumanian Commander-in-Chief found himself compelled to send reinforcements to the Dobrudja from the forces engaged in his operations against Transylvania. At the same time, by bringing up other fresh troops, he tried to take Mackensen's offensive in the rear from Rahovo, downstream from Rustchuk. A fine plan on paper! Whether it was a Rumanian inspiration or that of one of her allies is still unknown, even to-day. After the experiences which the Rumanians had had of us before the day of this Rahovo interlude, I regarded the enterprise as more than bold, and not only thought to myself but said openly: 'These troops will all be caught!' This desire, clothed in appropriate orders, was fulfilled by the Germans and Bulgarians in the best possible style. Of the dozen Rumanian battalions which reached the southern bank of the Danube at Rahovo, not a single man saw his home again during the war.

Disaster now overtook Rumania because her army did not march, her military leaders had no understanding, and at long last we succeeded in concentrating sufficient forces in Transylvania before it was too late. We took the offensive against the Rumanian Army, and on September 29 General von Falkenhayn destroyed the Rumanian western wing at Hermannstadt.

After the battle of Hermannstadt the general threw his army eastward. Disregarding the danger of the Rumanian numerical superiority and their favourable position north of the Upper Aluta, he swept his main columns south of this river, along the foot of the mountains, towards Kronstadt. The Rumanians hesitated, lost confidence in their numerical superiority, as in their own capabilities, made no attempt to exploit the situation which was still favourable to them, and halted on the whole front. Even as they did so they took the first steps in retreat. General von Falkenhayn had now secured the initiative completely, overcame the enemy's resistance south of the Geisterwald, and marched on. The Rumanians were now in full retreat at all points from Transylvania, not without suffering another bloody defeat at Kronstadt on October 8. They thus retired to the protecting wall of their country. Our next task was to get over this wall. At first we had great hopes of strategically exploiting our previous tactical successes by forcing our way directly to Bucharest from Kronstadt. Though the rugged mountains and the enemy superiority set our few weak divisions a very heavy task, the advantages of a break-through from this direction were much too obvious for us to neglect the attempt. It did not succeed, though our troops fought stoutly for every peak, every cliff, and every boulder. Our advance was completely held up when a severe early winter laid a mantle of snow on the mountains and turned the roads into icy streams. In spite of unspeakable privations and sufferings, our troops held all the ground they had gained, ready to press on when time and opportunity should allow.

Our previous experiences showed us that we must find another road into the Wallachian Plain than that which led from Kronstadt across the broadest part of the Transylvanian Alps. General von Falkenhayn proposed an irruption through the Szurduk Pass, farther west. Of course, this direction was less effective from a strategic point of view, but under existing circumstances it was the only one possible from a tactical and technical point of view. We thus invaded Rumania through this pass on November 11.

Meanwhile General von Mackensen had been ready, south of the Danube, to join hands with the invasion from the north. On October 21 he had thoroughly beaten the Russo-Rumanian army south of the Constanza–Cernavoda line. On the 22nd Constanza had fallen into the hands of the Bulgarian 3rd Army. The enemy retired north at top speed.

However, we broke off our pursuit as soon as a line of defence had been reached north of the railway which could be held with comparatively small forces. All the troops that could possibly be spared were sent to Sistova. Alluring was the prospect of occupying the whole of the Dobrudja, and then forcing our way to the rear of the Rumanian main armies in the region north of the Danube. The only question was – how were we to get the necessary bridging material to the northern Dobrudja? There were no railways there, and the Rumanian batteries on the northern bank of the Danube prevented us from using the river. We had to thank the gods that these batteries had not destroyed our one available heavy bridging-train at Sistova long before, although it had been within range of the enemy guns for months, and owed its escape solely to what we regarded as an inexplicable omission on their part. We were thus able to contemplate the crossing of the river, at any rate at that point.

In the grey morning hours of November 23 Field-Marshal von Mackensen gained a footing on the northern bank of the Danube. The direct co-operation between him and General von Falkenhayn, for which we had been working, was achieved. It was crowned by the destruction of the Rumanian main force on the battlefield of the Argesch. The curtain came down on the last act on December 3. Bucharest fell into our hands without resistance.

In the evening of that day I concluded my general report on the military situation with the words, 'A splendid day'. When I stepped out into the winter night later on, the church tower of the town of Pless was already pealing forth for the great new victory. For a long time I had been thinking of nothing else but the wonderful achievements of our brave Army and hoping that these feats would bring us nearer to the conclusion of the terrible struggle and its great sacrifices.

2
The Fighting on the Macedonian Front

The difficulties of our military situation had been materially increased in the autumn of 1916 by the course of the fighting on the Macedonian front.

Sarrail's army would have lost its very *raison d'être* if it had not taken the offensive itself at the time of the Rumanian declaration of war. We expected it to attack in the valley of the Vardar. If it had done so, and reached the neighbourhood of Gradsko, it would have seized the central point of the most important Bulgarian communications and made it impossible for the Bulgarians to remain in the district of Monastir. Sarrail chose to make

a direct attack on Monastir, perhaps compelled by special political considerations. As the result of his offensive the Bulgarian Army on the right wing
was driven from its position, south of Florina, which it had won in the
August offensive. In the further course of the fighting it lost Monastir, but
then managed to hold fast. These events had compelled us to send reinforcements to the Bulgarians from our own battlefronts, reinforcements which
had nearly all been earmarked for the Rumanian campaign. If the amount
of help we sent – about twenty battalions and many heavy and field batteries – was not very large compared with our whole resources, this sacrifice
was imposed on us at an extremely critical moment in which every man and
gun had to be economised.

Like ourselves, Turkey willingly sent help to her Bulgarian Ally in her
hard struggle. In addition to the reinforcements promised for the Rumanian
campaign, Enver Pasha sent a whole Turkish Army Corps to relieve
Bulgarian troops on the Struma front. This reinforcement was not accepted
very willingly by the Bulgarians. They were afraid that it would form the
basis for unpleasant political claims on the part of Turkey. However, Enver
Pasha assured us expressly that he would prevent any such claims being for-
mulated.

In my opinion the loss of Monastir had no military importance. In a military sense it would have been a great advantage if the Bulgarian right wing
had been voluntarily withdrawn to the extraordinarily strong positions at
Prilep, as this would have materially facilitated the work of supply to the
Bulgarian Army and correspondingly hampered that of the enemy. It was
just the enormous difficulties the Bulgarians had had with their communications which had greatly contributed to the crises which had supervened
time after time in the recent battles. The troops had had to go hungry all
day, and occasionally suffered from lack of ammunition. Putting our own
interests on one side, we had done everything in our power to enable the
Bulgarians to overcome these difficulties. The length of the communications to the rear, and the nature of this rugged and barren mountain region
made the solution of this problem uncommonly difficult.

3
The Asiatic Theatres

When Enver Pasha visited our Headquarters at the beginning of 1916 our
estimate of the situation in Asia was as follows:

The Russian offensive in Armenia, after reaching the line Trebizond–
Erzingan had come to a standstill. The Turkish offensive, which in the

summer of this year had begun in the south from the direction of Diabekr against the left flank of this Russian advance, had made no progress owing to the extraordinary difficulties of the country and the wholly inadequate supply system. It was to be expected that in view of the early approach of winter in the Armenian mountain-plateau the Russians would soon suspend their further attacks for good.

The fighting value of the two Turkish armies in the Caucasus had sunk to an extremely low level, and some divisions were divisions in name only. Privations, heavy losses, and desertion had had devastating effects on the establishments. Enver Pasha was extremely anxious about the coming winter. His troops were without the necessary clothing. Moreover, this region, barren and for the most part unpopulated and desolate, made the supply of the armies extraordinarily difficult. Owing to the shortage of draught and pack animals the requirements of the Turkish soldier in the way of food and military material in the dreary roadless mountains had to be sat- isfied by carrier-columns, and involved several days' march.

The situation in Irak at this time was better. For the moment the English had not yet made sufficient progress with their communications to be able to embark on an offensive to revenge Kut-el-Amara. We had no doubt that they would take their revenge, but we were not in a position to judge whether the Turkish forces in Irak were strong enough to offer a victorious resistance to the English attack. In spite of the very optimistic view of the Turkish General Staff we warned them that they ought to reinforce the troops there. Unfortunately, Turkey allowed herself to be led by political and pan-Islam ambitions to send a whole Army Corps into Persia.

The third Asiatic theatre, Southern Palestine, gave cause for immediate anxiety. The second Turkish attempt on the Suez Canal had been defeated in August, 1916, in the heart of the northern part of the Sinai peninsula. Following on this occurrence, the Turkish troops had gradually been with- drawn from this region and were now in the neighbourhood of Gaza, on the southern frontier of Palestine. The question if and when they would be attacked here seemed to depend largely on the time which it would take the English to complete their railway from Egypt behind their front. The threat- ened attack on Palestine seemed far more dangerous for the military and political stability of Turkey than an attack in Mesopotamia, which was so far away. We must expect that the loss of Jerusalem – quite apart from the loss of the whole of Southern Arabia which it would presumably involve – would lay a burden on Turkish statesmanship which it would not be able to carry.

Unfortunately, the strategic conditions in Southern Syria were not materially better for the Turkish operations than those in Mesopotamia.

In both theatres the Turks, in striking contrast to their enemy, suffered from such extraordinary difficulties in their communications that a material increase of their forces beyond the existing figure meant hunger and even thirst for everyone. In Syria, too, the situation as regards food supply was occasionally desperate. To add to the bad harvest and involuntary or voluntary failures of the responsible authorities, the attitude of the Arab population was generally hostile.

In the course of the war many well-meant representations were made to me in the hope of convincing me that Mesopotamia and Syria ought to be defended with stronger forces, indeed that we ought to pass to the offensive in both theatres. There was a great deal of interest in many German circles in these regions. Without saying as much, the thoughts of these gentlemen were probably straying beyond Mesopotamia to Persia, Afghanistan and India, and beyond Syria to Egypt. With their fingers on the map men dreamed that by these routes we could reach the spinal cord of British world power, our greatest peril. Perhaps, too, such ideas were an unconscious return to earlier Napoleonic schemes. But we lacked the first elements – sufficient really effective lines of supply – required for the execution of such far-reaching plans.

4
The Eastern and Western Fronts to the End of 1916

While we were occupied in overthrowing Rumania the Russians had continued their operations in the Carpathians and Galicia. On the Russian side there had been no intention of giving the new ally direct assistance in her attack on Transylvania, but the continuation of the previous Russian attacks on the Galician front was to facilitate the Rumanian operations. On the other hand, the Russians gave Rumania direct help in the Dobrudja. The reasons for this were as much political as military. Russia no doubt placed high hopes in the Russophile sentiment in the Bulgarian Army. With this idea in view, when the battles in the Southern Dobrudja began Russian officers and men tried to fraternise with the Bulgarians, and were bitterly deceived when the Bulgarians replied by firing at them. Another reason was that the occupation of Transylvania by Rumania aroused no political jealousy in Russia, but Russia could not suffer the new ally to bring Bulgaria to her knees by her own efforts and then possibly force her way to Constantinople or at least open the way there. For the capture of the Turkish capital had been the historic and religious preserve of Russia for centuries.

But even though we survived the critical situation and brought our campaign against Rumania to a successful conclusion, it cannot be said that the Russian relief attacks had completely failed to achieve their great strategic purpose. It is certainly true that Rumania's allies were not responsible for her downfall. On the contrary, the Entente did everything that their situation and resources permitted, not only in direct association with the Rumanian Army but indirectly through Sarrail's attacks in Macedonia, the Italian offensive on the Isonzo, and lastly the continuation of the Anglo-French onslaught in the West.

As has already been said, we anticipated at the start that, with the entry of Rumania into the war, the enemy would renew his attacks on the Western Front also with all his might – English stubbornness and French *élan*. That is exactly what happened.

Our rôle as supreme directors of these battles was simple. For lack of men we could not contemplate the idea of a relief attack either at Verdun or the Somme, however strong were my own inclinations for such a measure. Very soon after I took over my new post I found myself compelled by the general situation to ask His Majesty the Emperor to order the offensive at Verdun to be broken off. The battles there exhausted our forces like an open wound. Moreover, it was obvious that in any case the enterprise had become hopeless, and that for us to persevere with it would cost us greater losses than those we were able to inflict on the enemy. Our forward zone was at all points exposed to the flanking fire of superior hostile artillery. Our communications with the battle-line were extremely difficult. The battlefield was a regular hell and regarded as such by the troops. When I look back now, I do not hesitate to say that on purely military grounds it would have been far better for us to have improved our situation at Verdun by the voluntary evacuation of the ground we had captured. In August, 1916, however, I considered I could not adopt that course. To a large extent the flower of our best fighting troops had been sacrificed in the enterprise. The public at home still anticipated a glorious issue to the offensive. It would be only too easy to produce the impression that all these sacrifices had been incurred in vain. Such an impression I was anxious to avoid in the existing state of public opinion, nervous enough as it already was.

We were disappointed in our hopes that with the breaking-off of our offensive at Verdun the enemy would more or less confine himself to purely trench warfare there. At the end of October the French opened a largely-conceived and boldly-executed counter-attack on the eastern bank of the Meuse, and overran our lines. We lost Douaumont, and had no longer the strength to recover that field of honour of German heroism.

For this attack the French commander had abandoned the former practice of an artillery preparation extending over days or even weeks. By increasing the rate of fire of the artillery and trench-mortars to the extreme limit of capacity of material and men, only a short period of preparation had preceded the attack, which had then been launched immediately against the physically exhausted and morally shaken defenders. We could only hope that in the coming year he would not repeat the experiment on a greater scale and with equal success.

It was not until December that the actions at Verdun died down. From the end of August the Somme battle too had taken on the character of an extremely fierce and purely frontal contest of the forces on both sides. The task of Main Headquarters was essentially limited to feeding the armies with the reinforcements necessary to enable them to maintain their resistance. Among us battles of this kind were known as 'battles of material'. From the point of view of the attacker they might also be called 'battering-ram tactics', for the commanders had no higher ideal. The mechanical, material elements of the battle were put in the foreground, while real generalship was far too much in the background.

If our western adversaries failed to obtain any decisive results in the battles from 1915 to 1917 it must mainly be ascribed to a certain unimaginativeness in their generalship. The necessary superiority in men, war material and ammunition was certainly not lacking, nor can it be suggested that the quality of the enemy troops would not have been high enough to satisfy the demands of a more vigorous and ingenious leadership. Moreover, in view of the highly-developed railway and road system, and the enormous amount of transport at their disposal, our enemies in the West had free scope for far greater strategic subtlety. But notwithstanding all this, the demands which had to be made on our commanders and troops on this battlefield remained enormous.

At the beginning of September I visited the Western Front with my First Quartermaster-General. We had to familiarise ourselves with the conditions there if we were to render any effective help. On the way there His Imperial and Royal Highness the German Crown Prince joined us and honoured me at Montmédy by parading a Storm Company at the station. At Cambrai, on orders from His Majesty the Emperor, I met two other tried Army Commanders, the Crown Princes of Bavaria and Würtemberg, and the Prussian Staffs which had been lent to them, and held quite a long conference with the Chiefs of Staff on the Western Front. Their statements showed that rapid and ruthless action was urgently necessary if our terrible inferiority in aircraft, arms and munitions were at all to be made good.

General Ludendorff's immense capacity for work overcame this serious crisis. To my great joy officers from the front told me subsequently that the results of the conference at Cambrai had soon made themselves felt among the troops.

The extent of the demands which were being made on the army in the West was brought before my eyes quite vividly for the first time during this visit to France. I will not hesitate to admit that it was only now that I fully realised all that the Western Armies had done hitherto. What a thankless task it was for the commanders and troops, on whom pure defence was imposed and who had to renounce the vision of a tangible victory!

It was only when the arrival of the wet season began to make the ground impossible that things became quieter in the battle area of the Somme. The millions of shell-holes filled with water or became mere cemeteries. Neither of the contending parties knew the exaltation of victory. Over everyone hovered the fearful spectre of this battlefield which for desolation and horror seemed to be even worse than that of Verdun.

Chapter Eleven

My Attitude on Political Questions

I
Foreign Policy

When holding my high posts of command in the East, and even after I was appointed Chief of the General Staff of the Field Army, I had never felt either necessity or inclination to mix myself up in current political questions more than was absolutely necessary. Of course I believed that in a coalition war, with its innumerable and complicated problems that affect the conduct of operations, it was impossible for the military leaders to have absolutely no say in political affairs. Nevertheless, I recognised that the standard which Bismarck had laid down for the relations between military and political leadership in war was thoroughly sound as applied to our case also. Moltke himself was adopting the Bismarckian point of view when he said: 'The commander in his operations has to keep military victory as the goal before his eyes. But what statesmanship does with his victories or defeats is not his province. It is that of the statesman.' On the other hand, I should never have been able to account to my conscience if I had not brought forward my own views in all cases in which I was convinced that the efforts of others were leading us on doubtful paths, if I had not applied driving power where I thought I detected inaction or aversion to action, and if I had not made the very strongest representations when the conduct of operations and the future military security of my country were affected or endangered by political measures.

It will be allowed that the border-line between politics and the conduct of operations cannot be drawn with exact precision. The statesman and the soldier must have co-operated previously in peace time, as their different spheres unconditionally demand mutual understanding. In war, in which their threads are inextricably intertwined, they have to be mutually complementary the whole time.

One of the first political questions in which I was concerned, shortly after I assumed control of operations, was the future of Poland. In view of the great importance of this question during and after the war I think I ought to treat more fully of the manner in which it was handled.

From whatever side a solution of the Polish problem was sought, Prussia – Germany – was bound to be the unhappy party who had to pay the bill. Austro-Hungarian statesmanship appeared to see no dangers to her own existence in the creation of a free, united Poland. In view of the thoroughly Germanophobe attitude of the Poles, this policy of Austria was pregnant with danger for us. It could not be ignored that it meant that the strength of our alliance would in future be put to a test which could not be borne in the long run. In no circumstances could Main Headquarters, anxious about our future military situation on the Eastern frontier, leave this political point of view out of sight.

In my view all these political and military considerations showed Germany that she should touch the Polish question as little as possible, or at any rate deal with it in a very dilatory fashion, to use an expression employed in such cases. Unfortunately this was not done on the German side. The reasons why we did not act with the caution that was required are unknown to me. However that may be, the fact is that in the middle of August, 1916, a compact was made at Vienna between the statesmen of Germany and Austria-Hungary, a compact which provided for the speediest possible announcement of an independent Kingdom of Poland with an hereditary Constitutional Monarchy. Both the contracting parties had tried to make this agreement more palatable to us Germans by undertaking not to make over any part of their ancient Polish districts to the new Polish State, and by guaranteeing that Germany should have the right to command the future army of United Poland. I considered both concessions Utopian.

The political situation behind our Eastern Front would have been completely changed by this public announcement. For that reason my predecessor had immediately, and rightly, raised his voice against it. His Majesty the Emperor decided in favour of General von Falkenhayn. However, it was now clear to everyone who knew the conditions in the Danube Monarchy that the compact made in Vienna would not remain a secret. It might be kept an official secret for a short time still, but could not be got rid of altogether. As a matter of fact, it was known everywhere by the end of August. So when I went to Main Headquarters I was faced with a *fait accompli*. Shortly afterwards the Governor-General of Warsaw, who was not officially responsible to me, asked me on behalf of our Government to announce the Polish Kingdom as an act which could no longer be postponed. He gave me the choice between difficulties in the country and the certain prospect of a reinforcement of our armies by Polish troops, a reinforcement which would amount to five trained divisions in the spring of 1917 and one million men on the introduction of universal military service.

In our military situation, how could I have taken the responsibility of declining this reinforcement which was promised so definitely? But if I decided to accept it no time must be lost if we were to put fully-trained troops into the front lines by the time the next spring battles began. A victorious Germany would be able to settle the Polish question after the peace. At this point, greatly to my surprise, we met with objections on the part of the Government. It was about this time that the Government thought that they had discovered threads leading to a separate peace with Russia, and therefore considered it bad policy to compromise the steps they had taken by proclaiming an independent Poland. Political and military views were thus in conflict.

The conclusion of the whole business was that the hopes of a separate peace with Russia broke down, that the manifesto was published in the early days of November, and that the recruiting of Polish volunteers, to which it referred, was entirely without results.

As soon as the manifesto was published, the opposition between the interests of Austria and those of Germany in the Polish problem was at once revealed. Our Allies were aiming more and more openly at the union of Congress Poland with Galicia, the whole being subject to their own suzerainty. As a reply to these efforts, and failing the ability of our Government to bring them to naught, I considered that the least we could ask for was a corresponding ratification of our Eastern frontier from the purely military point of view.

Of course, the fact was that all these questions could only be decided by the result of the war. I therefore sincerely regretted that they took up so much of our time during the operations. But I cannot sufficiently insist that the friction between our allies and ourselves in political matters never had the slightest influence on our military co-operation.

The rôle that was played by Poland in our relations with Austria-Hungary was played by the Dobrudja in our political and military dealings with Bulgaria. At bottom the Dobrudja question amounted to whether Bulgaria was to secure possession of the Cernavoda–Constanza railway by her acquisition of the whole province. If she did so, she would control the last and, after the Orient Railway, the most important land route between Central Europe and the near Orient. Of course Bulgaria realised that the favourable moment to wring concessions from us in this direction was during the war. Turkey, on the other hand, as the country most immediately affected, asked for our political support against these Bulgarian plans. We gave her that support. Thus began diplomatic guerilla warfare in military guise, and lasted nearly a year. Put shortly the position was as follows:

The alliance concluded between us and Bulgaria provided, in case of war with Rumania, for a return to our ally of that part of the southern Dobrudja which had been lost in 1912, as well as for frontier adjustments in that region; but it said nothing about the assignment of the whole Rumanian province to Bulgaria. In accordance with this compact, as soon as the Rumanian campaign was virtually over, we had handed over the original Bulgarian portions of the southern Dobrudja to be administered by the Bulgarian Government, but established a German administration in the central Dobrudja in agreement with all our allies. As the result of a special economic agreement this German administration worked almost exclusively on behalf of Bulgaria. The northern Dobrudja, being in the military zone, was controlled by the 3rd Bulgarian Army there. As far as one could see, the matter seemed to have been arranged entirely satisfactorily. However, the satisfaction did not last for long.

The gauntlet was thrown down to us by the Bulgarian Minister-President. Even before the Rumanian campaign was over he had mooted to his Ministers the idea of the cession of the whole of the Dobrudja to Bulgaria, and represented the German General Staff as the obstacle in the way of these ambitions. The result was a strong political agitation against us. At first King Ferdinand had not agreed with the proceedings of his Government, but at length he felt himself compelled to yield to the general excitement. In the same way, at the outset the Bulgarian General Staff had not let themselves be drawn into the affair. They fully realised the danger of a new element of unrest being added to the political currents within their army which them-selves flowed strongly and diversely. However, before long even General Jekoff felt that he could resist the pressure of the Minister-President no longer. The Bulgarian Government lost control of the movement they had started, and the result was a general political outcry against the German General Staff, an outcry which was mainly the work of irresponsible agitators and had no respect for the relations between brothers-in-arms.

This incident betrayed the consequences of a defective side of our compact with Bulgaria. When that compact was made, we had given the Bulgarians the most far-reaching assurances possible with regard to the aggrandisement of the country and the unification of the Bulgarian race. We should have been able to give effect to those assurances only if we had won a complete victory. Bulgaria, however, was not satisfied with these assurances. She was continually advancing fresh claims without stopping to consider whether such a small State would be able, later on, to manage her new acquisitions, politically and economically.

The purport of our compact with Turkey was quite different from that with Bulgaria. As regards the Turkish Government we had only pledged ourselves before the war to maintain Turkey's territorial integrity. Now the Turks had lost an important part of their possessions in Asia during the first two years of the war. A very heavy burden had thus been laid on our treaty obligations. It did not seem impossible that these unhappy failures would have a harmful reaction on the conduct of operations. The Turkish Government could base claims in this direction which we should possibly not be in a position to disregard owing to political reasons. In these circumstances Enver Pasha's lofty conception of our common purpose and its decisive issues was of the very greatest value. Moreover, for the time being, the political views of the other Turkish statesmen seemed to offer a guarantee that Turkey's previous losses would not involve an excessive overdraft on our military account. We were thus certain that in case peace negotiations were opened, the Turkish Government would not tie us down to the strict letter of our compact, but would accept the recognition of a more or less formal suzerainty over a large part of the lost territory so long as we succeeded in finding a formula which would preserve the prestige of the present Government.

It was thus a very important task, both for our statesmen and our military commanders, to support the existing Ottoman Government; it would not be easy to find a substitute for Enver or Talaat Pasha, who were completely and absolutely loyal to us. Of course, this does not mean that we attempted to check political currents in Turkey which had an adverse influence on the military task of the nation within the framework of the combined operations. I am referring here to my previous remarks about the Pan-Islam movement. From the military point of view it always tended to deflect Turkey into wrong paths. After the collapse of Russia, Pan-Islam sought its conquests in the direction of the Caucasus. Indeed, it cast its eye beyond them to the Transcaspian region, and finally lost itself in the distant areas of Central Asia, inspired by the fantastic ambition of uniting all men of its own culture and faith under the Ottoman sway.

It was obvious that we could not lend military support to such Oriental political dreams, but that we must demand the abandonment of these far-reaching schemes for the sake of existing military realities. Unfortunately, all our efforts failed.

How much more difficult than our efforts to exercise influence on the problems of Turkish foreign policy must be those to obtain some influence on her domestic affairs. And yet we could not refrain from making at least an attempt to acquire such influence. It was not only her primitive economic condition that impelled us. Ordinary human feelings worked in the same direction.

The surprising revival of Ottoman military power and the renascence of her ancient heroism in this fight for existence also showed up the darkest side of Turkish domination. I mean her attitude to the Armenian portions of her Empire. The Armenian question embodied one of Turkey's most difficult problems. It affected both the Pan-Turkish and the Pan-Islam ideals. The whole world took a deep interest during the war in the methods with which the fanatical Turk attempted to solve it. Attempts have been made to associate us Germans with the horrible occurrences in the whole Turkish Empire, and, towards the end of the war, even in Armenian Trans-Caucasia. I therefore feel it my duty to touch on this question here, and indeed have no reason to pass over the part we played in silence. We never hesitated, both verbally and in writing, to exercise a deterrent influence on the savage and licentious methods of warfare which were traditional in the East, thanks to racial hatreds and religious animosities.

2
The Peace Question

It was in the very middle of our preparations for the Rumanian campaign that the peace question came to my notice. So far as I know, it was first brought up by the Austro-Hungarian Foreign Minister, Baron Burian. Those who know me and my views on war will require no further assurance that my natural human feelings welcomed such a step. I considered it my duty in this matter to strive for such a solution that neither the Army nor the Homeland should suffer any injury. Main Headquarters had to co-operate in settling the wording of our peace offer. It was a difficult and thankless task to avoid creating an impression of weakness at home and abroad while giving all provocative expressions a wide berth. I was able to see with what a devout sense of duty to God and man my All-Highest War Lord devoted himself to the solution of this peace problem, and I do not think that he regarded a complete failure of this step as probable. On the other hand, my own confidence in its success was quite small from the outset. Our adversaries had vied with one another in putting forward excessive claims, and it appeared to me out of the question that any of the enemy Governments could and would voluntarily go back on the promises which they had made to each other and their peoples. However, this view did not in any way affect my honest intention to co-operate in this work for the good of humanity.

On December 12 our readiness to conclude peace was announced to our enemies. Our answer from enemy propaganda, as well as the hostile camps, was only scorn and a rebuff.

Hot on the heels of our own peace step came a similar effort on the part of the President of the United States. Main Headquarters was informed by the Imperial Chancellor of the suggestions which the President had made through the medium of our ambassador in the United States. I myself considered that President Wilson was not exactly suited to the rôle of an unprejudiced intermediary as I could not overcome my feeling that the President had strong leanings towards our enemies, and more particularly England. That was indeed a perfectly natural consequence of his Anglo-Saxon origin. Like millions of my countrymen, I could not consider Wilson's previous attitude as neutral, although, possibly, it did not contravene the strict letter of neutrality. In all questions of breaches of International Law the President treated England with all possible consideration. In so doing, he had received some very severe rebuffs. On the other hand, in the question of submarine warfare, which was our only reply to England's arbitrary actions, Wilson had shown the greatest touchiness and immediately taken to threats of war. Germany signified her assent to the principle of Wilson's proposals. The reply of our enemies to Wilson was a recital of their demands, which to all intents and purposes comprised the permanent economic and political paralysis of Germany, the dismemberment of Austria-Hungary and the destruction of the Ottoman State. To anyone who judged the military situation at that time dispassionately, it must have been obvious that the enemy's war aims had no prospect of acceptance except by a hopelessly defeated foe, and that we had no reason to regard ourselves in that position. In any case, as things were then, I should have regarded it as a crime to my country and a betrayal of our Allies if I had taken any other course but absolutely refuse to consider enemy demands of that kind.

In contrast to our view, President Wilson's message of January 22 to the American Senate saw in our enemies' declaration of war aims of January 10 a more suitable basis for peace efforts than our diplomatic note, which merely expounded the principles on which we agreed to the continuation of his steps for peace. This behaviour on the part of the President shook my confidence in his impartiality even further. I should not have refused my approval of the lofty and to a certain extent praiseworthy humanitarian note in his message if I had not searched it in vain for any rejection of the attempt of our enemies to hold us up as men of a lower order. Moreover, the sentence about the restoration of a single free and independent Poland aroused my distrust. It seemed to me to be aimed directly at Austria-Hungary and ourselves, to compel the Danube Monarchy to renounce Galicia, and would mean the loss of territory or suzerainty for Germany as well. For us, the message was a Declaration of War rather than a peace proposal. If we had once committed ourselves into the hands of the President we should have found ourselves on a steep slope which threatened in the long run to bring us to a peace which would have meant the renunciation of our whole political, economic and military position.

In October, 1918, I learned from certain publications that immediately after his message to the Senate of January 22, 1917, President Wilson had informed the German Ambassador in Washington of his willingness to take official steps for peace. The news had reached Berlin on January 28. Until the autumn of 1918 I had never heard of this step of Wilson which apparently went pretty far to meet us. I do not know, even today, whether mistakes or a chain of adverse circumstances were responsible. In my view, war with America was inevitable at the end of January, 1917. At that time Wilson knew of our intention to start unrestricted U-boat warfare on February 1. There can be no doubt that, thanks to the English practice of intercepting and deciphering our telegrams on this subject to the German Ambassador in Washington, Wilson was as well informed about this matter as about the contents of all our other cables. The message to the Senate of January 22, and the offer of mediation which accompanied it, were thus branded for what they were at the outset. Disaster was on its way. It could therefore no longer be averted by our declaration of January 29 that we were prepared to stop U-boat warfare out of hand if the President were successful in his efforts to establish a basis for peace negotiations.

3
Home Politics

During the war Main Headquarters had to take an active interest in several internal problems, especially in the economic sphere. We did not seek these problems; they thrust themselves on our attention much more than we wished. The close relations between the Army and industry made it impossible for us to draw a hard-and-fast line between industrial questions at home and the conduct of operations.

I take full responsibility for the form of the great industrial programme which bears my name. The one principle which I laid down for its working-out was that the needs of our fighting troops must be supplied at any cost.

I should have regarded any other foundation as a crime against our Army and my country. It is true that our demands meant that the figures would reach gigantic proportions compared with what had gone before, but I did not venture to judge whether they could be attained.

I had devoted myself wholeheartedly to the introduction of the Auxiliary Service Law. It was my wish that in the crisis facing our Fatherland, not only every man fit to fight, but every man fit to work, and even women, should place themselves or be placed at the disposal of our great cause. I was convinced that by a law of this kind, moral as well as personal forces would be released which we could throw into the scales of war. The final form of the law certainly produced somewhat modest results which indeed differed materially from those we had had in view. Disillusioned as I was, I almost regretted that we had not tried to achieve our purpose by utilising existing legislation, as had been proposed in other quarters. The idea of presenting the acceptance of the law as a powerful and impressive manifesto by the whole German people had made me overlook the influence of the currents of domestic politics. In the long run, the law was passed, not through the pressure of public opinion, but on the grounds of industrial necessities.

The absence of an Industrial General Staff, trained for war, made itself very severely felt in the course of the struggle. Experience showed that such a Staff could not be procured by magic during the war. Though our military and financial mobilisation was brilliantly carried out, there was no industrial mobilisation at all. What proved essential in this last respect, and therefore had to be introduced, exceeded all previous calculation. As a result of our virtually complete loss of foreign imports and the enormous consumption of material and ammunition as the result of the long duration of the war, we saw ourselves faced with quite new problems which human fancy had hardly ventured even to contemplate in peacetime. As a result of the colossal problems which affected both the Army and the nation, the closest co-operation of all the State authorities revealed itself as an absolute necessity if affairs were to be conducted with a minimum of friction. Indeed, it was really vital to create a common central authority, to which all demands should be made and from which all supplies should flow. Some such authority alone would have been able to take far-seeing economic and military decisions; it would have had to act with an open mind and be assisted by economic experts who were in a position to foresee the consequences of their decisions. There was no such authority. I need not try to explain that only an unusually gifted intelligence and exceptional organising powers could have been equal to such a task. Even if all these preliminary requirements had been fulfilled, there would still have been considerable friction.

Chapter Twelve

Preparations for the Coming Campaign

I
Our Tasks

When the results of the fighting in the year 1916 could be more or less realised, we had to get some clear idea of how the war was to develop in the year 1917. We had not the slightest doubt about what our enemies would do in the coming year. We had to anticipate a general hostile offensive, as soon as their preparations and the weather permitted it. It was to be assumed that, warned by the experiences of the past year, our enemies would endeavour to co-ordinate their attacks on all fronts, if we left them time and opportunity to do so.

Nothing could commend itself more strongly, or be more in accordance with our desires and feelings, than to anticipate this general offensive, and in so doing blow the enemy's plans sky high and secure the initiative at the outset. I can certainly claim that with this end in view I had neglected nothing in the past campaigning year, as soon as the necessary resources, on a scale at all adequate, had been put at my disposal. Now, however, we had to be careful that this ambition did not cloud our views of the tactical situation.

There was no doubt that, at the end of 1916, the position as regards relative numbers between us and our enemies had developed even more to our disadvantage than had been the case at the beginning of the year. Rumania had joined our enemies, and in spite of her heavy defeat remained a serious factor with which we had still to reckon. Behind the Russian lines the Rumanian Army found shelter and time for reorganisation, a process for which she could rely on the co-operation of the Entente in the fullest measure.

It was a fateful thing for us that throughout the whole war our High Command never succeeded in forcing even one of our smaller opponents, with the exception of Montenegro, to desert the ranks of our enemies. In 1914 the Belgian Army had escaped from Antwerp and was now facing us, though practically inactive, and thus imposing on us a certain wastage which was not unimportant. Our experiences with the Serbian Army in 1915 had been only superficially better for us. It had avoided our enveloping movements, though its condition was very pitiful. In the summer of 1916 it reappeared, once more in fighting trim, in the Macedonian theatre, and its units were being continually reinforced and increased from all kinds of countries, of late more particularly by Austro-Hungarian deserters of Slav nationality.

We were in considerable doubt as to whether our main danger would come from the West or the East. From the standpoint of numerical superiority only, the danger appeared greater on the Eastern Front. We had to anticipate that in the winter of 1916–17, as in previous years, Russia would succeed in making good her losses and renewing the offensive powers of her armies. No intelligence came through to us which revealed any particularly striking indications of the disintegration of the Russian Army. Besides, experience had taught me to accept reports of this kind with extreme caution, whenever and from whatever source they originated.

Faced with this Russian superiority, we could not regard the condition of the Austro-Hungarian Army without anxiety. Reports which we received did not reveal much confidence that the favourable issue of the Rumanian campaign, and the relatively favourable if still tense situation on the Italian front, had had a really uplifting and far-reaching influence on the *morale* of the Austro-Hungarian troops. We had further to anticipate that attacks by the Russians might once again mean the collapse of the Austrian lines. It was in any case impossible to withdraw direct German support from the Austrian front. On the contrary, we had to be ready to send further reinforcements to our allies' front in case of emergency.

It was equally uncertain how things would shape on the Macedonian front. In the course of the last battle a German Army Group Headquarters had taken over the command of the right and centre Bulgarian armies – in short, the front from Ochrida to Lake Doiran. German officers were occupied in giving the Bulgarian armies the benefit of their wealth of experience on all our fronts. The result of this work would only be revealed when fighting was resumed. For the time being, it seemed advisable not to pitch our hopes too high. In any case, we had to be ready to send help to the Macedonian front also.

On our Western Front we had to expect that in the coming spring our enemies would reappear in the arena in full strength, in spite of the heavy losses they undoubtedly had suffered in the past year. I use the expression 'full strength' in the conditional sense only, for though the troops could be brought up to their old level numerically in the course of a few months, it was not the same with their quality. In this respect the enemy was subject to the same hard laws as ourselves.

The tactical situation on the most important part of this front was much as follows. In a fierce and obstinate conflict on the Somme, which lasted five months, the enemy had pressed us back to a depth of about six miles on a stretch of nearly twenty-five miles. This success which had been bought at the price of hundreds of thousands of lives was truly small when compared with the length of our whole front. However, the salient in our lines affected the neighbouring fronts north and south. It was urgently necessary that the position should be improved, otherwise we ran a risk of being enveloped in this salient by enemy attacks there combined with secondary attacks north and south of it. An enveloping attack of our own against the enemy at the point where he had broken through was the most obvious remedy, but in view of our general situation it was almost the most doubtful. Could we venture to devote all our resources to a great attack in the Somme region, alive with enemy troops, while running the risk of a breakthrough on some other part of the Western Front or the Eastern Front?

If an improvement in the configuration of the front bequeathed by the Somme battle could not be effected by an attack, it only remained to adopt the necessary alternative and withdraw our lines. We therefore decided to adopt that expedient, and transferred our line of defence, which had been pushed in at Péronne at one point and bulged out to west of Bapaume, Roye and Noyon at others, to the chord position Arras–St. Quentin–Soissons. This new line is known as the Siegfried Line.

So it was a case of retreat on the Western Front instead of attack! It was a dreadful disappointment for the army in the West; worse, perhaps, for the public at home; and worst – as we had good reason to fear – for our allies. Loud rejoicings among our enemies! Could more suitable material for propaganda be imagined? The brilliant, if somewhat belated, visible result of the bloody battle, the collapse of German resistance, the impetuous unceasing pursuit, the paroxysms about our methods of warfare! We could hear all the stops being drawn out beforehand. What a hail of propagandist literature would now descend on and behind our lines!

Our great retirement began on March 16, 1917. The enemy followed us into the open, generally speaking, with considerable caution. Where this caution was inclined to give place to greater haste our rearguards knew how to cool down the enemy zeal.

The measure we took not only gave us more favourable local conditions on the Western Front, but improved our whole situation. The shortening of our lines in the West made it possible for us to build up strong reserves. We were attracted by the idea of throwing at least a part of those reserves upon the enemy at the very moment when he was following our retreat to the Siegfried position across the open country, where we felt ourselves absolutely superior to him. However, we renounced the idea and kept our powder dry for the future.

The situation which we created for ourselves by the spring of 1917 may perhaps be described as a great strategic 'stand to', a stage in which we abandoned the initiative to the enemy for the time being, but from which we could emerge at any time to attack any of the enemy's weak points.

In connection with these dispositions I must mention two plans to which we had to devote our attention in the winter of 1916–17. These were proposals for attacks in Italy and Macedonia. In the former case the initiative was taken by General Conrad von Hötzendorff during that winter. He promised himself a far-reaching effect on our entire military and political situation as a result of a great victory over Italy. What General Conrad mainly had in mind in his proposal was the favourable effect of a successful campaign against Italy on public opinion in Austria-Hungary. He relied on the great relief of the military strain which such a victory would mean for Austria-Hungary. I could readily enough admit the justice of these points of view. Without strong German help – it was a matter of about twelve German divisions – General Conrad considered he could never again undertake an attack on the Italians from the Southern Tyrol. On the other hand, I did not think I could take the responsibility of allowing so many German troops to be locked up for an unlimited time in an enterprise which, in my opinion, lay too far from our Eastern and Western fronts, which were the most important and the most imperilled.

The same considerations applied to the question of an attack on the Entente troops in Macedonia. Bulgaria was toying with this plan, and very naturally from her own point of view, for if we had won a decisive victory it would have compelled the Entente to evacuate this region. By that means Bulgaria would have been practically completely relieved, in a political as well as a military sense. Further, the enterprise was dear to the heart of the nation and its Government, for the Bulgarians were always casting greedy eyes at the fine harbour of Salonica which had been so great a bone of contention. I admit that this last point of view had no weight with me, and in my opinion at that time the military relief of Bulgaria would have been of no advantage to our general situation. If we had compelled the Entente forces to withdraw from Macedonia we should have had them on our necks again on the Western Front.

From all I have said it must be perfectly clear that the strain on the German armies was so great, as a result of the general situation, that we could not allow it to be increased by further undertakings except such as were imperatively required for military and political reasons. Even the most splendid plans, which might offer certain prospects of great military victories, could not be allowed to turn us aside from our most important and immediate military task. This task was the fighting in the East and West, and indeed on both fronts, against overwhelming enemy superiority.

Turkey could be given no special instructions for 1917. Her task was to defend her territorial possessions and keep the armies facing her away from us. If she succeeded in accomplishing this she would be doing all that was required of her within the framework of our combined operations.

With a view to preserving the efficiency of the troops thus employed, in the autumn of 1916 we had suggested to the Turkish General Staff that they should withdraw the bulk of their two Caucasus armies from the sparsely populated and barren Armenian plateau with a view to making it easier for the troops to get through the winter. The necessary orders were issued too late, and as a result large numbers of troops were killed off by hunger and cold, as we had foreseen.

2
The U-boat Warfare

The desire to employ the U-boat weapon in full force with a view to a speedy delivery of our homeland from its sufferings and the relief of the Army in the terrible contest, was in existence before I took over the conduct of operations. In the pitiless blockade battle against our non-combatants at home, it was a question of an eye for an eye and a tooth for a tooth. Everything else seemed callousness towards our own flesh and blood.

But though we had the weapon and the will to use it, we must not lose sight of the consequences which might flow from the ruthless employment of this destructive instrument. If we need not have any regard for the stony-hearted enemy, we must have regard for the interests of maritime nations which had hitherto remained neutral. As a result of the employment of this weapon, the nation must not be faced with greater dangers and anxieties than those from which we proposed to deliver it. There was thus a considerable amount of hesitation, a hesitation comprehensible enough, to which ordinary human feelings also contributed.

Such was the situation when I appeared at Main Headquarters. To all the serious crises on land was now added a troublesome and fateful problem at sea. At first sight the decision of this question was the province of the Civil Government and the Naval Staff. Yet the General Staff was also seriously concerned. It was perfectly obvious that on purely military grounds we should desire the commencement of the U-boat campaign. The advantages which it would bring to our operations on land was plain to every eye. It would have been an immense relief to us if the enemy's manufacture of war material, or its transport over sea, could be materially hampered. It would be equally valuable if we succeeded at any rate in partially paralysing their overseas operations. What an immense relief that would mean not only to Bulgaria and Turkey, but to ourselves! And it would not have cost us a drop of German blood! Further, there would be a chance of restricting the imports of raw material and food into the Entente countries to an intolerable degree, and placing England, if not her Allies, before the fateful alternative either of holding out the hand of reconciliation to us or losing her place in world trade. The U-boat campaign seemed likely to have a decisive effect on the course of the war; indeed, at the beginning of 1917 it appeared to be the only means we could employ to secure a victorious conclusion to the war if we were compelled to fight on.

The most difficult question was and remained: 'Within what time would U-boat warfare produce decisive results?' On this question the Naval Staff could, of course, make no definite promises. But even what they alleged was an estimate based on the most conservative calculations was so favourable to us, that I considered that we were entitled to face the risk of finding that we had brought another adversary into the field as the result of employing the new weapon.

But even though the Navy was very insistent, political and military considerations demanded that the commencement of the unrestricted U-boat campaign should be postponed over the autumn of 1916. In the critical military situation in which we found ourselves at that time we dared not bring a new opponent into the field. In any case, we had to wait until the Rumanian campaign had ended victoriously. If it did so, we should find ourselves strong enough to prevent any neutral States on our frontiers from joining the ranks of our enemies, to whatever extent England might intensify her economic pressure upon them.

To considerations of a political nature were added others of a military nature. We did not wish to resort to the intensified use of the U-boat weapon until our peace step had proved a complete failure. When this peace measure collapsed, however, military considerations alone had any weight with me. The development of the military situation, especially in Rumania, in my opinion now permitted the most drastic use of this very effective weapon.

On January 9, 1917, our All-Highest War-Lord decided in favour of the proposals of the Naval and General Staffs and against the Imperial Chancellor, von Bethmann. Not one of us was in doubt about the seriousness of the step. But the adoption of unrestricted U-boat warfare, with its alluring prospects, increased the moral resolution of both the army and nation to continue the war on land for a long time to come.

I cannot close this section without questioning the view that has been put forward that with the entry of America into the ranks of our enemies our cause was finally lost. But let us first take a glance at the predicament in which we put our enemies, both by our U-boat operations and, at times, by our great successes on land in the spring of 1917. We shall then be in a position to realise that we were several times within an ace of wearing the victor's laurels ourselves, and will perhaps appreciate that other than military reasons are responsible for the fact that the war did not end victoriously, or at least tolerably, for us.

3
Kreuznach

After the victorious conclusion of the Rumanian campaign and the relief it brought to our situation in the East, the centre of gravity of our next operations must be sought in the West. In any case it was here that we must anticipate an early commencement of the fighting in the next campaigning year. We wanted to be close to the battlefield. If we established our headquarters in the West it would be easier and take less time to get into direct personal touch with the headquarters of the Army Groups and Armies. A further reason was that the Emperor Charles wished to be near the political authorities of his country, and was, moreover, unwilling to dispense with direct personal intercourse with his Commander-in-Chief. Accordingly, in the early months of 1917 the Headquarters of the Austro-Hungarian Army was transferred to Baden near Vienna. The result was that there was no longer any reason why His Majesty our Emperor and Main Headquarters should remain at Pless. In February we moved our Headquarters to Kreuznach.

The district in which we now settled was associated in my mind with memories of my previous activities as Chief of Staff in the Rhine Province. I had made the acquaintance of the town of Kreuznach itself at that time. Its inhabitants now vied with one another in giving us proofs of quiet hospitality. Among other ways this hospitality was shown in the fact that our quarters and common dining-room were decorated with fresh-cut flowers every day by young ladies.

Chapter Thirteen

The Hostile Offensive in the First Half of 1917

I
In the West

As soon as the best season of the year began, we awaited the opening of the expected general enemy offensive with the greatest anxiety. We had made strategic preparations to meet it by re-grouping our armies, but in the course of the winter we had also taken tactical measures to deal with what would in any case be the greatest of all the efforts of our enemies.

Not the least important of these measures were the changes we introduced into our previous system of defence. They were based on our experiences in the earlier battles. In future our defensive positions were no longer to consist of single lines and strong points but of a network of lines and groups of strong points. In the deep zones thus formed we did not intend to dispose our troops on a rigid and continuous front but in a complex system of nuclei and distributed in breadth and depth. The defender had to keep his forces mobile to avoid the destructive effects of the enemy fire during the period of artillery preparation, as well as voluntarily to abandon any parts of the line which could no longer be held, and then to recover by a counter-attack all the points which were essential to the maintenance of the whole position. These principles applied in detail as in general.

We thus met the devastating effects of the enemy artillery and trench-mortar fire and their surprise infantry attacks with more and more deeply distributed defensive lines and the mobility of our forces. At the same time we developed the principle of saving men in the forward lines by increasing the number of our machine-guns and so economising troops.

So far-reaching a change in our defensive system undoubtedly involved an element of risk. This element lay primarily in the fact that in the very middle of the war we demanded a break with tactical practices and experiences with which our subordinate commanders and the men had become familiar, and to which many of them naturally ascribed some particular virtue. A change from one tactical method to another provoked a mild crisis even in peace time. On the one hand it involved a certain amount of exaggeration of the new features, and on the other a very stubborn adhesion to the old. Even the most carefully worded instructions left room for misunderstandings.

But it was not for these reasons only that our tactical innovations were a risky step. It was much more difficult to give ourselves an affirmative answer to the question whether, in the middle of war, our army, constituted as it was now, was in a position to adopt the new measures and translate them into the reality of the battlefield. Additionally our new defensive system made heavy demands on the moral resolution and capacity of the troops because it abandoned the firm external rigidity of the serried lines of defence, and thereby made the independent action, even of the smallest bodies of troops, the supreme consideration. Tactical co-operation was no longer obtained by defences that were continuous to the eye, but consisted of the invisible moral bond between the men engaged in such tactical co-operation.

The first storm in the West broke just after the beginning of spring. On April 9 the English attack at Arras gave the signal for the opening of the enemy's great spring offensive. The attack was prepared for days with the whole fury of masses of enemy artillery and trench-mortars. There was nothing of the surprise tactics which Nivelle had employed in the October of the previous year. Did not the English believe in these tactics, or did they feel themselves too inexperienced to adopt them? For the moment the reason was immaterial. The fact alone was sufficient and spoke a fearful language. The English attack swept over our first, second and third lines. Groups of strong points were overwhelmed or silenced after a heroic resistance. Masses of artillery were lost. Our defensive system had apparently failed!

A ray appeared, though a tiny flickering ray. The English did not seem to have known how to exploit the success they had gained to the full. This was a piece of luck for us, as so often before. After the report I pressed the hand of my First Quartermaster-General with the words: 'We have lived through more critical times than today together.' Today! It was his birthday! My confidence was unshaken. I knew that reinforcements were marching to the battlefield and that trains were hastening that way. The crisis was over. Within me it was certainly over. But the battle raged on.

Another battle picture. After the first weeks of April the French guns were thundering at Soissons, and from there far away eastwards to the neighbourhood of Rheims. Here Nivelle commanded, the reward of the fame he had won at Verdun. Apparently he, too, had not drawn the inferences we expected from his recent experiences at Verdun. The French artillery raged for days, nay weeks. Our defensive zone was to be converted into a waste of rubble and corpses. All that was lucky enough to escape physical destruction was at any rate to be morally broken. There seemed little doubt that such a consummation would be attained in this fearful conflagration. At length Nivelle supposed our troops to be annihilated, or at any rate sufficiently cowed. On April 16 he sent forward his battalions, pretty confident of victory. Then the incredible happened. From the shattered trenches and shell-holes rose German manhood, possessed of German strength and resolution, and scattered death and desolation among the advancing ranks and the masses behind them which were already flinching under the storm of our artillery fire and tending to herd together. The German resistance might be overcome at the points where destruction had been fiercest, but in this battle of giants what did the loss of small sectors mean compared with the triumphant resistance of the whole front?

In the very first day it was clear that the French had suffered a downright defeat. The bloody reverse proved the bitterest, indeed the most overwhelming disappointment to the French leaders and their men.

The battles of Arras, Soissons and Rheims raged on for weeks. After the first few days our adversaries won not a single success worth mentioning, and after a few weeks they sank back exhausted on the battlefield and resumed trench warfare. So our defence measures had proved themselves brilliantly, after all.

Now for a third picture. The scene was changed to the heights of Wytschaete and Messines, north-west of Lille and opposite Kemmel Hill. It was June 7, a moment at which the failure of the battles I have just mentioned was already obvious. The position on the Wytschaete hills, the key to the salient at that point, was very unfavourable for a modern defence. The comparatively restricted back area did not permit the employment of a sufficiently deep defensive zone. Our forward trenches lay on the western slope and were a magnificent target for hostile artillery. The wet soil sank in summer and winter; below ground were mines innumerable, for this method of warfare had been employed earlier on in extremely bitter fighting for the possession of the most important points. Yet it was long since any sounds of underground burrowing had been heard. Our trenches on the heights of St Eloi as well as at the corner-stone of Wytschaete and Messines were exposed to hostile artillery fire not only from the west but from north and south as well.

The English prepared their attack in the usual way. The defenders suffered heavily, more heavily than ever before. Our anxious question whether it would not be better voluntarily to evacuate the heights had received the manly answer: 'We shall hold, so we will stand fast.' But when the fateful June 7 dawned the ground rose from beneath the feet of the defenders, their most vital strong-points collapsed, and through the smoke and falling débris of the mines the English storm troops pressed forward over the last remnants of the German defence. Violent attempts on our part to restore the situation by counter-attacks failed under the murderous, hostile artillery fire which from all sides converted the back-area of the lost position into a veritable inferno. Nevertheless, we again succeeded in bringing the enemy to a halt before he had effected a complete breach in our lines. Our losses in men and war material were heavy. It would have been better to have evacuated the ground voluntarily.

In my judgment the general result of the great enemy offensive in the West had not been unsatisfactory hitherto. We had never been defeated. Even our worst perils had been surmounted. Though gaining a good deal of ground, our enemies had never succeeded in reaching more distant goals, much less in passing from the breakthrough battle to open warfare. Once more we were to exploit our successes in the West on other fronts.

2
In the Near and Far East

Even before the wild dance had begun on our Western Front, Sarrail had renewed his attacks in Macedonia with his centre of gravity at Monastir. These events, too, commanded our full attention. Once more our enemy had far-reaching objectives. Simultaneously with this onslaught on the Bulgarian front, our enemy had instigated a rising in Serbia with a view to menacing our communications with the Balkan peninsula. The rising was suppressed at its critical point, Nish, before it had extended over the whole of Old Serbia, an eventuality which was much feared by Government circles in Bulgaria. The fighting on the Macedonian front was marked by great bitterness, but the Bulgarian Army succeeded in maintaining its position practically intact without our having to send further German reinforcements. A very satisfactory result for us! Our allies had fought very well. They had plainly realised that the work we had done in their ranks had been brilliantly justified. I felt convinced that the Bulgarian Army would remain equal to its task in future, and this opinion was confirmed when the Entente renewed their attacks in May. Once more their onslaught along the whole front from Monastir to Lake Doiran was an utter failure.

The front on the Armenian plateau had remained inactive. Occasional small raids during the winter seemed to be inspired far more by anxiety to secure booty than by any revival of the offensive spirit on either side. Under the influence of their great supply difficulties, the Russians had withdrawn the bulk of their troops from the wildest and most desolate parts of the mountains to more fertile districts in the interior. The complete pause in the Russian activity was certainly surprising. The Turks sent us no news which could in any way explain it.

On the Irak front the English attacked in February, and were in possession of Bagdad by March 11. They owed this success to their skilful envelopment of the strong Turkish positions. In Southern Palestine the English attacked at Gaza in great superiority, but purely frontally and with little tactical skill. Their onslaught collapsed completely in front of the Turkish lines. It was only the failure of a Turkish column which had been sent out to envelop their wing that saved the English from utter defeat.

3
On the Eastern Front

Even before the French and English opened their general offensive in the West the foundations of the Russian front were already trembling. Under our mighty blows the framework of the Russian State had begun to go to pieces.

The process of disintegration had undoubtedly begun in the Russian State. If a dictatorship, with powers to be employed as ruthlessly as those which had just been overthrown, did not arise, this process would continue, though perhaps slower than normally in the mighty and ponderous Russian Colossus with its unwieldy movements. From the outset our plan was to leave this process alone. We must, however, take care that it left us alone, and did not perhaps destroy us too.

For me personally to wait quietly while the process of Russian disintegration developed was a great sacrifice. If for political reasons I was not allowed to consider an offensive in the East, all my soldierly feelings urged me towards an attack in the West. Could any notion be more obvious than that of bringing all our effective fighting troops from the East to the West and then taking the offensive? I was thinking of the failure of the English attack at Arras and the severe defeat of France between Soissons and

Rheims. America was still far away. If she came after the strength of France was broken, she would come too late!

However, the Entente too recognised the peril with which they were menaced, and worked with all their might to prevent the collapse of Russian power, and with it the great relief that collapse would mean to our Eastern Front. Russia must remain in the war, at least until the new armies of America were on French soil; otherwise the military and moral defeat of France was certain. For this reason the Entente sent politicians, agitators and officers to Russia in the hope of bolstering up the shattered Russian front. Nor did these missions forget to take money with them, for in many parts of Russia money is more effective than political argument.

Once more we were robbed of the brightest prospect of victory by these counter-measures. The Russian front was kept in being, not through its own strength, but mainly through the work of the agitators whom our enemies sent there, and who achieved their purpose, even against the will of the Russian masses.

Our relations to the Russian Army on the Eastern Front at first took the form of an ever more obvious approach to an armistice, although there was nothing in writing. By degrees the Russian infantry everywhere declared that they would fight no more. Yet with the apathy of the masses they remained in their trenches. If the relations between the two sides led to too obviously amicable an intercourse, the Russian artillery intervened every now and then. This arm of the service was still in the hands of its leaders, not out of any natural conservative instinct, but because it counted fewer independent heads than its sister arm. The agitators of the Entente and the officers still had great influence with the Russian batteries. It was true that the Russian infantry grumbled about the way in which this long-desired armistice was thus disturbed, and indeed occasionally turned on their artillery sister and openly rejoiced when our shells fell among the gun-pits. But the general situation I have described remained unchanged for months.

The Russian disinclination to fight was most patent on the northern wing. From there it extended to the south. The Rumanians were apparently unaffected by it. After May it appeared that the commanders had got the reins in their hands again, even in the north. Friendly relations between the two trench lines gradually stopped. There was a return to the old method of intercourse, weapon in hand. Before long there was no doubt that in the areas behind the Russian front the work of discipline was being carried on at top pressure. In this way parts, at any rate, of the Russian Army were once more made capable of resistance, and indeed capable of attack. The war current had set strongly, and Russia advanced to a great offensive under Kerensky.

It was difficult to say whether Kerensky adopted the idea of an offensive of his own free will, or was induced or compelled to do so by the Entente. In either case it was entirely to the interest of the Entente that Russia should be driven into an offensive once more. In the West they had already offered up in vain a good half of their best fighting troops; perhaps more than half. What other alternative had they but to send in what they had left, as American help was still far away? It was in these very months that the U-boat warfare was encroaching on the margin of existence of our bitterest and most irreconcilable foe to such a degree that it appeared questionable whether shipping would be available for the American reinforcements in the coming year. German troops must therefore be held down fast in the East, and for that reason Kerensky must send Russia's last armies to the attack. It was a venturesome game, and for Russia most venturesome of all! Yet the calculation on which it was based was an accurate one, for if the game suc-ceeded, not only would the Entente be saved, but a dictatorship in Russia could be created and maintained. Without such a dictatorship Russia would lapse into chaos.

It must be admitted that the prospects of Kerensky's offensive against the German front were hardly more inviting than on previous occasions. Good German divisions might have been sent to the West, but those that were left were sound enough to hold up a Russian onslaught. A large number of Russian apostles of freedom were roving the back areas of the army for loot, or streaming homewards. Even good elements were leaving the front, inspired by anxiety for their relatives and possessions in view of the inter-nal catastrophe which was threatening. But, on the other hand, the situa-tion on the Austro-Hungarian front gave cause for anxiety. It was to be feared that once more, as in 1916, the Russian onslaught would find weak spots. In the spring of this year a representative of our ally had given us a very grave description of the state of things on this part of the front, and told us his general impression that 'the great majority of the Austro-Slav troops would offer even less resistance to a Russian attack than they had in 1916.' The fact was that the process of political disintegration was affecting them simultaneously with the Russian troops. The same authority gave us Kerensky's plan which had been told him by deserters. It was this: local attacks against the Germans in order to tie them down, while the main blow was dealt at the Austro-Hungarian wall. And that is exactly what happened.

The Russians attacked the German lines at Riga, Dvinsk and Smorgon and were driven off. The wall in Galicia proved to be stone only where Austro-Hungarian troops were stiffened by German. On the other hand the

Austro-Slav wall near Stanislau collapsed under Kerensky's simple tap. But Kerensky's troops were not like Brussiloff's. So notwithstanding fairly favourable prospects, the Russian offensive did not get right through at Stanislau. The Russian grain was now ripe for reaping. The reaper too was ready.

Chapter Fourteen

Our Counter-attack in the East

Counter-attack! No troops, no leader in the field can ever have received such news with more joyous satisfaction than I felt when I realised that the time for such a measure had at length arrived.

The defensive battles in the West had been a heavy drain on our available reserves. A comparison of numbers and the difficulties of this front made a counter-offensive there with what was left out of the question. On the other hand these reserves seemed sufficient to enable us to turn the situation in the East once and for all in our favour, and thereby precipitate the political collapse of our adversary on that side. Russia's foundations had become rotten. The last manifestations of force of the now Republican Army were only the result of an artificially produced wave, a wave which no longer welled up

At the time we made the decision we had to face a good many anxieties and risks. It was even then clear that the English attack of June 7 at Wytschaete and Messines was but the prelude to a much greater military drama which, carrying on the work then begun, would have its background in the great stretch of Flanders on the north. We had also to anticipate that France, too, would resume her attack as soon as her army had recovered from the serious disaster of the spring offensive.

It was undoubtedly a risk to take troops from the West – it was a question of six divisions – but a risk similar to that we had taken in 1916 in our attack on Rumania. On that occasion, of course, it had been a case of imperious necessity. Now we did it of our own free will. But in both cases the venture had been based on our unshakable confidence in our troops. Dissentient voices were raised against our plan on other grounds besides that of the general military situation. As a result of the enemy's experiences with our defence, some among us doubted the possibility of a really great offensive victory. I remember how, just before the opening of our counter-offensive on the Galician front, we were warned that with the troops we had concentrated we could not hope for more than a local success – that means the production of a salient in the enemy lines such as our opponents had so often created in their offensives at the first rush. Was that our goal? Then had we not better renounce the whole operation?

Among opinions on this side there was another that was quite plausible: we ought to keep our land forces principally on the defensive and otherwise wait until our U-boats had fulfilled our hopes. There was something very alluring in this idea. According to such reports as we had then received, the result of the U-boat warfare had already exceeded all expectations. Its effects must therefore soon make themselves felt. Yet I was not able to give my consent to that proposal. The military and political situation in the East now demanded something more than that we should stand still for months and simply look on. We feared that if our counter-blow did not follow hard on the heels of Kerensky's attack, the war party in Russia would once more get the upper hand. There is no need for me to describe the reaction such an event would have on our country and our Allies.

While Kerensky strove in vain to get the mass of his still effective troops to break through the Austro-Hungarian lines – which had meanwhile been propped up by German troops – we concentrated a strong force south-west of Brody, that is on the flank of the Russian breakthrough, and on July 19 attacked in a south-easterly direction towards Tarnopol. Our operation struck a part of the Russian line which had little capacity for resistance, and, indeed, had been exhausted in the previous attack. The Russian troops were quickly scattered to the winds, and Kerensky's whole offensive collapsed at a blow.

Our offensive came to a standstill on the frontier of Moldavia. No one regretted it more than I did. We were in the most favourable strategic position imaginable to effect the occupation of this last part of Rumania by continuing our advance. Judging by the political situation in Russia at the moment, the Rumanian Army would unquestionably have dissolved if we had compelled it to abandon the country altogether. However, thanks to the destruction of the stations by the retreating Russians, our communications had become so difficult that with a heavy heart we had to renounce the further prosecution of the operations at this point. A later attempt on our part to shatter the Rumanian Army in Moldavia was unsuccessful. We adhered to our decision not to let go of Russia until she had been finally eliminated in a military sense, even though the commencement of the drama in Flanders was claiming our attention and, indeed, filling us with increasing anxiety. If we could not destroy the Russian Army in Wolhynia and Moldavia we must do so at some other part of the front. Riga seemed a peculiarly favourable point, a militarily and politically sensitive point, at which Russia could be hit. At Riga the Russian northern wing formed a mighty flank position, more than forty miles deep and only twenty wide along the coast to the western bank of the Dvina. It was a position which threatened our whole front, both strategically and tactically. This situation had irritated us in previous years when I was Commander-in-Chief in the East. Both in 1915 and 1916 we had planned to break through this salient somewhere near its base, and thereby deal a great blow at its defenders.

On paper this seems a simple enough operation, but it was not so simple in practice. The spear-head must be driven northwards across the broad Dvina above Riga. It is true that in the course of the war great rivers had certainly not lived up to their imposing reputation as obstacles. Had not General von Mackensen crossed the mighty Danube in full view of the enemy? We could therefore face the prospect of crossing the smaller Dvina with a light heart; but the great drawback to the operation lay in the fact that the strongly-held Russian trenches lay on the far bank, so that the Dvina formed a kind of moat.

However, on September 1 our bold attack succeeded, as the Russians abandoned their trenches on the bank during our artillery preparation. Moreover, the occupants of the great flanking salient west of the river withdrew, marching day and night, through Riga to the east, thus for the most part evading capture.

Our attack at Riga aroused the liveliest fears in Russia for the safety of Petersburg. The capital of the country was in a panic.

Even among us there were great illusions about an advance on Petersburg. It goes without saying that no one would have been more pleased to carry out such an advance than I. I well understood the anxiety of our troops and their leaders to continue our invasion, at least as far as Lake Peipus. But we had to renounce all these ideas, alluring though they undoubtedly were. They would have tied down too many of our troops – and for too long – in a region with which our future plans were not concerned.

But if we could not continue our advance to Petersburg and thereby keep the nerve-centre of Russia at the highest tension until collapse was inevitable, there was still another way by which we could attain that end – the way of the sea. At our instigation our Fleet accepted our suggestion with loyal devotion. Thus originated the decision to capture the island of Oesel lying at the entrance to the Gulf of Riga. From that point we should directly threaten the Russian naval harbour of Reval and intensify our pressure on nervous Petersburg without employing any large forces.

The operation against Oesel stands out in this war as the one completely successful enterprise on either side in which an army and a fleet co-operated. The execution of our plans was rendered so doubtful by bad weather at the outset that we were already thinking of disembarking the troops on board. The arrival of better weather then enabled us to proceed with the venture. From that point everything went like clockwork. The Navy answered to the high demands which we had to make on it in every direction. We succeeded in possessing ourselves of Oesel and the neighbouring islands. In Petersburg nerves were more shaken than ever. The structure of the Russian front became ever looser. It became clearer with every day that passed that Russia was too shaken by internal agitation to be capable of any military demonstration within a measurable time. Everything that still held fast in this turmoil was gradually being swept away by the red flood. The pillars of the State were crumbling stone by stone.

Chapter Fifteen

The Attack on Italy

Although the situation in Flanders this autumn was extremely serious, we decided on an offensive against Italy. In view of my previous attitude of aversion to such an enterprise, it may cause surprise that I should now obtain the consent of my All-Highest War Lord to the employment of German troops for an operation from which I promised myself little effect on our general situation. On the contrary, I must maintain that I had not changed my views on this question. In August, 1917, I still considered that even if we won a wholesale success we should not succeed in forcing Italy out of her alliance with our enemies. I believed that it was as inadvisable to draw German troops from our imperilled Western Front, mainly for the glory of a successful campaign against Italy, in the autumn of 1917 as it had been when the year opened. The reasons why I now approved our co-operation in such an operation were to be ascribed to other considerations. Our Austro-Hungarian allies had told us that they no longer felt themselves strong enough to resist a twelfth Italian attack on the Isonzo front. This news was equally significant to us from the military and political point of view. What was at stake was not only the loss of the line of the Isonzo, but, in fact, the entire collapse of the Austro-Hungarian resistance. The Danube Monarchy was far more sensitive to defeat on the Italian front than to any reverse in the Galician theatre. No one in Austria had ever fought with much enthusiasm for Galicia. 'He who loses the war will keep Galicia anyhow,' was an Austro-Hungarian joke that was often heard during the campaign. On the other hand, the interest of the Danube Monarchy in the Italian theatre was always particularly strong. In Galicia – that is, against Russia – Austria-Hungary was fighting only with her head, whereas against Italy she was fighting with her whole soul. It was very significant that in the

war against Italy all the races of the Dual Monarchy co-operated with practically equal devotion. Czecho-Slovak troops which had failed against
Russia did excellent work against Italy. The war on this side formed to a
certain extent a military bond of unity for the whole Monarchy. What
would happen if even this bond were severed?

The danger of such an eventuality at the time at which I am writing was
great. To begin with, at the end of August Cadorna had gained a considerable amount of ground in the eleventh Isonzo battle. All previous losses of
ground had been misfortunes we could survive. Our multifarious experiences had taught us that they were a natural consequence of the destructive
effect of offensive weapons against even the strongest defences. But by now
the Austro-Hungarian line of defence had been brought as far back as it
could be. If the Italians resumed their artillery preparation and won further
ground, Austria-Hungary would not be able to maintain any line in front
of Trieste. The threat to Trieste was therefore absolutely critical. But woe
betide if that city fell. For the Danube Monarchy it was not only the symbol
of greatness, but of the very highest practical value. The economic independence of the country in the future largely depended on its possession.
Trieste must therefore be saved, with German help if not otherwise.

If we succeeded in bringing as much relief to our Allies by a joint and
far-reaching victory on the South-western front as we had just done on her
Eastern front, as far as we could see Austria-Hungary would be in a position
to continue the war by our side.

For an operation against Italy the most obvious idea was to break out from
the Southern Tyrol. From there the bulk of the Italian armies could be
destroyed or dissolved in the great cauldron of Venetia. On no other of our
fronts did the strategic contour of the opposing lines offer such favourable
prospects for a mighty victory. Compared with this, every other operation
must appear practically an open confession of strategic failure. And yet we
had to renounce the idea!

In judging our new plan of campaign we must not leave out of sight the
intimate connection between our fighting on the Western Front and the war
against Italy. Bearing in mind our position in the West, we could spare for
the Italian campaign not more than half the number of divisions which
General Conrad had considered essential for a really decisive attack from the
Southern Tyrol in the winter of 1916–17. We were quite unable to put
stronger forces at the disposal of our ally, even though, as actually happened,
we considered it possible that our foes on the Western Front might find
themselves compelled by their Ally's serious defeat to send a few divisions
to Italy, divisions which they could spare in view of their great numerical

superiority. Another objection to an operation from the Southern Tyrol was the consideration that an early winter might set in before our concentration there was complete. All those reasons compelled us to satisfy ourselves with a more modest objective and to attempt to break through the Italian front on the obviously weak northern wing of the Isonzo Army, and then deal an annihilating blow at the main Italian army in the south before it could retire behind the defences of the Tagliamento. Our attack began in the region of Tolmino on October 24. Cadorna had great difficulty in getting his southern armies, which were threatened with destruction, into safety behind the Piave, and then only by leaving thousands of prisoners and a vast amount of war material behind. It was only there that the Italians, supported by French and English divisions which had been rushed up, found themselves strong enough to renew their resistance. The left wing of the new front clung desperately to the last peaks of the Venetian Alps. We failed in our attempt to capture these heights, which commanded the whole plain of Upper Italy, and therefore to ensure the collapse of the enemy resistance in the Piave front also. I had to convince myself that our strength was insufficient for the execution of this task. The operation had run itself to a standstill.

Chapter Sixteen

Further Hostile Attacks in the Second Half of 1917

I
In the West

While we were delivering the final blows against Russia and bringing Italy to the very brink of military collapse, England and France were continuing their attacks on the Western Front. There lay the greatest danger of the whole year's campaign for us.

The Flanders battle flamed up at the end of July. I had a certain feeling of satisfaction when this new battle began, in spite of the extraordinary difficulties it involved for our situation on the Western Front and the danger that any considerable English successes might easily prejudice our operations in the other theatres. As we anticipated, England was now making her supreme effort in a great and decisive attack upon us even before the assistance coming from the United States could in any way make itself felt. I thought I could detect the effects of the U-boat campaign, which were compelling England to obtain a military decision this year and at any cost.

From the point of view, not of scale, but of the obstinacy which the English displayed and the difficulties of the ground for the defenders, the battles which now began in Flanders put all our battles on the Somme in 1916 completely in the shade. The fighting was now over marshes and mud instead of the hard chalk of the Artois. These actions, too, developed into one of the long-drawn-out battles with which we were already so familiar, and in their general character represented an intensification of the sombre scenes peculiar to such battles. It is obvious that these actions kept us in great and continual anxiety. In fact, I may say that with such a cloud hanging over our heads we were seldom able to rejoice wholeheartedly over our victories in Russia and Italy.

It was with a feeling of absolute longing that we waited for the beginning of the wet season. As previous experience had taught us, great stretches of the Flemish flats would then become impassable, and even in firmer places the new shell-holes would fill so quickly with ground water that men seeking shelter in them would find themselves faced with the alternative: 'Shall we drown or get out of this hole?' This battle, too, must finally stick in the mud, even though English stubbornness kept it up longer than otherwise.

As the Flanders battle was drawing to a close, a fierce conflict unexpectedly blazed up at a part of the line which had hitherto been relatively inactive. On November 20 we were suddenly surprised by the English near Cambrai. The attack at this point was against a portion of the Siegfried Line which was certainly very strong from the point of view of technical construction, but was held by few troops and those exhausted in previous battles. With the help of their tanks, the enemy broke through our series of obstacles and positions which had been entirely undamaged. English cavalry appeared on the outskirts of Cambrai. At the end of the year, therefore, a breach in our line appeared to be a certainty. At this point a catastrophe was averted by German divisions which had arrived from the East, and were more or less worn out by fighting and the long journey. Moreover, after a murderous defensive action lasting several days we succeeded in quickly bringing up comparatively fresh troops, taking the enemy's salient in flank by a counter-attack, and almost completely restoring the original situation at very heavy cost to the enemy. Not only the Army Headquarters Staff on the spot, but the troops themselves and our railways had performed one of the most brilliant feats of the war.

The first considerable attack on our side in the West since the conduct of operations was entrusted to me had come to a victorious conclusion. Its effect on me personally was as strong and invigorating as on our troops and their leaders. I felt it as a release from a burden which our defensive strategy on the Western Front had placed upon my shoulders. For us, however, the success of our counter-attack involved far more than mere satisfaction. The element of surprise which had led to our success contained a lesson for the future.

With the Battle of Cambrai the English High Command had departed from what I might call the routine methods which hitherto they had always followed. Higher strategy seemed to have come into its own on this occasion. The pinning down of our main forces in Flanders and on the French front was to be used to facilitate a great surprise blow at Cambrai. It must be admitted that the subordinate commanders on the English side had not been equal to the demands and possibilities of the situation. By neglecting to exploit a brilliant initial success they had let victory be snatched from them, and indeed by troops which were far inferior to their own, both in numbers and quality. From this point of view our foe at Cambrai deserved his thorough defeat. Moreover, his High Command seemed to have failed to concentrate the resources required to secure the execution of their plans and their exploitation in case of success. Strong bodies of cavalry assembled behind the triumphant leading infantry divisions failed, even on this occasion, to overcome the last line of resistance, weak though it was, which barred the way to the flanks and rear of their opponents.

The English attack at Cambrai for the first time revealed the possibilities of a great surprise attack with tanks. We had had previous experience of this weapon in the spring offensive, when it had not made any particular impression. However, the fact that the tanks had now been raised to such a pitch of technical perfection that they could cross our undamaged trenches and obstacles did not fail to have a marked effect on our troops. The physical effects of fire from machine-guns and light ordnance with which the steel Colossus was provided were far less destructive than the moral effect of its comparative invulnerability. The infantryman felt that he could do practically nothing against its armoured sides. As soon as the machine broke through our trenchlines, the defender felt himself threatened in the rear and left his post. I had no doubt that though our men had had to put up with quite enough already in the defence, they would get on level terms even with this new hostile weapon, and that our technical skill would soon provide the means of fighting tanks, and, moreover, in that mobile form which was so necessary.

As was to be expected, the French did not stand idly by and watch the attacks of their English Ally in the summer and autumn. In the second half of August they attacked us at Verdun and on October 22 north-east of Soissons. In both cases they captured a considerable portion of the trench systems of the armies at those points and caused them important losses. But, speaking generally, the French High Command confined themselves to local attacks in the second half of the year. They were undoubtedly compelled to do so by the appalling losses they had suffered in the spring, losses which made it seem inadvisable to subject their troops to any similar disastrous experiences.

2
Asia

I will now turn to the course of events in Asiatic Turkey. The general military situation was not further affected by events in Mesopotamia, but the loss of Bagdad was a sore point for German foreign policy. We had guaranteed the Turkish Government the territorial integrity of the Empire, and now felt that, in spite of the generous interpretation of this contract, our political account was heavily overdrawn by this new great loss.

Enver Pasha's request for German help in order to recover Bagdad was therefore welcomed by all of us, not the least because the Turkish High Command had always shown itself willing to assist us in the European theatre. At Enver's suggestion the conduct of the new campaign was to be put in German hands, not because the assistance of German troops was contemplated on any considerable scale, but because the Turkish Generalissimo considered it essential that the military prestige of Germany should preside over the enterprise. But the success of the scheme was inconceivable unless we managed to overcome the enormous difficulties of supply due to the appalling length of the lines of communication. A Turkish commander would have come to grief over this essential preliminary.

On the suggestion of the Turks, His Majesty the Emperor entrusted the conduct of this extraordinarily difficult operation to General von Falkenhayn. In May, 1917, the general, to familiarise himself with the elements of his problem, visited Mesopotamia and Syria, as well as Constantinople. The visit to Syria was necessary because General von Falkenhayn could not possibly operate against Bagdad unless he had an absolute guarantee that the Turkish front in Syria would hold. For there could be no doubt that the Bagdad enterprise would soon be betrayed to England, and that such news must provoke an English attack on Syria.

General von Falkenhayn came to the conclusion that the operation was possible. We therefore met the demands he made upon us. We restored to Turkey all the Ottoman troops which we were still employing in the European theatre. The Ottoman Corps in Galicia left the German Army just as Kerensky's troops were withdrawing eastwards before our counteroffensive. It returned homewards accompanied by expressions of the liveliest gratitude on our part. The Turk had once more revived his ancient military fame in our ranks and proved himself a thoroughly effective instrument of war in our hands.

I had hoped that the Ottoman Corps would form a particularly valuable element in the force earmarked for the expedition against Bagdad. Unfortunately these expectations were not fulfilled. No sooner were these troops out of range of our influence than they went to pieces again, thus proving what little effect our example had had on the Turkish officer. In comparison with the great mass of insufficiently trained and ineffective elements only a few individuals proved particularly brilliant exceptions.

The Turkish Army would have required complete reorganisation if it was really to become capable of the achievements which the sacrifices of the country required. The defects of its present condition were revealed most strikingly in an extremely high rate of wastage. This phenomenon was characteristic of every army which was insufficiently trained and had not been properly prepared for war.

Apart from a number of officers who were lent for special employment, the German reinforcements for the Bagdad enterprise comprised the so-called 'Asiatic Corps'. There has been a certain amount of criticism in our country on the ground that we placed so splendid a corps at the disposal of the Turks for a distant objective instead of using these precious troops in Central Europe. However, the corps consisted of only three infantry battalions and a few batteries. The name 'Asiatic Corps' was chosen in order to mislead the enemy. With regard to this help it was less a question of the material reinforcement of our Allies than of giving them moral and intellectual support – that is, resolution and experience. The peculiar character of the help we rendered was hit off exactly in an expression of the Tsar Ferdinand when, after the autumn battles of 1916 in Macedonia, he warned us against withdrawing all the German troops from the Bulgarian front: 'My Bulgarians like to see spiked helmets, for the sight gives them confidence and a sense of security. They have everything else themselves.'

The operations against Bagdad never materialised. Before the summer months were over it appeared that the English had completed all their preparations to attack the Turkish forces at Gaza before the wet season set in. General von Falkenhayn, who was now permanently stationed in the East, became more and more convinced that the Syrian front would not prove equal to the strain of an English attack, which would doubtless be made in great superiority. Turkish divisions which had been earmarked for the operations against Bagdad had to be diverted to the south. The result of this was that the chance of a successful enterprise in Mesopotamia had vanished. At Enver Pasha's suggestion I accordingly agreed that all available reserves should be sent to Syria with the idea of taking the offensive ourselves before the English attacked. The German command hoped to improve the capacity of the railway and the administration of the Turkish districts to such an extent that a substantially larger number of troops could be supplied in this theatre and provided with all the war material required.

Thanks to both political and military causes of friction, General von Falkenhayn lost a lot of precious time. At the beginning of November the English succeeded in taking the offensive at Beersheba and Gaza. The Turkish armies were driven north, and Jerusalem was lost at the beginning of December. It was not until the middle of this month that the Turkish lines were re-established north of the line Jaffa–Jerusalem–Jericho.

Although we had feared that these Turkish defeats, and especially the loss of Jerusalem, would have a regrettable political reaction on the position of the existing government in Constantinople, nothing of the kind happened – at least, not to outward appearance. A remarkable atmosphere of indifference took the place of the agitation we feared.

I myself had no doubt that Turkey would never recover possession of Jerusalem and the holy places. This view was shared, though tacitly, at the Golden Horn also. Ottoman eyes were now turned in deeper longing than ever to other regions of Asia, seeking compensation for the lost provinces. Unfortunately, this was premature from the military point of view.

Part IV

The Fight for a Decision in the West

Chapter Seventeen

The Question of an Offensive in the West

I
Our Intentions and Prospects for 1918

In view of the military helplessness of Russia and Rumania, as well as the heavy defeat of Italy, I considered that the burden on Austria-Hungary had been relieved to such an extent that it would not be difficult for the Danube Monarchy to carry on the war on her own fronts by herself. I believed that Bulgaria was in every sense capable of dealing with the armies of the Entente in Macedonia, all the more so as the Bulgarian forces which had been employed against Russia and Rumania could very shortly be entirely released for Macedonia. Turkey, too, had been immensely relieved in Asia Minor by the collapse of Russia. So far as I could see the result was that she had sufficient troops at her disposal materially to reinforce her armies in Mesopotamia and Syria.

In my view the further resistance of our allies depended, apart from their own resolution, mainly upon the effective employment of the resources available, which were in any case sufficient for their task. I asked nothing more than that they should hold out. We ourselves would secure a decision in the West. For the purposes of such a decision our armies in the East were now available, or we could, at any rate, hope to have them available by the time the best season began. With the help of these armies we ought to be able to secure a preponderance of numbers in the West. For the first time in the whole war the Germans would have the advantage of numbers on one of their fronts! Of course it could not be as great as that with which England and France had battered our Western Front in vain for more than three years. In particular, even the advent of our forces from the East did not suffice to cancel out the immense superiority of our enemies in artillery and aircraft. But in any case we were now in a position to concentrate an immense force to overwhelm the enemy's lines at some point of the Western Front without thereby taking too heavy a risk on other parts of that front.

Even with the advantage of numbers on our side, it was not a simple matter to decide on an offensive in the West. It was always doubtful whether we should win a great victory. The course and results of the previous attacks of our enemies seemed to offer little encouragement. What had our enemies achieved in the long run with all their numerical superiority and their millions of shells and trench-mortar bombs, not to mention the hecatombs of corpses? Local gains of ground a few miles in depth were the fruits of months of effort. Of course we too had suffered heavy losses in the defence, but it was to be assumed that those of the attacker had been materially higher. A decision was not to be reached merely by these so-called 'battles of material'. We had neither the resources nor the time for battles of that kind, for the moment was coming nearer when America would begin to come on the scene fully equipped. If before that time our U-boats had not succeeded in making the transport of large masses of troops with their supplies highly questionable, our position would become serious.

The question that pressed for an answer was this: What was there that entitled us to hope for one or more real victories such as our enemies had always failed to secure hitherto? It is easy to give an answer but difficult to explain it. The answer is the word 'confidence'. Not confidence in our lucky star or vague hopes, still less confidence in numbers and the outward show of strength. It was that confidence with which the commander sends his troops forward into the enemy fire, convinced that they will face the worst and do the seemingly impossible. It was the same confidence which inspired me in 1916 and 1917 when we had subjected our Western Front to an almost superhuman test in order to be able to carry out great attacks elsewhere; the same confidence which had enabled us to keep superior enemy forces in check in all the theatres of war, and even to overthrow them.

Moreover, if the necessary numbers were in existence, it seemed to me that the necessary resolution was everywhere present likewise. I seemed to feel the longing of the troops to get away from the misery and oppression of pure defence. I knew that the German 'rabbit' – which one of our bitterest enemies had held up to the derision of the English as 'driven from the open into its holes' – would become the German soldier in his steel helmet who would rise from his trenches in great and overwhelming anger to put an end by attack to the years of torment he had suffered in defence.

Moreover, I thought that the summons to attack would have even greater and more far-reaching consequences. I hoped that with our first great victories the public at home would rise above their sullen brooding and pondering over the times, the apparent hopelessness of our struggle and impossibility of ending the war otherwise than by submission to the sentence of tyrannical powers. My hopes soared even beyond the frontiers of our homeland. Under the mighty impression of great German military victories, I saw the revival of the fighting spirit in hard-pressed Austria-Hungary, the rekindling of all the political and national hopes of Bulgaria and the strengthening of the will to hold out even in far-away Turkey.

We had now to make up our minds how and where we should seek it. The 'how' might in general be summed up in the words, 'we must avoid a deadlock in a so-called battle of material.' We must aim at a great and if possible surprise blow. If we did not succeed in breaking the enemy resistance at one stroke, this first blow must be followed by others at different points of the enemy lines until our goal was reached.

Of course from the start the ideal objective for my purposes was a complete break-through the enemy lines, a break-through to unlock the gate to open warfare. This gate was to be found in the line Arras–Cambrai–St Quentin–La Fère. The choice of this front for attack was not influenced by political considerations. We had no idea of attacking there merely because we had the English against us at this point. It is true that I still regarded England as the main pillar of the enemy resistance, but at the same time it was clear to me that in France the desire to injure us to the point of annihilation was no less strong than in England.

Moreover, from the military point of view it was of little importance whether we attacked the French or English first. The Englishman was undoubtedly a less skilful opponent than his brother-in-arms. He did not understand how to control rapid changes in the situation. His methods were too rigid. He had displayed these defects in attack, and I had no reason to think it would be otherwise in defence. Phenomena of that kind are regarded as inevitable by those who have much knowledge of military training. They are due to the lack of appropriate training in peace time. Even a war that lasts years cannot wholly make good the effects of insufficient preparation. But what the Englishman lacked in skill he made up, at any rate partially, by his obstinacy in sticking to his task and his objective; and this was true both of attack and defence. The English troops were of varying value. The élite consisted of men from the Colonies – a fact which is undoubtedly to be attributed to the circumstance that the colonial population is mainly agrarian.

The average Frenchman was a more skilful fighter than his English comrade. On the other hand, he was not so obstinate in his defence. Both our leaders and their men regarded the French artillery as their most dangerous opponent, while the prestige of the French infantryman was not very high. But in this respect also the French units varied with the part of the country from which they were recruited. In spite of the apparent lack of close co-operation on the Anglo-French front, it was certainly to be anticipated that either of the Allies would hasten to the help of the other in case of need. I considered it obvious that in this respect the French would act more promptly and ruthlessly than the English, in view of the political dependence of France on the goodwill of England and our previous experiences in the war.

At the time of our decision to attack, the English army was massed, and had been since the battles in Flanders, mainly on the northern wing of its front which extended from the sea to south of St Quentin. Another and somewhat weaker group appeared to have remained in the neighbourhood of Cambrai after the battle there. Apart from that, the English forces were apparently distributed pretty evenly. The least strongly held part of their line was that south of the Cambrai group. The English salient in our lines near this town had been somewhat flattened as the result of our counter-attack on November 30, 1917, but it was marked enough to permit of the application of tactical pincers – to use a phrase in vogue – from north and east. By so doing we should be able to cut off the English troops there. Of course it was always doubtful whether the English would keep their forces distributed in the way to which I have referred until our attack began. This depended very largely on whether we should be able to conceal our intentions. All our experience negatived such a possibility. We ourselves had known of the enemy's preparations in all his attempts to break through our Western Front, and generally long before the battles themselves began. We had been able to prevent the extension of the enemy's attacks to the wings practically every time. His months of preparation had never escaped the eagle eye of our scouting planes. Moreover, our ground reconnaissance had developed an extreme sensitiveness to any changes on the enemy's side. The enemy had patently renounced the element of surprise in his great attacks, in view of the apparent impossibility of concealing his extensive preparations and the concentration of troops. We, on the other hand, believed that quite special importance must be attached to surprise. Our efforts in that direction naturally meant that to a certain extent thorough technical preparation had to be sacrificed. To what extent it must be sacrificed was left to the tactical instinct of our subordinate commanders and their troops.

Our great offensive involved tactical training as well as technical preparation. As for defence in the previous year, new principles were now laid down for attack and issued to the troops in comprehensive pamphlets. In our confidence in the offensive spirit of the troops, the centre of gravity of the attack was to be found in thin lines of infantry, the effectiveness of which was intensified by the wholesale employment of machine-guns and by the fact that they were directly accompanied by field artillery and battle-planes. Of course, the offensive powers of these infantry waves were entirely dependent on the existence of a strong offensive spirit. We were completely renouncing the mass tactics in which the individual soldier finds the driving force in the protection given him by the bodies of the men around him, a form of tactics with which we had become extremely familiar from the practice of the enemy in the East and with which we had had to deal occasionally even in the West.

On December 15 an armistice had been concluded on the Russian front. In view of the progressive disruption of the Russian Army, we had previously made a beginning with the transport of a large number of our troops from that theatre. Yet some divisions, effective and suitable for manœuvre warfare, had had to remain in Russia and Rumania until we had finally settled with these two countries. Of course it would have entirely corresponded to our military desires if peace bells could have rung in the year 1918 in the East. The place of these bells was taken by the wild, inflammatory speeches of revolutionary doctrinaires with which the conference room in Brest-Litovsk resounded. The great masses of all countries were summoned by these political agitators to shake off the burden of slavery by establishing a reign of terror. Peace on earth was to be ensured by the wholesale massacre of the bourgeoisie. The Russian negotiators, especially Trotsky, degraded the conference table, at which the reconciliation of two mighty opponents was to be effected, to the level of a muddle-headed tub-thumper's street corner.

In these circumstances it was hardly surprising that the peace negotiations made no progress. It seemed to me that Lenin and Trotsky behaved more like the victors than the vanquished, while trying to sow the seeds of political dissolution in the rear as well as the ranks of our army. As events were shaping, peace seemed likely to be worse than an armistice. The representatives of our Government indulged in a good deal of false optimism in their dealing with the peace question. Main Headquarters can at any rate claim that it recognised the danger and gave warning of it.

However great may have been the difficulties under which our German Commission at Brest-Litovsk laboured, it was unquestionably my duty to insist that for the sake of our proposed operations in the West peace should be attained in the East at the earliest possible moment. However, affairs only came to a head when on February 10 Trotsky refused to sign the Peace Treaty, but for the rest declared the state of war at an end. In this attitude of Trotsky, which simply flouted all international principles, I could see nothing but an attempt to keep the situation in the East in a state of perpetual suspense. I cannot say whether this attempt revealed the influence of the Entente. In any case the situation which supervened was intolerable from a military point of view. The Imperial Chancellor, Count von Hertling, agreed with this view of the General Staff. On February 13 His Majesty decided that hostilities should be resumed in the East on the 18th.

Our operations met with practically no resistance anywhere. The Russian Government realised the peril with which it was threatened. On March 3 the Treaty of Peace between the Quadruple Alliance and Great Russia was signed at Brest-Litovsk. The military power of Russia was thus out of the war in the legal sense also. Great tracts of country and many peoples were separated from the former united Russian organism, and even in the heart of Russia there was a deep cleavage between Great Russia and the Ukraine. The separation of the border states from the old Empire as a result of the peace conditions was in my view mainly a military advantage. It meant that a broad forward zone was created against Russia on the far side of our frontiers. From the political point of view I welcomed the liberation of the Baltic Provinces, because it was to be assumed that from henceforth the German elements there would be able to develop in greater freedom, and the process of German colonisation in that region would be extended.

I need hardly give any assurance that to negotiate with a Russian terrorist Government was extremely disagreeable to a man of my political views. However, we had been compelled to come to some final agreement with the authorities that now held sway in Great Russia. In any case Russia was in a state of the greatest ferment at this time, and personally I did not believe that the reign of terror would last for long.

In spite of the conclusion of peace it was even now impossible for us to transfer all our effective troops from the East. We could not simply abandon the occupied territories to Fate. It was absolutely necessary for us to leave behind strong German forces in the East, if only to maintain a barrier between the Bolshevist armies and the lands we had liberated. Moreover, our operations in the Ukraine were not yet at an end. We had to penetrate into that country to restore order there. Only when that had been done had we any prospect of securing food from the Ukraine, mainly for Austria-Hungary, but also for our own homeland, as well as raw materials for our war industries and war materials for our armies. In these enterprises political considerations played no part so far as Main Headquarters were concerned.

Of very different import was the military assistance which in the spring of that year we sent to Finland in her war of liberation from Russian domination. The Bolshevik Government had not fulfilled the promise it had made us to evacuate this country. We also hoped that by assisting Finland we should get her on our side, and thus make it extremely difficult for the Entente to exercise military influence on the further development of events in Great Russia from the vantage points of Murmansk and Archangel. Further, we were thus gaining a foothold at a point which immediately menaced Petersburg, and this would have great importance if Bolshevik Russia attempted to attack our Eastern Front again. The part played by the small force that was required – it was only a matter of about a division – was a very profitable investment. My frank sympathies with the Finnish nation in its struggle for liberty were, in my opinion, easily reconciled with the demands of the military situation.

The troops which we had left in Rumania were practically wholly available when the Government of that country saw itself compelled to come to terms with us as the result of the conclusion of peace with Russia. The rest of our fighting troops which still remained in the East formed the source from which our Western armies could to a certain extent be reinforced in the future.

The transport of the German divisions which we had employed in the campaign against Italy could be begun at once in the course of the winter. I considered that Austria-Hungary was unquestionably in a position to deal with the situation in Upper Italy by herself.

One important question was whether we could approach Austria-Hungary with the request to place part of her available forces in the East and Italy at our disposal for the approaching decisive battle. As the result of reports I received, however, I came to the conclusion that these forces would be better employed in Italy than in the mighty conflict in the West. If by an impressive threat to the whole country Austria-Hungary succeeded in tying down the whole Italian Army, and perhaps also the English and French troops in the line in the North, or if she kept these away from the decisive front by a successful attack, the corresponding relief which we in the West would enjoy would perhaps be greater than the advantage of direct assistance. We confined ourselves to securing the transfer of some Austro-Hungarian artillery.

I regarded it as elementary that we should make an attempt to recover for our Western offensive all the effective troops which we had hitherto employed in Bulgaria and Asiatic Turkey. I have already shown how violent was the political opposition to such a step in Bulgaria. General Jekoff was too sensible a soldier not to realise the justice of our demands, but apparently he shared his Sovereign's opinion that the German spiked helmet was indispensable in Macedonia. Thus the transfer of the German troops from the Macedonian front was a very slow process. It was with great reluctance, and after repeated representations on our part, that General Jekoff decided to relieve them by Bulgarian troops from the Dobrudja. The serious reports about the *morale* and attitude of the Bulgarian troops on the Macedonian front which we received from our German commanders on that front finally compelled us to leave behind the rest of the German infantry, three battalions and some of our numerous artillery units.

Efforts in the same direction had a similar result in Turkey. In the autumn of 1917 our Asiatic Corps had been transferred to Syria with the Turkish divisions which had originally been earmarked for the campaign against Bagdad. The uncertain position on that front compelled us at the beginning of 1918 to increase that corps to double its size. Most of the troops thus required were taken from our forces in Macedonia. Before these reinforcements reached their new destination we thought that a material improvement in the position on the Syrian front had taken place, and therefore negotiated with Enver Pasha for the return of all German troops in that theatre. Enver approved. Urgent military and political representation on the part of the German commander in Syria, as well as the German Government which had been influenced by that commander, compelled us to cancel the recall.

To sum up, I am entitled to claim that on our side nothing was neglected to concentrate all the fighting forces of Germany for the decision in the West. We had at last attained the object of three years' strivings and longings. No longer threatened in the rear, we could turn to the great decision in the West and must now address ourselves to this passage of arms. We should perhaps have been spared the trouble if we had only overthrown the Russians once and for all in 1915.

I have already shown how much more difficult our task had become by 1918. France was still a mighty opponent, though she might have bled more than we ourselves. At her side was an English army of many millions, fully equipped, well trained and hardened to war. We had a new enemy, economically the most powerful in the world, an enemy possessing everything required for the hostile operations, reviving the hopes of all our foes and saving them from collapse while preparing mighty forces. It was the United States of America and her advent was perilously near. Would she appear in time to snatch the victor's laurels from our brows? That, and that only, was the decisive question! I believed I could answer it in the negative.

2
Spa and Avesnes

Approving our suggestion, His Majesty gave orders that our headquarters were to be transferred to Spa, and the removal was carried out on March 8. The change had been necessitated by the coming operations in the West. From our new headquarters we could reach the most important parts of our Western Front in far shorter time than we could have done from Kreuznach. As we wished to be in the closest possible touch with coming events we also selected Avesnes as a kind of advanced headquarters of Main Headquarters. We arrived there on March 19 with the greater part of the General Staff, and found ourselves in the very centre of the headquarters of the Army Groups and armies which were to play the principal parts in the forthcoming battle for a decision.

His Majesty did not take up residence in Avesnes, but lived in his special train during the period of the great events which followed. The train was moved about according to the military situation. This residence of several weeks in the restricted quarters on the train may serve as an example of the simple ways of our War Lord. At such a time he lived entirely with his army. Regard for danger, even from enemy airmen, was quite beyond the range of our Emperor's thoughts.

Our stay at Avesnes during the next few months gave me more frequent opportunities than I had previously enjoyed to come into direct personal touch with the commanders of our Army Groups and armies as well as officers of other higher Staffs. I was particularly glad of the chance of seeing regimental officers. Their experiences and stories, which were usually told in touchingly simple language, were of extreme interest to me, not only from the military but from the purely human point of view.

It was a quite peculiar and special pleasure to be able to pay an occasional visit to the Masurian Regiment which bore my name, the Guards Regiment in which I had served as a young officer through two wars, and the Oldenburg Infantry which I had once commanded. Of course there was little left of the original regiment, but I found the old soldierly spirit in the new men. I was seeing most of the officers and men for the first time – and in many cases the last also. Honour to their memory!

Chapter Eighteen

Our Three Great Offensive Battles

I
The 'Great Battle' in France

Shortly before we left Spa His Majesty issued the Order for the first great battle. I will quote the material portion of this order in full to save a detailed description of our plans. By way of explanation I may remark that the preparations for the great battle are indicated by the rubric 'Michael', and that the day and hour of the attack were only inserted when we knew for certain that our preparations were complete.

MAIN HEADQUARTERS
10-3-18

BY HIS MAJESTY'S ORDERS:

1. The Michael attack will take place on the 21.3. The first attack on the enemy's lines is fixed for 9.40 A.M.
2. The first great tactical objective of the Crown Prince Rupprecht's Army Group is to cut off the English in the Cambrai salient and reach the line Croisilles (south-east of Arras)–Bapaume–Péronne. If the attack of the right wing (17th Army) proceeds favourably this army is to press on beyond Croisilles.

   The further task of this Army Group is to push forward in the general direction Arras–Albert, keep its left wing on the Somme at Péronne and intensifying its pressure on the right wing, compel the retirement of the English front facing the 6th Army also, and release further German troops from trench warfare for the general advance. . . .

3. The German Crown Prince's Army Group will first gain the line of the Somme south of the Omignon stream (this flows into the Somme south of Péronne) and the Crozat Canal (west of La Fère). By pushing on rapidly the 18th Army (right wing of the Crown Prince's Army Group) is to secure the crossings of the Somme and the Canal. . . .

The tension in which we had left Spa in the evening of March 18 had increased as we arrived at our new headquarters at Avesnes. The beautiful bright weather of early spring which we had been enjoying had changed. Violent rain-storms swept over the country. In themselves clouds and rain were by no means unwelcome to us in these days. They would probably shroud our final preparations. But had we really any grounds for hoping that the enemy had not got wind of what we were about? Here and there the hostile artillery had been particularly wide-awake and lively. But the firing had then died down. From time to time enemy airmen at night had tried to observe the most important of our roads with the help of light-balls and turned their machine-guns on all suspected movements. But all this supplied no definite data on which to answer the question: 'Can our surprise succeed?'

The reinforcements earmarked for the attack entered the assembly trenches in the final few nights; the last trench-mortars and batteries were brought up. The enemy did not interfere to any appreciable extent! At different points parties volunteered to drag heavy guns right up to our wire and there conceal them in shell-holes. We believed that we ought to be venturesome if we could thereby guarantee that the attacking infantry should have artillery support in their passage through the whole enemy defensive system. No hostile counter-measures hindered this preparatory work.

The weather was stormy and rainy almost the whole day on March 20. The prospects for the 21st were uncertain. Local mist was probable. But at midday we decided definitely that the battle should begin in the morning of the following day.

The early morning hours of March 21 found the whole of Northern France, from the coast to the Aisne, shrouded in mist. The higher the sun mounted into the sky the thicker the fog became. At times it limited the range of vision to a few yards. Even the sound waves seemed to be absorbed in the grey veil. In Avesnes we could only hear a distant indefinite roll of thunder coming from the battlefield, on which thousands of guns of every calibre had been belching forth fury since the early hours of the morning.

Unseeing and itself unseen, our artillery had proceeded with its work. It was only our conscientious preparation which offered any guarantee that our batteries were being really effective. The enemy's reply was local, fitful and of varying violence. It looked as if he were groping about for an unseen enemy rather than systematically fighting a troublesome foe.

It was therefore still uncertain whether the English were not fully prepared with their defence and expecting our attack. The veil which hid everything did not lift. About 10 A.M. our brave infantry advanced into the very heart of it. At first we received only vague reports, recitals of objectives reached, contradictions of previous reports, recalls. It was only gradually that the atmosphere of uncertainty cleared and we were in a position to realise that we had broken through the enemy's first line at all points. About midday the mist began to dissolve and the sun to triumph.

By the evening hours we were able to piece together a definite picture of what had been accomplished. The armies on the right wing and the centre of our battle front were to all intents and purposes held up in front of the enemy's second position. The army on the left had made immense progress beyond St Quentin. There was no doubt that the right wing was faced with the stoutest opposition. The English had suspected the danger which was threatening them from the north and brought up all their available reserves to meet it. On the other hand the left wing had had relatively the easiest task, apparently as the result of a wholesale surprise. In the north our losses had been larger than we expected; otherwise they were in accordance with anticipation.

The results of the day seemed to me satisfactory. Such was also the opinion of the General Staff officers who had followed the troops and were now returning from the battlefield. Yet only the second day could show whether our attack would now share the fate of all those which the enemy had made upon us for years, the fate of finding itself held up after the first victorious break-through.

The evening of the second day saw our right wing in possession of the second enemy position. Our centre had even captured the third enemy line, while the army on the left wing was in full career and now miles away to the west. Hundreds of enemy guns, enormous masses of ammunition and other booty of all kinds were lying behind our lines. Long columns of prisoners were marching eastwards. The destruction of the English troops in the Cambrai salient could not be achieved, however, as, contrary to our expectations, our right wing had not pushed on far and quickly enough.

The third day of the battle made no change in the previous impressions of the course of events; the heaviest fighting was on our right wing, where the English defended themselves with the greatest obstinacy and were still maintaining themselves in their third line. On the other hand we had gained more ground in our centre and also on the left wing. This day the Somme had been reached south of Péronne, and indeed crossed at one point.

It was this day, March 23, that the first shells fell into the enemy's capital.

In view of the brilliant sweep of our attack to the west, a sweep which put into the shade everything that had been seen on the Western Front for years, it seemed to me that an advance on Amiens was feasible. Amiens was the nodal point of the most important railway connections between the two war zones of Central and Northern France (the latter being mainly the English sphere of operations) which had the line of the Somme as a definite boundary. The town was thus of very great strategic importance. If it fell into our hands, or even if we succeeded in getting the town and its neighbourhood under effective artillery fire, the enemy's field of operations would be cleft in twain and the tactical breakthrough would be converted into a strategical wedge, with England on one side and France on the other. It was possible that the strategic and political interests of the two countries might drift apart as the result of such a success. We will call these interests by the names of Calais and Paris. So forward against Amiens!

We did indeed go forward, and with giant strides. And yet it was not quick enough for active imaginations and glowing wishes. For we had to fear that the enemy also would realise the peril in which he now stood, and would do everything in his power to avert it. English reserves from the northern wing, French troops drawn from the whole of Central France were hastening to Amiens and its neighbourhood. It was also to be expected that the French High Command would take our advance in flank from the south.

The evening of the fourth day saw Bapaume in our hands. Péronne and the line of the Somme south of it was already well behind our leading divisions. We were once more treading the old Somme battlefield. For many of our men it was rich in proud, if serious memories, and for all who saw it for the first time it spoke straight to the heart with its millions of shell-holes, its confused medley of crumbling and overgrown trenches, the majestic silence of its desolate wastes and its thousands of graves.

Whole sections of the English front had been utterly routed and were retiring, apparently out of hand, in the direction of Amiens. It was the progress of the army on our right wing which was first held up. To get the battle going again at this point we attacked the hills east of Arras. The attempt only partially succeeded, and the action was broken off. Meanwhile our centre had captured Albert. On the seventh day our left wing, guarding against French attacks from the south, pressed forward through Roye to Montdidier.

The decision was therefore to be sought more and more in the direction of Amiens. But here also we found the resistance stiffening, and our advance became slower and slower. The hopes and wishes which had soared beyond Amiens had to be recalled. Facts must be treated as facts. Human achievements are never more than patchwork. Favourable opportunities had been neglected or had not always been exploited with the same energy, even where a splendid goal was beckoning. We ought to have shouted into the ear of every single man: 'Press on to Amiens. Put in your last ounce. Perhaps Amiens means decisive victory. Capture Villers-Brétonneux whatever happens, so that from its heights we can command Amiens with masses of our heavy artillery!' It was in vain; our strength was exhausted.

The enemy fully realised what the loss of Villers-Brétonneux would mean to him. He threw against our advancing columns all the troops he could lay hands on. The French appeared, and with their massed attacks and skilful artillery saved the situation for their Allies and themselves.

With us human nature was urgently voicing its claims. We had to take breath. The infantry needed rest and the artillery ammunition. It was lucky for us that we were able to live to a certain extent on the supplies of the beaten foe; otherwise we should not even have been able to cross the Somme, for the shattered roads in the wide shell-hole area of the first enemy position could only have been made available after days of work. Even now we did not give up all hope of capturing Villers-Brétonneux. On April 4, we made another attempt to drive the enemy from the village. The first reports of the progress of our attack on that day were very promising, but the next day brought a reverse and disillusionment at this point.

Amiens remained in the hands of the enemy, and was subjected to a long-range bombardment which certainly disturbed this traffic artery of our foe but could not cut it.

The 'Great Battle' in France was over!

2
The Battle on the Lys

Among the battle proposals for the opening of the 1918 campaign we had contemplated and worked out an attack on the English positions in Flanders. The fundamental idea behind this plan was that we should attack the great easterly bulge of the English northern wing on both sides of Armentières, and by pressing forward in the general direction of Hazebrouck cause the whole line to collapse. The prospects which opened for us if we made good progress in such an operation were very alluring, but the execution of the attack was faced with most serious obstacles. In the first place, it was clear that we were dealing with the strongest English group at this point. This group, concentrated in a comparatively confined area, was quite in a position to bring our attack to a standstill after it had made but little progress. Such an enterprise would therefore face us with the very danger we were most anxious to avoid. To that must be added the difficulties of the ground on either side of Armentières over which we had to attack. In the first place, there were the low-lying meadows of the Lys, several miles broad, and then the river itself to be crossed. In winter this low-lying area was to a large extent flooded, and in spring it was often nothing but a marsh for weeks on end – a real horror for the troops holding the trenches at this point. North of the Lys the ground gradually rose, and then mounted sharply to the great group of hills which had its mighty pillars at Kemmel and Cassel.

It was perfectly hopeless to think of carrying out such an attack before the valley of the Lys was to some extent passable. In normal circumstances of weather, we could only expect the ground to become dry enough by the middle of April. But we thought we could not wait until then to begin the decisive conflict in the West. We had to keep the prospects of American intervention steadily before our eyes. Notwithstanding these objections to the attack, we had the scheme worked out, at any rate in theory. In this working out we provided for the eventuality that our operation at St Quentin would compel the enemy's leaders to withdraw large reserves from the group in Flanders to meet our break-through there.

This eventuality had materialised by the end of March. As soon as we saw that our attack to the west must come to a standstill, we decided to begin our operations on the Lys front. An inquiry addressed to the Army Group of the Crown Prince Rupprecht elicited the reply that, thanks to the dry spring weather, the attack across the valley of the Lys was already feasible. The enterprise was now taken in hand by the Army Headquarters Staff and the troops with amazing energy.

On April 9, the anniversary of the great crisis at Arras, our storm troops rose from their muddy trenches on the Lys front from Armentières to La Bassée. Of course they were not disposed in great waves, but mostly in small detachments and diminutive columns which waded through the morass which had been upheaved by shells and mines, and either picked their way towards the enemy lines between deep shell-holes filled with water or took the few firm causeways. Under the protection of our artillery and trench-mortar fire, they succeeded in getting forward quickly in spite of all the natural and artificial obstacles, although apparently neither the English nor the Portuguese, who had been sandwiched in among them, believed it possible. Most of the Portuguese troops left the battlefield in wild flight, and once and for all retired from the fighting in favour of their Allies, It must be admitted that our exploitation of the surprise and the Portuguese failure met with the most serious obstacles in the nature of the ground. It was only with the greatest difficulty that a few ammunition wagons were brought forward behind the infantry. Yet the Lys was reached by the evening and even crossed at one point. Here again the decision was to be expected only in the course of the next few days. Our prospects seemed favourable. On April 10 Estaires fell into our hands and we gained more ground north-west of Armentières. On the same day our front of attack was extended to the region of Wytschaete. We again stormed the battered ruins of the much-fought-for Messines.

The next day brought us more successes and fresh hopes. Armentières was evacuated by the enemy and we captured Merville. From the south we approached the first terrace of the great group of hills from which our opponent could see our whole attack and command it with his artillery. From now on progress became slower. It soon came to a stop on our left wing, while our attack in the direction of Hazebrouck was slowly becoming paralysed. In our centre we captured Bailleul and set foot on the hills from the south. Wytschaete fell into our hands, but then this first blow was exhausted.

The difficulties of communication across the Lys valley which had to be overcome by our troops attacking from the south had been like a chain round our necks. Ammunition could only be brought up in quite inadequate quantities, and it was again only thanks to the booty the enemy had left behind on the battlefield that we were able to keep our troops properly fed.

Our infantry had suffered extremely heavily in their fight with the enemy machine-gun nests, and their complete exhaustion threatened unless we paused in our attack for a time. On the other hand, the situation urgently exacted an early decision. We had arrived at one of those crises in which the continuation of the attack is extremely difficult, but when the defence seems to be wavering. The release from such a situation can only come from a further attack and not by merely holding on.

We had to capture Mount Kemmel. It had lain like a great hump before our eyes for years. It was only to be expected that the enemy had made it the key to his positions in Flanders. The photographs of our airmen revealed but a portion of the complicated enemy defence system at this point. We might hope, however, that the external appearance of the hill was more impressive than its real tactical value. We had had experiences of this kind before with other tactical objectives. Picked troops which had displayed their resolution and revealed their powers at the Roten-Turm Pass, and in the fighting in the mountains of Transylvania, Serbian Albania and the Alps of Upper Italy, might once more make possible the seemingly impossible. A condition precedent to the success of our further attacks in Flanders was that the French High Command should be compelled to leave the burden of the defence in that region to their English Allies. We therefore first renewed our attacks at Villers-Brétonneux on April 24, hoping that the French commander's anxiety about Amiens would take precedence of the necessity to help the hard-pressed English friends in Flanders. Unfortunately this new attack failed. On the other hand, on April 25 the English defence on Mount Kemmel collapsed at the first blow. The loss of this pillar of the defence shook the whole enemy front in Flanders. Our adversary began to withdraw from the Ypres salient which he had pushed out in months of fighting in 1917. Yet to the last Flemish city he clung as if to a jewel which he was unwilling to lose for political reasons.

But the decision in Flanders was not to be sought at Ypres, but by attacking in the direction of Cassel. If we managed to make progress in that quarter, the whole Anglo-Belgian front in Flanders would have to be withdrawn to the west. Just as our thoughts had soared beyond Amiens in the previous month, our hopes now soared to the Channel Coast. I seemed to feel how all England followed the course of the battle in Flanders with bated breath. After that giant bastion, Mount Kemmel, had fallen, we had no reason to flinch from the difficulties of further attacks. It is true that we had received reports about the failure of certain of our units. Mistakes and omissions had occurred on the battlefield. Yet such mistakes and omissions are inherent in human nature. He who makes the fewest will remain master of the battlefield. We were now the master and intended to remain so. Victories such as we had gained at Kemmel not only elate the troops who actually win them, but revitalise the spirits of whole armies. Therefore on! We must have Cassel at least! From that vantage point the long-range fire of our heaviest guns could reach Boulogne and Calais. Both towns were crammed full with English supplies, and were also the principal points of debarkation of the English armies. The English army had failed in the most surprising fashion in the fight for Kemmel. If we succeeded in getting it to ourselves at this point, we should have a certain prospect of a great victory. If no French help arrived, England would probably be lost in Flanders. Yet in England's dire need this help was once more at hand. French troops came up with bitter anger against the friend who had surrendered Kemmel, and attempted to recover this key position from us. It was in vain. But our own last great onslaught on the new Anglo-French line at the end of April made no headway.

On May 1 we adopted the defensive in Flanders, or rather, as we then hoped, passed to the defensive for the time being.

3
The Battle of Soissons–Rheims

After the conclusion of the battles in Flanders, we still adhered to the plans we had chosen for the attainment of our great goal. Of course we intended to proceed with our task of 'shaking the hostile edifice by closely connected partial blows in such a way that sooner or later the whole structure would collapse'. Thus were our plans described in a memorandum drawn up at that time. Twice had England been saved by France at a moment of extreme crisis. Perhaps the third time we should succeed in gaining a decisive victory over this adversary. The attack on the English northern wing remained as before the *leitmotiv* of our operations. I believed that the war would be decided if this attack were successfully carried through. If we reached the Channel Coast we should lay hands directly on England's vital arteries. In so doing we should not only be in the most favourable position conceivable for interrupting her maritime communications, but our heaviest artillery would be able to get a portion of the South Coast of Britain under fire. The mysterious marvel of technical science, which was even now sending its shells into the French capital from the region of Laon, could be employed against England also. The marvel need only be a little greater to get the heart of the English commercial and political world within its range from the coast near Calais. That would be a serious prospect for Great Britain, not only for the moment, but for her whole future!

In May, 1918, it was our immediate business to attempt to separate the two friends in Flanders once more. England was easier to beat when France was far away. If we faced the French with a crisis on their own front, they would withdraw the divisions which were now in line on the English front in Flanders. The greatest possible haste was necessary, or the reinforced enemy might snatch the initiative from us. A dangerous enemy irruption into our defensive fronts, which were not very strong, would have thrown out our calculations and perhaps upset them altogether. The sensitive point of the French front was the direction of Paris. At the time the political atmosphere of Paris seemed to be heavily charged. Our shells and attacks from the air had hitherto not produced the explosion, but we had reason to hope that there would be an explosion if we advanced our lines nearer to the city. From the information at our disposal the French defences in the region of Soissons were particularly lightly held, yet here the ground was extremely unfavourable for attack.

When I paid my first visit to Laon at the beginning of the year 1917, I walked on the terrace of the Préfecture which is in the southern part of this peculiarly sited hill-town. The whole region around me was exposed to full view on this splendid spring morning. Bounded by two groups of hills on the west and east, the landscape stretched away to the south and there ended in a mighty wall, the Chemin des Dames. One hundred and three years before, after days of violent fighting south of the Marne, Prussian and Russian forces under the command of Blücher had crossed the heights of the Chemin des Dames from the south, and after the murderous action at Craonne had been drawn up for battle against the great Corsican in the immediate neighbourhood of Laon. In the night of March 9–10, 1814, the battle on the eastern slopes of the steep hills of Laon had been decided in favour of the Allies.

It was on the heights of the Chemin des Dames that the French spring offensive of 1917 had been brought to naught. Fighting had raged on this position for weeks with varying fortune, and then silence had reigned. In October, 1917, however, the right shoulder of this ridge, north-east of Soissons, had been stormed by the enemy and we were forced to evacuate the Chemin des Dames and establish our defences behind the Ailette.

Our troops had now to attack once more over the slopes of the Chemin des Dames. The success of this enterprise depended even more on surprise than had been the case with our previous offensives. If we failed in this respect, our attack would break down on the northern face of the high ridge.

The battle began on May 27, and everything went brilliantly. At the outset we were bound to anticipate that our attack would come to a halt on the Aisne–Vesle line and would be unable to get beyond that sector. We were therefore not a little surprised when we received a report about midday on the opening day that smoke from German shrapnel could already be seen on the southern bank of the Aisne and that our infantry would cross the same day.

The centre of our complete tactical break-through reached the Marne from Château-Thierry to Dormans in a few days. Our wings wheeled towards Villers-Cotterêts on the west, and on the east against Rheims and the hilly region south of that city. Our booty was colossal, for the whole area of concentration of the French spring offensive of 1917 was in our hands with its immense supplies of all kinds. The construction of new roads and hutments for thousands of men, as well as much else, furnished a proof of the immense scale on which the French had then prepared their attack in many months of strenuous labour. We had made short work of the affair!

With a view to broadening our front of attack we had extended the right wing of our attack west to the Oise even while the battle in the Marne salient was still in progress. The attack was only partially successful. Another which we made from the Montdidier–Noyon line in the direction of Compiègne on June 9 only got half-way to that town. Moreover, our effort in the direction of Villers-Cotterêts yielded no better results. We were thus led to the conclusion that in the Compiègne–Villers-Cotterêts region we had the main enemy resistance before us, to break which we had not the resources at our disposal.

By way of conclusion, let me sum up my description of the Soissons–Rheims battle with the comment that the fighting had carried us much farther than had originally been intended. Once more unexpected successes had filled us with fresh hopes and given us fresh objectives. That we had not completely attained these objectives was due to the gradual exhaustion of the troops we employed. It was not in keeping with our general intentions that we should employ more divisions in the operation in the region of the Marne. Our gaze was still directed steadfastly at Flanders.

4
Retrospect and Prospects at the End of June, 1918

From the military point of view, what we had accomplished in the three great battles completely put in the shade everything that had been done in offensive operations in the West since August, 1914. The greatness of the German victories was clearly shown by the extent of the ground gained, the amount of booty, and the bloody losses inflicted on the enemy. We had shaken the structure of the enemy resistance to its very foundation. Our troops had shown themselves in every respect equal to the great demands we had made upon them. In weeks of offensive fighting the German soldier had proved that the old spirit had not been paralysed in the years of defence, but that it had risen to the heights of the moral elation of 1914 as soon as the word 'Forward' was given. The impetuosity of our infantry had not failed to produce its effect on the foe.

Unfortunately everything we had done had not hitherto been enough to wound our adversaries to death in a military and political sense. There was no sign of surrender on the enemy's part. On the contrary, each military defeat seemed only to strengthen the enemy's lust for our destruction. This impression was in no wise diminished by the fact that here and there the voice of moderation was heard in the hostile camp. The dictatorial authority of the political organisms against which we were fighting was on the whole in no way injured. They held the wills and the resources of their nations together as if with iron bands, and by more or less autocratic methods suppressed the capacity for harm of all who dared to think differently from the tyrants in power. To me there was something very impressive in the working of these autocratic powers. They kept their own hopes alive and turned the attention of their peoples mainly to the gradual relaxation of our efforts. In their opinion, these efforts were gradually bound to collapse. Hunger in the German homeland, the fighting at the front, the poison of propaganda, bribery, pamphlets from the air, internal dissensions had hitherto failed to bring us to destruction. Now another factor was at work: the help of America. We had made the acquaintance of her first trained troops at Château-Thierry. They had attacked us there, and had proved themselves clumsily but firmly led. They had taken our weak units by surprise, thanks to their numerical superiority.

With the appearance of the Americans on the battlefield the hopes which the French and English had so long cherished were at length fulfilled. Was it remarkable that the enemy statesmen were now less inclined than ever for a peaceful compromise with us? The destruction of our political and economic existence had long been decided upon, even though they tried to conceal this intention under threadbare and sophistical professions of moderation. They used such phrases only when it served their propagandist ends, either of making the necessary bloodshed tolerable to their own peoples or of destroying the resolution of our nation. Thus for us the end of the war was not in sight.

In the middle of June the general military situation had materially changed for the worse for the Quadruple Alliance. After a promising beginning the Austro-Hungarian offensive in Italy had failed. Although our adversaries there were not strong enough to turn the failure of the Austro-Hungarian enterprise to greater advantage, the collapse of the offensive was accompanied by consequences which were worse than if it had never been attempted. Our ally's misfortune was also a disaster for us. The enemy knew as well as we did that with this attack Austria-Hungary had thrown her last weight into the scales of war. From now onwards the Danube Monarchy ceased to be a danger for Italy. We must certainly anticipate that Italy would now be unable to refuse the urgent solicitations of her allies and would herself send troops to the decisive theatre in the West, not only to prove the existence of a political united front, but to play a really effective part in the coming battle. If we were not to take this fresh burden on our own shoulders, we must make efforts to get Austro-Hungarian divisions sent to our Western Front. For us, this was the main motive for our request for immediate direct reinforcements from Austria-Hungary. We did not expect any great effect from these reinforcements, at any rate at first. The fate of the whole Quadruple Alliance hung more than ever on the strength of Germany.

The question was whether our resources would be sufficient to secure a victorious conclusion of the war. I have already spoken of the brilliant achievements of our troops; before I can answer that question I must turn to another and less pleasing side.

With all my affection for our soldiers and gratitude for what they had done, I could not entirely close my eyes to those defects in the structure of our army which had been revealed in the course of the long war. The lack of a sufficient number of well-trained commanders of the lower ranks had made itself very much felt in our great offensive battles. Battle discipline had occasionally gone to pieces. It was natural enough in itself that a private, finding himself in the middle of plentiful supplies in an enemy depôt, should thoroughly enjoy food and other delicacies which he had not tasted for a very long time. But he should never have been allowed to do so at the wrong time, and thereby neglect his duties. Quite apart from the damaging effect of such behaviour on the spirit of the troops, there was also the danger that favourable situations would not be exploited, and indeed would be allowed to turn to our disadvantage.

The battles had made further great gaps in our ranks, gaps that could not be filled up. Many an infantry regiment needed reconstruction from top to bottom. Generally speaking the material available was no longer of the same value as the old. The weaknesses of the situation at home were frequently mirrored in the *morale* of the recruits who came to us in the field. It is true that public opinion at home had been greatly revitalised in many quarters by the influence of our military victories. The news from the front was followed with the greatest anxiety, and the public hoped for a rapid and successful conclusion of the fearful conflict. Hunger, the loss of life and the feeling of apprehension seemed not to have been in vain, and much was forgotten or endured with manly stoicism as long as a happy end of the colossal trial seemed to be approaching. Thus the victories of the army made good many of the omissions of our political leadership. But the starting-point for the process of demoralisation which was to destroy our whole national organism was provided by the unpatriotic passions of a certain section of the German people who were permeated by political notions which had degenerated as the result of self-interest and self-seeking.

These were men whose shaken nerves and moral depravity prompted them to regard the victory of the enemy as the herald of peace and happiness for the Fatherland, men who could see nothing but good in the camp of the enemy and nothing but evil in our own. Trotsky had certainly not wasted his words on the desert air of Brest-Litovsk. His political heresies had swarmed over our frontier posts and found numerous admirers among all classes and from the most varying motives. Enemy propaganda continued its work in public and private. It invaded every department of our activities. Thus the diminution of the will to resist in our people and army threatened to join with the enemy's lust for our destruction to compass our ruin. Military victory seemed to provide the only way out of so critical a situation. To reach a successful end by that means was not only my unshakable resolve but also my sure hope. For such a triumph it was essential that we should not lose the initiative. That meant we must remain on the offensive.

Chapter Nineteen

Our Attack Fails

The Plan of the Rheims Battle

The situation in the Marne salient after the June action came to an end gave me the impression of an imperfect and uncompleted task. Although we occupied this salient from the middle of June, we could not remain there permanently. The lines of communication in the mighty semicircle were defective. They were just good enough for a state of relative inactivity, but threatened serious complications if a great battle lasting any length of time should flame up. We had only one railway, of very slight capacity, at our disposal as the principal line of supply of our great mass of troops to an area which was relatively confined. Moreover, the deep salient obviously invited our enemy to attack it from all sides.

A real improvement of our supply system as well as our tactical situation was only possible if we captured Rheims. In the battles of May and June we had not managed to get possession of the town. We had then exercised our main pressure principally to the west of it. The capture of Rheims must now be the object of a special operation, but the operation thus required fitted into the general framework of our plans.

I have already emphasised that after we broke off the Lys battle we did not abandon our goal of dealing the English a decisive blow in Flanders. Our offensive at Soissons had been in keeping with that idea, for it had compelled the enemy High Command to withdraw the French reinforcements from the English front in Flanders.

In the interval we had proceeded with our preparations for the new Flanders battle. While the work was proceeding on the future fronts of attack the divisions earmarked for the execution of our plans were billeted in Belgium and Northern France for the purpose of rest and training.

I had no fear of any offensive counter-measures on the part of the English. Even though the larger portion of the English Army had now had several months in which to recover the fighting qualities which had been so seriously affected, it appeared improbable that the English would venture on an offensive in view of the dangers threatening them in Flanders.

Our former experiences enabled me to hope that we should soon settle with the English main armies in Flanders when once we had succeeded in keeping the French away from that battlefield for all time. The resumption of the attack at Rheims would therefore serve our greater and further purpose of seeking a decision against the English main armies.

The situation on the French front at the beginning of July was more or less as follows: General Foch kept the bulk of his reserves in the region of Compiègne and Villers-Cotterêts. From a strategical point of view this position was very favourable. They were prepared to meet any further attack of ours in the direction of these two towns, but they were also in a position, thanks to their extraordinarily good railway communications, to be transferred rapidly from their present concentration area to any part of the French and English front. It seemed to me highly improbable that Foch would attempt a great offensive before strong American reinforcements arrived, unless he found himself driven to such a step by a particularly inviting situation or urgent necessity.

There were apparently no large bodies of enemy troops south of the Marne. On the other hand, there was unquestionably a strong hostile group at Rheims and in the hills south of it, a group which comprised English and Italian units as well as French. On the rest of the French front the situation was not materially different from what it had been at the time of our spring offensive. The position on these fronts was not essentially changed by the perpetual replacement of worn-out divisions by troops from other parts of the line. We were not absolutely clear about the arrival of the American reinforcements, but it was obvious that the American masses would now be poured out uninterruptedly on the soil of France. Our U-boats were unable to hinder or limit these movements, just as they had previously failed to reduce the shipping available to the enemy to a figure which made this mass transport impossible.

We had to find some way of dealing with this situation. If we worked the intended attack on Rheims in close strategic co-operation with our plans in Flanders we had still to decide the question what extension we should wish and have to give to the operation at Rheims. We had originally intended to be satisfied with the capture of the town. The possession of Rheims would be settled by the occupation of the hilly district between Epernay and Rheims. The main purpose of our attack was the capture of these hills. To facilitate our advance at that point – and that meant to eliminate the danger of a hostile flank attack from the south bank of the Marne – a considerable force was to cross to the south side of this river on both sides of Dormans, and then also press on to Epernay. The crossing of the river in the teeth of an opponent prepared to dispute it was certainly a bold operation. However, in view of our successive experiences in crossing various rivers and streams, we did not regard such an attempt as too hazardous in this case. Our principal difficulty was not in mastering the river sector, but in proceeding with the action on the far side of the obstacle. Artillery and all war material and supplies for the troops engaged could only be brought up by temporary bridges, which naturally offered easy targets for the long-range guns and bombing squadrons of the enemy. After we had originally decided to limit our operation practically to the capture of Rheims, our plan was extended in the course of various conferences by adding an attack eastwards and right into Champagne. On the one hand our motive was an intention to cut off the Rheims salient from the south-east also. On the other we believed that, in view of our recent experiences, we might perhaps reach Châlons-sur-Marne, attracted as we were by the prospect of great captures of prisoners and war material, if an operation on such a scale succeeded. We therefore decided to face the risk of weakening our forces at decisive points for the sake of securing a broad front of attack.

Of course it was of great importance to us that our new operation should begin soon. Thanks to the arrival of American reinforcements, time was working not for but against us. To find a proper balance between the requirements of preparation and the demands of the general situation was our special problem, and certainly not the easiest element in our decision. Quite apart from purely tactical preparations, such as bringing up and assembling everything required for the attack to the appropriate front, and in spite of the claims of the general situation, we could not ignore the difficulties which the proper rest and recuperation of our troops would put in the way of fresh operations. Thus in the case in question we could not fix the date of the attack for earlier than July 15.

2
The Rheims Battle

In the early hours of July 15 our thousand-stringed artillery began to play its battle tune on the new front of attack. It was equally active on our side of the Marne. At the outset the reply of the enemy was not particularly violent, though it gradually became more so. We had noticed nothing which seemed to indicate that the enemy front had been reinforced or special counter-measures taken. Our infantry succeeded in crossing to the southern bank of the Marne. Enemy machine-gun nests were destroyed; we mounted the heights on the far side of the river and captured a number of guns. The news of this first advance reached us very soon in Avesnes. It relieved our natural anxiety and increased our hopes.

As on the Marne, the battle flamed up in a wide circle round Rheims without actually touching the town itself and its immediate neighbourhood. The town was to fall into our hands by being cut off from both sides. In Champagne and away to the Argonne the first enemy defensive system had been destroyed by the fire of our artillery and trench mortars. Behind the enemy's front lines there was a great maze of trenches which were the legacy of earlier battles. No one could say whether we should find them occupied, wholly or partially. In any case they offered the enemy innumerable strong points, and very little work would have been required to make them service-able again and suitable to play a part in some new defensive scheme. On the other hand our opponents here in Champagne appeared to be quite unprepared to resist, judging by first impressions. The reply of their artillery was not very strong. It was apparently loosely and remarkably deeply distributed.

After concentrating our heaviest fire on the first enemy lines, as in previous offensive battles, these tightly-packed storm clouds began their devastating march across the hostile defences. Our infantry followed. The first enemy lines were stormed, practically without resistance, along the whole front. The attack was continued, but as soon as our barrage lifted from the second objective, in order to make way for the infantry, an unexpected and violent resistance on the part of the enemy was encountered. The enemy's artillery fire began to swell mightily. Our troops nevertheless attempted to struggle on. In vain! The infantry guns were brought up. They arrived partly horse-drawn and partly man-handled, for horses were of little use in this wilderness of shell-holes. Scarcely were the guns in position before they lay in fragments on the ground. The enemy had obviously used his second position as his principal line of defence. Our most effective artillery preparation had, therefore, been practically without result. A new system of defence against the destructive effects of our massed artillery had been introduced and employed by the enemy – thanks to a German traitor, as the enemy subsequently announced in triumph to the whole world!

Our operations south-west of Rheims and on both sides of the Marne took a more favourable course. South of the river our infantry pressed forward for nearly a league, exercising its main pressure in the direction of Epernay. By the evening we had got a third of the way, after very severe fighting. North of the river also our attack had made progress in the 'Mountain of the Forest of Rheims', greater than the chalk cliffs of the Chemin des Dames, a medley of heights cleft by deep gullies and for the most part crowned with dense forest. The whole district was eminently suited for the most obstinate defence, for it made it extremely difficult for the attacker to concentrate the full fury of his artillery on definite targets. Yet our infantry made progress. For the first time they had met Italian troops on the Western Front, troops who apparently fought with little enthusiasm on French soil.

By the evening of July 15 we had captured about fifty guns on the whole front of attack. Fourteen thousand prisoners were reported. The results certainly did not correspond to our high hopes. But we expected more on the following day. In Champagne the morning of July 16 passed without our troops making definite progress at any point. We were faced with the difficult alternative either of breaking off the attack at this point or renewing our attempts at a decision with our forces, which were not very numerous. We ran the risk of seeing our troops bleed to death in vain, or in the most favourable case suffer such heavy losses that they would hardly be in a condition thoroughly to exploit the advantages they had gained. Our goal at Châlons had, therefore, vanished into the dim distance. For these reasons I approved the suggestion that we should dig in at this point. On the other hand we adhered to our plan of continuing our attacks south of the Marne and in the Rheims hills. During the day we were gradually forced to the defensive on the far side of the river. The enemy counter-attacked us with strong forces. In the direction of Epernay, however, we gained more ground on both sides of the river. By the evening we were half-way to the town – that is, about six miles off. In the Rheims hills we were approaching the Epernay – Rheims road in spite of desperate counter-attacks on the part of the enemy. The fate of Rheims seemed to hang by a thread. Even if all the rest of our plan could now be regarded as a failure, Rheims at least would fall.

On July 17 the battle died down in Champagne. South of the Marne the situation began to change ever more to our disadvantage. It is true that we held the ground we had gained against severe enemy attacks, but our lines were so near to the river, and therefore had so little depth, that a reverse might prove fatal. Moreover, our temporary bridges across the Marne were increasingly in danger from the long-range fire of hostile artillery and French bombing squadrons. We had, therefore, to withdraw to the northern bank as we could not gain any more ground on the southern. Hard though it was for me, I ordered the withdrawal of our troops to the north bank of the Marne. The movement was carried out in the night of July 20–21.

We seemed to have very little left of all we had striven for. The operation had apparently failed and, so far as the French front was concerned, nothing definite had been gained. But it was not impossible that it might prove very valuable for our attack on the Flanders front. The battles had not been in vain if the only result we achieved was to keep the French forces away from the English defences.

With this thought in mind, General Ludendorff went to visit the Army Group of Crown Prince Rupprecht on the evening of July 17 in order to discuss the proposed attack on the English northern wing in greater detail.

For the execution of our plans in the region of Rheims it was essential that the western flank of the great Marne salient between Soissons and Château-Thierry should stand firm. It was to be assumed that our offensive would provoke counter-measures on the part of the French reserves concentrated in the neighbourhood of Compiègne and Villers-Cotterêts. If General Foch were in a position to embark on active operations at all, he would have to abandon his previous attitude of passivity as soon as our plan of attack across the Marne and at Rheims was revealed.

In the case of a French attack from the general direction of Villers-Cotterêts the task of our troops in line between the Aisne and the Marne was therefore not a simple one. We had disposed a number of divisions behind our forward lines and believed consequently that we could proceed in full confidence to the great attack on Rheims which I have described. It is true that the troops between Soissons and Château-Thierry were not all fresh, but they had fought so brilliantly in the previous battles that I regarded them now as fully equal to their task. The main consideration, in my view, was that every part of our defences there should keep the probability of a strong enemy attack continuously in mind. Whether there were omissions in this respect on the Soissons–Château-Thierry front will probably always remain a subject of debate. In view of later information, I myself believe that the initial successes which were gained in our operations on the Marne and near Rheims from July 15 to 17 made some of our troops on the Soissons–Château-Thierry front inclined to ignore the seriousness of the position on their own front. During those days these troops could hear the thunder of the guns on the battlefield. They knew of our crossing of the Marne and the success it promised. Exaggerated accounts of our victories reached them, as happened so often, through irregular channels. There was talk of the capture of Rheims and of great victories in Champagne. However, on their own front everything was quiet for these three days, unnaturally quiet to an expert observer, but agreeably quiet to anyone who liked to enjoy the sensation and had no intimate knowledge of the situation.

On the morning of July 18 some of our troops, who were not in line at the time, went out on harvest work in the cornfields. Suddenly a violent hail of shells descended upon the back areas. Harassing fire? Our own artillery replied but feebly, apparently because a pretty thick haze veiled everything. The *tat-tat* of machine guns began on a broad front and showed that it was a question of more than harassing fire. Before the situation was definitely ascertained enemy tanks appeared in the high corn. The enemy was undoubtedly attacking on the whole front from the Aisne to the Marne. Our first lines had already been broken through in places. The sector between the Ourcq and Soissons appeared to be the greatest danger point. While what was left of our decimated and isolated troops in the front lines were fighting with the fury of despair, our reserves farther back attempted to form and hold a new line of resistance until the divisions in support could be brought up for a counter-attack. Many a heroic deed was done. In parts of the line which were temporarily recovered, our troops found German machine-gun nests in which every single man of the guns' crews lay dead surrounded by whole circles of fallen opponents. Yet even heroism such as this could no longer save the situation; it could only prevent an utter catastrophe. The enemy had penetrated particularly deeply towards Soissons and farther south; that is, at our most sensitive point, the western pillar of the Marne salient south of the Aisne. The enemy pressed down from here on the rest of our line of defence as far as Château-Thierry. What was worse, he was approaching the single line of railway communicating with the Marne salient at the point where it turns south from the valley of the Aisne east of Soissons into the centre of our great semicircle.

The position was thus serious for us from the very first moment. It threatened to become a real catastrophe unless we succeeded in restoring the original situation or, at any rate, preventing it from getting any worse. It was my desire and intention to take the enemy irruption in flank from the north across the Aisne near Soissons and destroy him where he stood. However, the necessary concentration would have taken too much time, and so I had to accept the counter-proposal that we should first completely secure the part of our front which had been attacked, in order to be masters of our own decisions once more. All the reserves which were available were therefore employed to that end. Unfortunately the crisis was not overcome but only postponed. The enemy broke through at other points and aggravated our situation in the Marne salient. How did it help us that, generally speaking, the enemy onslaught south of the Ourcq was a failure, and more particularly that the strong but unskilfully led American attacks collapsed before our weak lines, especially at Château-Thierry? We could not and must not allow the situation to hang in the balance for any length of time. It would have been madness. We therefore withdrew our left wing from Château-Thierry and at first retired a short distance eastwards while still keeping our flank on the Marne.

In conformity with our decision of July 17 we had withdrawn from the southern bank of this river in good time after very severe fighting. The splendid behaviour of our troops – thanks to which all the French attacks had failed – had enabled us successfully to overcome the critical situation at that point. The retirement had been carried out even more successfully than we expected. It was only on July 21 that, after powerful artillery preparation, the enemy attacked our evacuated lines – tanks in front and strong columns behind. Our troops watched this little piece of by-play from the northern bank of the Marne.

Owing to the hostile artillery fire from every side the conduct of operations in the salient, which was still very deep, was extremely difficult. The enemy artillery had the critical section of our railway east of Soissons under fire. A regular hail of enemy aeroplane-bombs descended upon it day and night. We were compelled to detrain the arriving reinforcements and reliefs in the neighbourhood of Laon and far away from the salient. They then proceeded to the battlefield by forced marches which took days. Often enough they reached their destination only just in time to take over the line from their exhausted comrades and save a complete collapse.

The situation could not be allowed to remain thus for long. The battle threatened to consume all our reserves. We must evacuate the salient and say good-bye to the Marne. It was a grievous decision, not from the purely military standpoint but from that of professional pride. How the enemy would rejoice if the word 'Marne' were to mean a revolution in the military situation for the second time! Paris, and indeed all France, would breathe again. What would be the effect of this news on the whole world? We realised how many eyes and hearts would follow us with envy, hatred – and hope.

But at such a time military considerations could alone prevail. Their warning rang out loud and clear: get out of this situation! There was no reason for precipitate action. General Foch might hurl all his armies at us from all sides, but a really deep breakthrough was a rare occurrence. We could thus retire step by step, save our precious war material from the clutches of the enemy, and withdraw in good order to the new line of defence which nature offered us in the Aisne–Vesle sector. The movement was completed in the first days of August. It was a masterpiece on the part of both commanders and men. It was not the power of the enemy's arms which forced us out of the Marne salient, but the hopelessness of our situation as the result of the difficult communications in the rear of our troops fighting on three sides. General Foch had thoroughly realised those difficulties. He had a great goal in sight. The magnificent behaviour of our men prevented him from reaching it. After the first surprise they had fought brilliantly. They had done everything that human beings could have done. The result was that our infantry left the battlefield in no way with the feeling of having been vanquished. Their sense of pride was partially due to their observation of the fact that their enemies' attacks had largely failed when they had been carried out without the protection or the moral support of tanks.

Where there were no tanks our enemy had sent black waves against us. Waves of black Africans! Woe to us when these waves reached our lines and massacred, or worse, tortured our defenceless men! It is not at the blacks who performed such atrocities that indignant humanity will point an accusing finger, but at those who brought these hordes to the soil of Europe to take part in the so-called struggle for Honour, Freedom and Justice. The blacks were led to the slaughter in thousands.

Though Englishmen, Americans, Italians, French and all their subject races swarmed round our infantry, when it came to fighting, man against man, our soldier felt and proved himself the lord of the battlefield. Even the feeling of helplessness against the enemy's tanks had to some extent been overcome. Our men had often made audacious attempts to lay low this troublesome foe and had been lustily supported by our own artillery. Once more the French artillery had been responsible for the worst crises with which our men had been faced. The employment for hours, and even days, of this destructive weapon, which was boldly brought out into the open and disdained even the cover of shell-holes, had shattered the lines of our infantry and put their nerves to the hardest test. The approach of the enemy storm troops had often been regarded as a release from the menace of inevitable destruction.

From the purely military point of view it was of the greatest and most fateful importance that we had lost the initiative to the enemy, and were at first not strong enough to recover it ourselves. We had been compelled to draw upon a large part of the reserves which we intended to use for the attack in Flanders. This meant the end of our hopes of dealing our long-planned decisive blow at the English Army. The enemy High Command was thus relieved of the influence which this threatened offensive had had on their dispositions. Moreover, the English armies, thanks to the battle in the Marne salient, were relieved from the moral spell which we had woven about them for months. It was to be expected that resolute generalship on the part of the enemy would exploit this change in the situation, which they could not fail to realise, to the full extent of their available forces. Their prospects were very favourable, as, generally speaking, our defensive fronts were not strong and had to be held by troops which were not fully effective. Moreover, these fronts had been considerably extended since the spring and were thus strategically more sensitive.

Of course, it was to be assumed that the enemy also had suffered very heavily in the recent fighting. Between July 15 and August 4, 74 hostile divisions, including 60 French, had been suffering losses while the English armies had been practically spared for months. In these circumstances the steady arrival of American reinforcements must be particularly valuable for the enemy. Even if these reinforcements were not yet quite up to the level of modern requirements in a purely military sense, mere numerical superiority had a far greater effect at this stage when our units had suffered so heavily.

The effect of our failure on the country and our Allies was even greater, judging by our first impressions. How many hopes, cherished during the last few months, had probably collapsed at one blow! How many calculations had been scattered to the winds!

But if we could only master the situation at the front once more we could certainly rely on the restoration of the political balance.

Part V

Beyond Our Powers

Chapter Twenty

On the Defensive

I
August 8

Our troops had taken up their new line on the Aisne. The last waves of the enemy attack flowed in and flowed out. In places there was desultory fighting from time to time.

Several of our divisions which had been exhausted in the recent fighting and required rest, were in billets behind our lines. Among other areas they were quartered in the region of Avesnes. I was thus able to see how quickly our soldiers recovered. When they had a day or two of good sleep, regular meals and rest, they seemed quickly to forget all they had suffered, even their mental torture. Of course, for this purpose the rest had to be real rest, undisturbed by enemy shells and bombs, and if possible somewhere where the thunder of the guns could not be heard. But how seldom and how few of our troops had a rest of that kind in the long years of fighting! Swept from one theatre of war to another, from battlefield to battlefield, they were practically subjected to an uninterrupted physical and moral strain. Herein lay the principal difference between the achievements of our men and those of all our opponents.

The roar of battle in the Marne salient had reached us at Avesnes like the rolling thunder of a heavy storm, now sharp and clear, now sullen. For the moment it had practically died down.

On the morning of August 8 this comparative peace was abruptly interrupted. In the south-west the noise of battle could clearly be heard. The first reports, which came from Army Headquarters in the neighbourhood of Péronne, were serious. The enemy, employing large squadrons of tanks, had broken into our lines on both sides of the Amiens–St Quentin road. Further details could not be given.

The veil of uncertainty was lifted during the next few hours, though our telephone lines had been broken in many places. There was no doubt that the enemy had penetrated deeply into our positions and that batteries had been lost. We issued an order that they were to be recovered and that the situation must everywhere be restored by an immediate counter-attack. We sent officers to ascertain precisely how matters stood, to secure perfect harmony between our plans and the dispositions of the various Staffs on the shaken front. What had happened?

In a very thick haze a strong English tank attack had met with immediate success. The tanks had met no special obstacles, natural or artificial. The troops on this front had certainly been thinking too much about continuing the offensive and not enough of defence.

In any case, it would have cost us heavy losses to dig trenches and construct obstacles when we were in direct contact with the enemy, for as soon as the hostile observers noticed any movement, even if it were a matter of a few individuals, their artillery immediately opened fire. It seemed our best plan to lie quietly in the high corn, without cover against enemy shells it is true, but at the same time safe from enemy telescopes. In this way we were spared losses for the time being but ran the risk of suffering even greater losses if the enemy attacked. It was not only that little work had been done on the first line; even less had been done on the support and rear lines. There was nothing available but isolated sections of trenches and scattered strong points.

On this August 8 we had to act as we had so often acted in equally menacing situations. Initial successes of the enemy were no new experience for us. We had seen them in 1916 and 1917, at Verdun, Arras, Wytschaete, and Cambrai. We had only quite recently experienced and mastered another at Soissons. But in the present case the situation was particularly serious. The great tank attack of the enemy had penetrated to a surprising depth. The tanks, which were faster than hitherto, had surprised divisional staffs in their headquarters and torn up the telephone lines which communicated with the battle front. The Higher Command posts were thus isolated, and orders could not reach the front line. That was peculiarly unfortunate on this occasion, because the thick mist made supervision and control very difficult. Of course our anti-tank guns fired in the direction from which the sound of motors and the rattle of chains seemed to come, but they were frequently surprised by the sight of these steel colossi suddenly emerging from some totally different quarter. The wildest rumours began to spread in our lines. It was said that masses of English cavalry were already far in rear of the foremost German infantry lines. Some of the men lost their nerve, left positions from which they had only just beaten off strong enemy attacks and tried to get in touch with the rear again. Imagination conjured up all kinds of phantoms and translated them into real dangers.

On this August 8 our order to counter-attack could no longer be carried out. We had not the men, and more particularly the guns, to prepare such an attack, for most of the batteries had been lost on the part of the front which was broken through. Fresh infantry and new artillery units must first be brought up – by rail and motor transport. The enemy realised the outstanding importance which our railways had in this situation. His heavy and heaviest guns fired far into our back areas. Various railway junctions, such as Péronne, received a perfect hail of bombs from enemy aircraft, which swarmed over the town and station in numbers never seen before. But if our foe exploited the difficulties of the situation in our rear, as luck would have it he did not realise the scale of his initial tactical success. He did not thrust forward to the Somme this day, although we should not have been able to put any troops worth mentioning in his way.

A relatively quiet afternoon and an even more quiet night followed the fateful morning of August 8. During these hours our first reinforcements were on their way.

The position was already too unfavourable for us to be able to expect that the counter-attack we had originally ordered would enable us to regain the old battle front. Our counter-thrust would have involved longer preparation and required stronger reserves than we had at our disposal on August 9. In any case we must not act precipitately. On the battle front itself impatience made men reluctant to wait. They thought that favourable opportunities were being allowed to slip, and proceeded to rush at unsurmountable difficulties. Thus some of the precious fresh infantry units we had brought up were wasted on local successes without advantaging the general situation.

The attack on August 8 had been carried out by the right wing of the English armies. The French troops in touch with them on the south had only taken a small part in the battle. We had to expect, however, that the great British success would now set the French lines also in motion. If the French pushed forward rapidly in the direction of Nesle our position in the great salient projecting far out to the south-west would become critical. We therefore ordered the evacuation of our first lines south-west of Roye, and retired to the neighbourhood of that town.

2

The Consequences of August 8 and Further Battles in the West up to the End of September

I had no illusions about the political effects of our defeat on August 8. Our battles from July 15 to August 4 could be regarded, both abroad and at home, as the consequence of an unsuccessful but bold stroke, such as may happen in any war. On the other hand the failure of August 8 was revealed to all eyes as the consequences of an open weakness. To fail in an attack was a very different matter from being vanquished on the defence. The amount of booty which our enemy could publish to the world spoke a clear language. Both the public at home and our allies could only listen in great anxiety. All the more urgent was it that we should keep our presence of mind and face the situation without illusions, but also without exaggerated pessimism.

The military situation had certainly become serious. We could only expect that, encouraged by his great victory, our enemy would now open similar attacks at other points. He had now found out that, in comparison with 1917, our present defence lines had many defects. In the sector east of Amiens, as on other parts of the front, too much had been said about continuing our offensive and too little about the requirements of defence. Moreover, the behaviour of very many of our troops in the battle must have convinced the enemy that on our defensive fronts the stubborn resolution of 1917 was no longer present at all points. Further, the enemy had learned a good deal from us since the spring. In the last operation he had employed against us those tactics with which we had soundly beaten him time after time. He had fallen upon us suddenly, and not after months of preparation, and had no longer tried to force a decision by driving a wedge into our defences. He had surprised us in an attack on a broad front. He was able to venture on such tactics now because he realised the weaknesses of our lines. If the enemy repeated these attacks with the same fury, in view of the present constitution of our army, there was at any rate some prospect of our powers of resistance being gradually paralysed. On the other hand, the fact that the enemy had once more failed to extract all possible advantages from his great initial successes gave me the hope that we should overcome further crises.

This line of reasoning enabled me, when I was summoned on August 13 to a political conference at Spa with the members of the Government to discuss the military situation, to affirm that this was certainly serious, but that it must not be forgotten that we were still standing deep in the enemy's country. I emphasised this point of view to my Emperor also on the following day, when I summarised affairs after a pretty lengthy conference. I agreed with the views of the Imperial Chancellor, Count Hertling, that no official steps in the direction of peace should be taken on our side until there had been some improvement in the existing military situation. This fact alone shows to what an extent we had had to renounce our former political goals.

I did not consider that the time had come for us to despair of a successful conclusion of the war. In spite of certain distressing but isolated occurrences in the last battle, I certainly hoped that the Army would be in a position to continue to hold out. I also believed that our public at home would be strong enough to survive even the present crisis. I fully realised what the homeland had already borne in the way of sacrifices and privations and what they would possibly still have to bear. Had not France, on whose soil the war had now been raging for four years, had to suffer and endure far more? Had that country ever been cast down by failure during the whole of that time? Did she despair when our shells fell into her capital? I believed that our own public would keep this in mind even in this serious crisis, and stand firm if only we at the front continued to stand firm too. As long as we did so I felt sure that it would have its effect on our Allies. Their military tasks, at any rate those of Austria-Hungary and Bulgaria, were simple enough.

In this process of reasoning, mere anxiety to uphold the honour of our arms played no predominant part. In the four years of war our Army had laid the foundations of that honour so deeply that the enemy could never remove them, come what might. The main motive for my decisions and proposals was regard for the welfare of my country and that alone. If we could not by victory on the battlefield force our enemies to a peace which gave us everything which once and for all secured Germany's future, we could at any rate make certain that the strength and resolution of our enemies would be paralysed during the campaign. It was to be assumed that even this would mean a tolerable political existence for the State.

After the battle in the Marne salient came to an end, General Foch had certainly realised that the success he had gained would be wasted if our troops were given time to recover. I felt convinced that the enemy High Command now believed that it must stake everything on one card.

On August 20 the French attacked between the Oise and the Aisne in the direction of Chauny. In three days of fighting they threw us back on that town. On August 21 and the following days the English extended their front of attack of August 8 to the north as far as north-west of Bapaume. The enemy broke through at several points and compelled us gradually to withdraw our line in this quarter. On August 26 the English hurled themselves at our line in the direction of Cambrai. They broke through, but were finally held. On September 2 a fresh hostile attack overran our lines once and for all on the great Arras–Cambrai road and compelled us to bring the whole front back to the Siegfried Line. For the sake of economising men we simultaneously evacuated the salient north of the Lys which bulged out beyond Mount Kemmel and Merville. All these were disagreeable decisions which had been carried out by the end of the first week of September. These movements did not ease the situation, as we had hoped. The enemy pressed forward at all points and the crisis continued.

On September 12 fighting flamed up on the hitherto inactive front southeast of Verdun and at Pont-à-Mousson. At this point we were holding lines which had solidified after our attacks in the autumn of 1914. They were a tactical abortion which invited the enemy to attempt a great blow. It is not easy to understand why the French left us alone for years in this great triangle which projected into their front. If they had made a mighty thrust along the line of the base a serious crisis for us would have been inevitable. It may possibly be made a matter of reproach to us that we had not evacuated this position long before, certainly as soon as our attack on Verdun was broken off. The only point was that it was the very conformation of our lines at this point which had had the most serious effect on the enemy's freedom of movement at Verdun and barred the valley of the Meuse, so important to him, south of the fortress. It was only at the beginning of September, when there seemed to be a certain liveliness on the part of the enemy between the Meuse and the Moselle, that we decided to evacuate this salient and withdraw to the lines we had long prepared along its base. Before the movement had been carried out in its entirety the French and Americans attacked and inflicted a serious defeat upon us.

Generally speaking, however, we managed more or less to hold up the enemy attacks upon our front. The extension of the enemy's attacks to Champagne on September 26 affected the general situation from the coast to the Argonne but little at first. On the other hand, the Americans this day penetrated our line between the Argonne and the Meuse. This was the first occasion on which the power of America, expressed through an independent army, made itself decisively felt on the battlefields of the last phase.

Although as a result of the enemy irruptions our Western Front had to be repeatedly withdrawn, it had not been broken through. It was shaking, but it did not fall. But at this moment a great gap was torn in our common front. Bulgaria collapsed.

Chapter Twenty-One

The Last Battles of Our Allies

I
The Collapse of Bulgaria

In the year 1918 there had been no material change in the domestic situation in Bulgaria. It was still serious, but on the other hand the country's foreign policy seemed to be in no way prejudiced by it. It is true that from time to time news reached us of unauthorised negotiations of certain Bulgarians with the Entente in neutral Switzerland. Moreover, there was no reason to doubt that the American Consulate-General in Sofia was a hotbed of schemes aiming at our ruin. We made a vain attempt to secure the removal of the Americans. Policy demands the use of the velvet glove even in the iron realities of war.

The furious strife between the political parties of Bulgaria continued. The Army, too, was compromised ever more deeply. Meanwhile pacifism was making great headway among the Bulgarian people. The question of food supply was becoming more difficult. The Army in particular suffered from this cause, or, I should perhaps say, was allowed to suffer from it. At times the soldiers practically starved, and moreover were so badly clad that for a time even the most essential things were lacking. Mutinies occurred, though these were generally kept quiet from us. The Army was permeated with foreign elements. Men from the occupied territories were forced into it to keep the units up to establishment. The result was that desertion occurred on an amazing scale. Was it surprising that in these circumstances the *morale* of the troops deteriorated? It apparently touched its lowest point in the spring. At that time, at the suggestion of the German Headquarters Staff of the Army Group, the Bulgarian General Staff had planned an attack

in Albania, west of Lake Ochrida. It was hoped that if this operation succeeded it would effectively close the Santa Quaranti–Koritza road, which
was so important for the enemy, and further have a favourable reaction on
the *morale* of the Army and the nation. In the end it proved impossible to
proceed with this undertaking, as Bulgarian officers declared that the troops
would refuse to attack. An even more serious condition of affairs was
revealed when, in May, the Bulgarian troops offered no resistance to the
attack of the Greeks and French in the centre of the Macedonian front, and
abandoned their positions practically without fighting. Most of the divisions
told off for the counter-attack mutinied.

In the course of the summer the internal condition of the Army seemed
to have improved. We gave such help as we could, sent food supplies as well
as clothing from our own stock. Moreover, our victories on the Western
Front at this time aroused intense enthusiasm in the Bulgarian Army. It was
none the less clear to us that this better spirit would soon vanish again if we
ourselves suffered any reverses.

As regards the comparative strength of the opponents on the Macedonian
front, there seemed to have been no material change in the course of 1918.
After the conclusion of peace with Rumania, Bulgaria was in a position to
concentrate all her forces on one front. Compared with this reinforcement
the withdrawal of a few German battalions from Macedonia did not really
affect the question of numbers. One English division had been transferred
to Syria, the French troops had sent their youngest classes back home, while
the so-called 'Royal Greek Divisions', which had just been mobilised,
showed little stomach for fighting. It was apparently for this reason that the
defence of the Struma sector had been entrusted to these troops. If we could
accept the reports of deserters, most of these men were quite ready to join
us if German troops were put in line on the Struma front. We therefore sent
out to Macedonia a few battalions which could not be used on the decisive
fronts in the West. They arrived at their destination at the very moment
when the war was decided, so far as Bulgaria was concerned.

In the evening of September 15 we received the first reports of the commencement of the attack of the Entente armies in Macedonia. There was
something very striking about this date. Had not Bulgarian soldiers declared
in the spring that they would abandon their lines on this day if the war were
not previously concluded?

On the other hand it was not less extraordinary that the enemy should select
for his attack a sector in the very centre of the rugged mountains in which his
advance would have been faced with critical difficulties if the Bulgarian troops
and their subordinate commanders had shown any inclination to resist.

For this reason we thought we could await the development of this battle with confidence, and continue to expect the serious and decisive effort of the enemy in the valley of the Vardar. At that point and in the neighbourhood of Lake Doiran, preparations to attack on the part of the English had been observed for some considerable time. Here again we thought that there could be no danger, in view of the extraordinary strength of the defences, so long as the Bulgarians took the necessary measures. The Bulgarian High Command certainly had the numbers required at their disposal.

The first reports of the course of the battle on September 15 gave no cause for alarm. The first lines had undoubtedly been lost, but there was nothing unusual in that. The main thing was that the enemy had not succeeded in getting right through on the first day. Later reports were more serious. The Bulgarians had been forced back farther north than had at first been thought. The troops which had first taken part in the battle had apparently made little resistance and shown even less resolution. The reserves which came up, or ought to have come up, displayed little inclination to face the enemy's fire. Apparently they preferred to abandon the battlefield to the enemy, and this at a point which was perilously close to Gradsko, the most important centre of all the communications in the Macedonian theatre.

If Gradsko fell, or the enemy were able to reach it with his guns, the Bulgarian right wing army in the neighbourhood of Monastir would be deprived of its most important line of communication, and in the long run it would be impossible to keep it supplied in its present position. Moreover, the Bulgarian army on both sides of the Vardar valley in the centre would find its railway connection with the homeland severed. It seemed incredible that the Bulgarian commanders should not realise the peril that was threatening them and bring up every man they had to avert an appalling catastrophe to their main armies.

In contrast to the behaviour of the Bulgarian army south of Gradsko, the Bulgarian troops between the Vardar and Lake Doiran had been fighting very strenuously since September 18. It was in vain that the English strove to force their way through at this point. Bulgarian courage and obstinacy had never been displayed to better advantage. But how could heroism at Lake Doiran help, if faint-heartedness held the field at Gradsko – indeed perhaps something worse than faint-heartedness?

Vain were the attempts of the German Staff to save the situation in the centre of the Bulgarian Army with German troops. What could the small and weak German nucleus do when the Bulgarians were running away on the right and left? Entire Bulgarian regiments streamed past the German battalions which were marching to meet the enemy, and openly refused to fight. It was an extraordinary scene. Still more extraordinary were the declarations of the Bulgarian troops. They were off home to their wives and children, for they wanted to see their houses and farms again and look after their fields. Most of them bore their officers no ill-will. If the officers liked to come back home with them they were welcome, but if they wanted to remain on the field of honour they would have to remain alone. The Bulgarians were ready enough to assist any German who got into difficulties while marching to meet the enemy. They helped to get the German guns over bad bits of road. But for the rest they left the fighting to the Germans.

Faced with facts such as these, the German Staff, which exercised command from Lake Ochrida to Lake Doiran, found themselves in a desperate position. Anything they could lay hands on in the way of German troops, units on the lines of communication, Landsturm and recruits, were scraped together to bolster up the Bulgarian centre and save Gradsko. The prospects of success became smaller every minute. In view of the speed in retreat shown by the Bulgarian centre, the only possibility of safety was to withdraw the wings of the army. Such a movement would in itself be of small tactical disadvantage, for in Macedonia great defensive positions lay one behind the other, and the farther north the enemy got the more difficult became his communications. It is true that the communications of the Bulgarians also became much worse when the valley of the Vardar was abandoned. However, it seemed likely that this measure would enable us to save the bulk of the army.

The Bulgarian leaders raised the most serious objections to the decision of the German Headquarters Staff of the Army Group. They believed that their troops would still hold on in their present lines and, indeed, fight. They were also convinced that their armies would dissolve altogether if an order to retreat were issued.

We at Main Headquarters were also faced with fateful problems. We had to try and save whatever could be saved in Bulgaria. We had to send reinforcements, and indeed at once, however hard it was for us. It was on September 18 that the full meaning of this necessity became clear. Just think how fearfully the battle was raging on our Western Front at this time. Only a few days before, the Americans had gained their great success between the Meuse and the Moselle and we were faced with an extension of the attack. The first reinforcements which we could make available were the troops – a mixed brigade – which had been earmarked for Trans-Caucasia and were even then in process of transport across the Black Sea. They were recalled by wireless and ordered to return by Varna and Sofia. But these troops would not be enough. A few more divisions could certainly be spared from our

Eastern Front. We had intended to bring them to a quiet part of the Western Front. But what kind of troops were they? Not a man was under thirty-five, and all the General Service men had already been brought to the West. Yet it had to be, for not only the Bulgarian Army but the Bulgarian Government and the Tsar must have German backing in this very critical situation.

We also sent reinforcements from the West. Our Alpine Corps, which had just been engaged in very severe fighting, was entrained for Nish. Austria-Hungary also joined in the attempt to help Bulgaria and made several divisions available. We had thus to renounce the prospect of further Austro-Hungarian reinforcements on our Western Front.

Until these German and Austrian reinforcements arrived the attempt had to be made to save the main Bulgarian armies at any rate. With that end in view, and in spite of Bulgarian opposition, the German Army Group Headquarters issued the order for retreat to the Bulgarian armies on the right wing and in the centre. Their lines on the Belashitza, north of Lake Doiran, were to form the pivot for the entire movement. During the whole of this time the Bulgarian army on the left wing had not been attacked. Its lines on the Belashitza and behind the Struma were extremely strong. A few machine guns and batteries would have been quite enough for their defence. Yet confusion overtook this army also. Courage and hard thinking went to a discount. Its commander considered his position untenable and begged the Tsar to conclude an armistice at once. The Tsar replied: 'Go and die in your present lines.' The remark shows that the Tsar was still master of the situation and that I had made no mistake about him.

On September 20 the centre army began its retreat in accordance with orders. This led to utter dissolution. Confusion was worse confounded by unskilful dispositions. The Staffs failed, the Army Staff worst of all. There was only one man, the Commander-in-Chief, who retained a clear vision and was inspired by firm resolution.

The right wing army had a difficult task. Its main line of retreat was through Prilep on Veles. As the enemy was already quite close to Gradsko, this line of retreat was very seriously threatened. Another road farther west led from the region of the lakes and Monastir through the rugged mountains of Albania to Kalkandelen. At Uskub it met the road through Veles. This tract through the Albanian mountains was safe but very difficult, and it was doubtful whether a large body of troops would find the necessary supplies in that region. In spite of these drawbacks large numbers of troops had to use it. Even larger bodies had to take this route when the enemy captured Gradsko and then pressed forward against the Prilep–Gradsko road from the south-east. Gradsko had fallen as early as September 21. From being a wretched little village it had become a regular hutted town and its appearance and size reminded one of a brand new American settlement. An immense quantity of supplies, sufficient for a whole campaign, was stored here. Judging by the depots there was nothing to account for the fact that the Bulgarian Army at the front had had to go short. The whole lot was now either destroyed by the Bulgarians or captured by the enemy. It was not only at Gradsko but at many other points that Bulgaria had large depots. Hitherto we had heard nothing about them, as they were guarded by a miserly bureaucracy which in Bulgaria, as in other lands, forms the crust of the national organism in spite of the most liberal laws and a free parliament.

Bulgaria could therefore continue the war as long as she did not, or would not, herself regard it as lost. Our plan, which met with the approval of the Bulgarian High Command, was as follows: The centre army was to fall back to the frontier of Old Bulgaria. The army on the right wing was to be concentrated at Uskub or farther north; it would be reinforced by the approaching German and Austrian divisions. These troops would be quite enough to restore the situation at Uskub; indeed if the Bulgarian units were not hopelessly ineffective, we might anticipate that from Uskub we should be able to embark on an offensive towards the south. It seemed impossible that without rest the enemy would be able to bring his strong columns forward to Uskub and the frontier of Old Bulgaria. How would he cope with his supply difficulties as we had utterly destroyed the railway and roads? Moreover, we hoped that the energy and sense of responsibility of the Bulgarian troops would revive when they stood on their own soil.

The proposed operation was only possible on the assumption that Uskub could be held until the Bulgarian troops from Kalkandelen arrived. This seemed to be an easy task, as the enemy was coming up from Gradsko with relatively weak forces.

There was no change at the front. The retirement of the Bulgarian masses continued uninterruptedly. It was in vain that we tried to get individual bodies – there was no longer any question of proper formations – to form a front against the enemy and offer a real resistance, at least in places. The moment the enemy approached the Bulgarians fired a few rounds and then left their lines. German troops were no longer able to provide a nucleus for the Bulgarian resistance. Equally impossible was it for German and Bulgarian officers, rifle in hand, to produce by their example any effect on the uncontrollable and indifferent mob.

Thus the enemy approached Uskub before fresh German and Austro-Hungarian troops could arrive there. On September 29 strong bodies of the right wing of the Bulgarian Army emerged from the mountain region and reached Kalkandelen. They had only to make for Uskub by a good road. We were told that the troops were thoroughly keen and fit to fight. The worst of the crisis, therefore, seemed to have been overcome. In a military sense that may have been true, but morally the cause was lost once and for all. That was soon to be proved beyond doubt. Weak Serbian units captured Uskub. The troops at Kalkandelen lost heart. They capitulated. In the evening of September 29 Bulgaria concluded an armistice.

2
The Overthrow of Turkish Power in Asia

The opening of 1918 marked a great revival of the war fever in Turkey. Even before the end of winter, in the highlands of Armenia Turkey opened an attack on the Russian armies there. Russian power in this region turned out to be simply a phantom. The bulk of the armies had already dissolved. The only resistance the Turks met with in their advance was offered by Armenian bands. The difficulties which the nature of this mountainous country placed in the way of the Turks at this season proved more formidable than this Armenian opposition. The Turks crossed the frontier of Turkish Armenia into the region of Trans-Caucasia urged on by various motives; Pan-Islam dreams, thoughts of revenge, hopes of compensation for the territory they had lost, and anticipation of booty. There was yet another reason, the search for manpower. The Empire, and more particularly the portion inhabited by the splendid Anatolian, was absolutely exhausted from the point of view of manpower. In Trans-Caucasian Adzerbaidjan and among the Mohammedans of the Caucasus new and great sources seemed to be available. Russia had not drawn on these Mohammedans for regular military service, and now they were to fight under the Crescent. The number of the prospective volunteers, as communicated to us, revealed all the wealth of Oriental imagination. Further, if the Turkish reports were to be believed, we had to assume that the Mohammedan peoples of Russia had for long had no more intense longing than to form one great and self-contained Mohammedan nation in the Turkish Empire. But we must not lose sight of the fact that Turkey found fresh resources at her disposal in these regions, and that England would find herself compelled to devote special attention to the development of these events. On the other hand it is just as well occasionally to have some regard for sober reality. We therefore attempted to calm the billows of Ottoman hopes and expectations, unfortunately not with the success that we could have wished. It was agreed, from the point of view of the whole war, that Turkey's principal task lay far more in Syria and Mesopotamia than in the Caucasus and on the Caspian. But what was the good of promises and good intentions in Constantinople when the commanders in the outlying theatres went their own way!

We sent troops to Georgia with a view to securing at least a share of the abundant supplies of raw material in Trans-Caucasia to be used in our joint war. We hoped to help the Georgian Government with the re-establishment of a proper economic system. However, the Pan-Islam fanatics and profiteers in Constantinople would not rest until Baku was in Turkish hands, and this at a time when the ancient structure of Turkish dominion in Asia was about to collapse.

The idea of exercising a paramount influence in Persia led Turkey even farther east. The Turks intended to use Persia as a starting-point for a flank attack on the English operations in Mesopotamia, a plan which was good enough in itself, but required time for its realisation. It was certainly doubtful whether we should be allowed that time. But it was always possible that the first Turkish movement in Northern Persia would tie down English troops and therefore save Mesopotamia for Turkey. England appeared to be anxious to influence the course of events in Russia through the Caspian Sea and Baku as much as from the White Sea and Archangel. From that point of view the execution of the Turkish plans in Persia and Trans-Caucasia was in our interests also. The only thing was that defence in Mesopotamia and especially in Syria must not be neglected. The formation of an effective Turkish reserve army in the neighbourhood of Aleppo would have been far more useful than great operations in Persia, in view of the strategic possibilities open to the English south of the Taurus.

Judging by the map, the situation in Mesopotamia had remained unchanged since the autumn of 1917; but, as a matter of fact, the Turkish armies south of Mosul had suffered a real catastrophe, and that not in battle. As in the Armenian highlands in the winter of 1916–17, Turkish soldiers succumbed in large numbers on the plains of Mesopotamia in the winter of 1917–18. There was talk of 17,000 men who were starving there or had died as the result of privations. Only fragments of the Turkish army in Mesopotamia survived the winter. It is very doubtful whether they could ever have been brought up to effective strength again. The question was, 'Why did not the English attack in Mesopotamia, or, rather, why did they not simply advance?'

While the Turkish armies were celebrating triumphs in the mountains of Armenia, the Syrian front had not remained inactive. There had been several frontal attacks on the part of the English which had led to no material change in the situation. In the spring of 1918 the English general seemed at length to have grown tired of this unending monotony. He adopted another line of action, and broke out through Jericho into the country east of the Jordan. He supposed that the Arabian tribes in this region were only waiting for the arrival of their liberators from the Turkish yoke to fall on the rear of the Ottoman armies. The enterprise failed pretty ingloriously against the resistance of weak German and Turkish forces, thanks to splendid Turkish generalship. For the summer the position in Syria was thus saved, for during this season inactivity was usually general in these sun-baked regions. It was all the more certain that in the autumn the English would renew their attacks somewhere or other. We believed that the interval would be long enough to enable us to secure this front by bringing up fresh Turkish forces.

The internal difficulties of Turkey continued during the year 1918. The death of the Sultan had at first no visible effect. At home matters began gradually to improve. The new Sultan was apparently a man of action. He displayed a firm resolve to rid himself of the ancient tutelage of the Committee and to set his face against the serious abuses in the State.

The land was completely exhausted by the war. It could hardly give the Army anything more. The result was that even during the summer the efforts to improve the situation on the Syrian front were a failure. It is difficult to estimate how much more could have been done in that quarter in view of the positively pitiable communications. The supply of the Army was still in a bad way. The troops were not actually starving, but they were practically continuously short of food, physically exhausted, and morally numb.

As I have said earlier on, we had had to renounce the idea of withdrawing the German troops from the Syrian front. The German commander there considered that the position could not be regarded as secure unless German help was at hand. It must be admitted that we did not regard the offensive spirit of the Anglo-Indian Army as very high, especially judging by the evidence we got from Mohammedan Indian deserters. Moreover, the previous achievements of English generalship had been so unimpressive that we felt we were justified in hoping that with the small force at our disposal it would, at any rate, be possible to delude the enemy into thinking that we were still capable of offering further resistance. How long we could keep up the illusion mainly depended on whether the enemy would ever bring himself to embark on a resolute and wholesale operation, and thereby bring down the whole structure of Turkish resistance, with its weak German supports, about our ears.

On September 19 the English opened a surprise attack on the right wing of the Turkish armies in the coast plain. They broke through the lines there practically without opposition. The rapid advance of the Indo-Australian cavalry squadrons sealed the fate of the two Turkish armies on the Syrian front.

It was just at this time that Turkey was robbed of her former land defences in Europe by the collapse of Bulgaria. Constantinople was thus immediately rendered defenceless on the land side. Of recent times the Turkish troops at the Dardanelles had become steadily worse. The armies in the outlying provinces had drained them of all men who were of any fighting value. Thrace was unprotected except for some weak coast-defence garrisons which were scarcely fit to fight. The fortifications of the far-famed Chataldja lines consisted of collapsed trenches which had been left by the Turkish troops after the battles of 1912–13. The rest of the Turkish army existed only in imagination or was engaged in the execution of plans which were will-o'-the-wisps.

As soon as the first reports of the threatening collapse of Bulgaria arrived certain formations were hastily scraped together and sent from Constantinople to man the Chataldja lines. No resistance worth mentioning, however, could have been expected of such troops. For *morale* rather than practical reasons we ordered the immediate transfer of German Landwehr units from the south of Russia to Constantinople. Turkey also decided to send all the divisions which had been recalled from Trans-Caucāsia to Thrace. A considerable time would elapse before any appreciable force could reach Constantinople. Everything which had been published hitherto leaves it uncertain why the enemy did not use this interval to occupy the capital. Once more Turkey found herself saved from a direct catastrophe. But at the end of September such an eventuality seemed only a matter of days.

3
Military and Political Issues in Austria-Hungary

After the failure of the attack of the Austro-Hungarian armies on Italy, it became ever clearer that the Danube Monarchy had employed her last and best resources in that enterprise. It no longer had the numerical and moral forces to be able to repeat such an attack. The plight of the Army was revealed to us by the condition of the divisions which were sent to us as reinforcements for our Western Front. Their immediate employment was quite out of the question if we were to get any good work out of them later on. They needed rest, training, and suitable equipment most of all. These facts were admitted by the troops themselves as freely as by the

Austro-Hungarian General Staff. In the relatively short time at their disposal all the Austro-Hungarian officers took the greatest pains to train the Austrian troops to be used in the West to the level of their coming task. If they did not achieve their aim, it was certainly not for want of energy and intelligence on the part of the officers. The men also showed themselves extremely willing.

The great losses of the Austro-Hungarian armies in Italy, their precarious situation as regards drafts, the political unreliability of some parts of the Army and the uncertain domestic situation, unfortunately made a really effective and striking reinforcement of our Western Front impossible.

During the summer nothing of any note occurred on the Austro-Hungarian front. The only military event worth mentioning at this time took place in Albania. In that region the opponents had faced one another inactively for years: the Italians in the strength of rather more than an army corps at and east of Valona, and the Austrians in the north of Albania. This theatre would have been without any military importance if it had not had a certain connection with the Macedonian front. Bulgaria was always afraid that if the enemy pressed forward west of Lake Ochrida the right flank of their front would be enveloped. From the military point of view it would have been a perfectly simple matter to meet such a move on the part of the enemy by withdrawing the western wing from the region of Ochrida in a north-easterly direction. As I have said before, it was solely due to considerations of Bulgarian domestic politics at this time that the withdrawal of the Bulgarian troops from this conquered district was impossible. To that must be added Austro-Bulgarian jealousies in Albania, which we had great difficulty in composing.

In their operations in Albania the Austro-Hungarians had played the part of a kind of Sleeping Beauty. The sleep had only been disturbed at intervals by raids on both sides, raids which were carried out with small bodies of troops and even less energy. The situation in Albania could be taken more seriously in the summer of 1918, when the Italians took the offensive on a broad front from the coast to the neighbourhood of Lake Ochrida. The weak, and to a certain extent very neglected, Austro-Hungarian detachments were driven north. There was great excitement in Sofia and on the Macedonian frontier immediately, and the Bulgarians demanded our intervention, as having supreme military control. This intervention took the form of a request to the Austro-Hungarian General Staff to reinforce their Albanian front so that they could continue to cover the Macedonian flank. The Austro-Hungarians at once decided on a counter-attack in Albania, and the Italians were thrown back again.

In the course of the year 1918 the domestic situation in Austria-Hungary had developed along the fateful lines which I have already discussed. The exceptional difficulties with the food supply occasionally threatened Vienna with a real catastrophe. It was thus hardly surprising that the Austro-Hungarian authorities, in their anxiety to lay hands on everything available, whether in Rumania or the Ukraine, proceeded to measures which very definitely conflicted with our own interests.

In the dismal political situation in which Austria-Hungary found herself, it was not a matter for wonder that we were informed again and again that it would be quite impossible for the Danube Monarchy to continue the war beyond the year 1918. Anxiety for the conclusion of hostilities found ever more frequent and stronger expression.

I felt convinced that the Austro-Hungarian attempt to suggest a peaceful compromise with the Entente in the middle of September was unfortunate. In practice the enemy too showed strong disinclination towards such a step. They realised our situation at this time too clearly to wish to take the path of a peace by negotiation. To them the question of further sacrifice of life played no part. The enemy's attitude was completely dominated by the fear that we Germans might easily recover if we were allowed a moment's respite, so powerful was the impression which our achievements had made on our foes, and perhaps still make. This may well fill us with a feeling of pride even in the midst of what we are now suffering and will still have to suffer!

Chapter Twenty-Two

Towards the End

I
September 29 to October 26

In the book of the Great War the chapter on the heroism of the German Army may only just have been written, but with regard to the last fearful struggle it is written with the blood of our sons in letters that can never fade. What terrible demands were made in these few weeks on the physical strength and moral resolution of the officers and men of all Staffs and formations! The troops had now to be thrown from one battle into another. It was seldom that the so-called days in rest billets were enough to allow us to reorganise the decimated or scattered units and supply them with drafts, or distribute the remains of divisions we had broken up among other formations. Both officers and men were certainly beginning to tire, but they always managed to find a new impulse whenever it was a question of holding up some fresh enemy attack. Officers of all ranks, even up to the higher Staffs, fought in the front lines, sometimes rifle in hand. The only order issued in many cases was simply 'Hold out to the last.'

We had not the men to form a continuous line. We could only offer resistance in groups, large and small. It was only successful because the enemy, too, was visibly tiring. He seldom attempted a large operation unless his tanks had opened a way or his artillery had extinguished every sign of German life. He did not storm our lines directly, but gradually slipped through their many gaps. It was on this fact that I based my hope of being able to hold out until the efforts of our enemies were paralysed.

Though German courage on the Western Front still denied our enemies a final break through, though France and England were visibly tiring and

America's oppressive superiority bled in vain a thousand times, our resources were patently diminishing. The worse the news from the Far East, the sooner they would fail altogether. Who would close the gap if Bulgaria fell out once and for all? We could still do much, but we could not build up a new front. It was true that a new army was in process of formation in Serbia, but how weak these troops were! Our Alpine Corps had scarcely any effective units, and one of the Austro-Hungarian divisions which were on their way was declared to be totally useless. It consisted of Czechs, who would presumably refuse to fight. Although the Syrian theatre lay far from a decisive point of the war, the defeat there would undoubtedly cause the collapse of our loyal Turkish comrades, who now saw themselves threatened in Europe again. What would Rumania, or the mighty fragments of Russia do? All these thoughts swept over me and forced me to decide to seek an end, though only an honourable end. No one would say it was too soon.

In pursuance of such thoughts, and with his mind already made up, my First Quartermaster-General came to see me in the late afternoon of September 28. I could see in his face what had brought him to me. As had so often happened since August 22, 1914, our thoughts were at one before they found expression in words. Our hardest resolve was based on convictions we shared in common.

In the afternoon of September 29 we held a conference with the Foreign Secretary. He described the situation in a few words. Hitherto all attempts at a friendly compromise with our enemies had failed, and there was no prospect of getting into touch with the leaders of the hostile States through negotiations or mediation on the part of neutral Powers. The Secretary of State then described the internal situation. Revolution was standing at our door, and we had the choice of meeting it with a dictatorship or concessions. A parliamentary Government seemed to be the best weapon of defence.

Was it really the best? We knew what an immense strain we should put on our country with the steps we took to secure an armistice and peace, steps which would very naturally cause extreme anxiety about the situation at the front and our future. At such a moment, which meant the death of so many hopes, a moment in which bitter disillusionment would go hand in hand with even deeper anger, and every man was looking for some nucleus of stability in the State organism, ought we to let political passions be converted into some more violent agitation?

What direction would that agitation take? Surely not the direction of stability, but that of further chaos! Those who had sown the unholy weeds in our soil would be thinking that the time of harvest had arrived. We were on the slippery path.

Was it possible to believe that by concessions at home we could make an enemy less exacting who had not yielded to our sword? Ask those of our soldiers who, trusting in the alluring promises of our foes, voluntarily laid down their arms! The enemy's mask fell at the same moment as the Germans lowered their weapons. The German who let himself be deceived was treated not a whit better than his comrade who defended himself to the last gasp.

We had also to fear that the formation of a new Government would further postpone a step which we had already delayed as long as possible. As a matter of fact, we had not taken it a moment too soon. Would it come too late as a result of the reorganisation of the State?

Such were my anxious thoughts. They were entirely shared by General Ludendorff.

As the result of our conference we placed our proposals for a peace step before His Majesty. It was my duty to describe the military situation, the seriousness of which was realised by the Emperor, to provide a foundation for the necessary political action. His Majesty approved our proposals with a strong and resolute heart.

As before, our anxieties for the Army were mingled with cares for the homeland. If the one did not stand firm the other would collapse. The present moment was to prove this truth more clearly than ever before.

My All-Highest War Lord returned home, and I followed him on October 1. I wanted to be near my Emperor in case he should need me in these days. Nothing was farther from my thoughts than to wish to control political developments. I was ready to explain the whole situation to the new government which was in process of formation and answer their questions to the full extent that I thought possible. I hoped I could fight down pessimism and revive confidence. Unfortunately, the State had already been shaken too greatly for me to achieve my purpose as yet. I myself was still firmly convinced that, in spite of the diminution of our forces, we could prevent our enemy from treading the soil of the Fatherland for many months. If we succeeded in doing so the political situation was not hopeless. Of course it was a tacit condition for this success that our land frontier should not be threatened from the east or south and that the public at home stood firm.

Our peace offer to the President of the United States went forth in the night of October 4–5. We accepted the principles he had laid down in January of this year for a 'just peace'.

Our next concern was with the further operations. The failing energies of the troops, the steady diminution of our numbers and the repeated irruptions of the enemy compelled us on the Western Front gradually to withdraw our troops to shorter lines. What I told the leaders of the Government on October 3 can be put in the following words: As far as possible we are clinging to enemy soil. The operations and actions are of the same character as all others since the middle of August. A diminution of the enemy's offensive capacity is accompanying the deterioration of our own fighting powers. If the enemy delude themselves into believing that we shall collapse, we ourselves may make the mistake of hoping that the foe may become completely paralysed. Thus there could be only one *finale* unless we succeeded in creating one last reserve from the resources of our people at home. A rising of the nation would not have failed to make an impression on our enemies and on our own army. But had we still enough life left in us for that? Would the mass still possess the spirit of self-sacrifice? In any case our attempt to bring such a reserve to the front was a failure.

The homeland collapsed sooner than the Army. In these circumstances we were unable to offer any real resistance to the ever-increasing pressure of the President of the United States. Our Government cherished hopes of moderation and justice. The German soldier and the German statesman went different ways. The gulf between them could no longer be bridged. My last effort to secure co-operation is revealed in the following letter of October 24, 1918:

I cannot conceal from your Grand-Ducal Highness* that in the recent speeches in the Reichstag I missed a warm appeal for goodwill to the Army, and that it caused me much pain. I had hoped that the new Government would gather together all the resources of the whole nation for the defence of our Fatherland. That hope has not been realised. On the contrary, with few exceptions they talk only of reconciliation and not of fighting the enemies which threaten the very existence of our country. This has had first a depressing and then a devastating effect on the Army. It is proved by serious symptoms.

If the Army is to defend the nation, it needs not only men but the conviction that it is necessary to go on fighting, as well as the moral impetus this great task demands.

Your Grand-Ducal Highness will share my conviction that realising the outstanding importance to be attached to the *morale* of the nation in arms, the Government and the representatives of the nation must inspire and maintain that spirit in both the army and the public at home.

To your Grand-Ducal Highness, as the Head of the new Government, I make an earnest appeal to rise to the height of this holy task.

---

* Prince Max of Baden who headed the new government and advocated a negotiated peace.

It was too late. Politics demanded a victim. The victim was forthcoming on October 25.

In the evening of that day I left the capital, whither I had gone with my First Quartermaster-General to confer with our All-Highest War Lord, and returned to Headquarters. I was alone. His Majesty had granted General Ludendorff's request to be allowed to resign and refused my own. Next day I entered what had been our common office. I felt as if I had returned to my desolate quarters from the graveside of a particularly dear friend. Up to the present moment – I am writing this in September, 1919 – I have never again seen my loyal helper and adviser during these four years. In thought I have visited him a thousand times and always found him present in my grateful heart.

2
October 26 to November 9

At my request my All-Highest War Lord appointed General Gröner as my First Quartermaster-General. The general had become well known to me through holding previous posts during the war. I knew that he possessed a wonderful organising talent and a thorough knowledge of the domestic situation at home. The time we were now to spend together brought me ample proofs that I was not mistaken in my new colleague.

The problems which faced the general were as difficult as thankless. They demanded ruthless energy, utter self-denial, and renunciation of all glories but that of duty faithfully done, and the gratitude of none but his colleagues for the time being. We all know how great and critical was the work which awaited him. Affairs began to go from worse to worse. I will attempt to describe them in outline only.

In the East the last attempts at resistance of the Ottoman Empire were collapsing; Mosul and Aleppo fell, practically undefended, into the hands of the enemy. The Mesopotamian and Syrian armies had ceased to exist. We had to evacuate Georgia, not under military pressure, but because our economic plans there could not be realised, or at any rate made profitable. The troops which we had sent to help with the defence of Constantinople were withdrawn. The Entente did not attack it from Thrace. Stamboul was not destined to fall by some mighty deed of heroism or impressive manifestation of military power. All our other German reinforcements which were in Turkey were drawn in the direction of Constantinople. They left the land we had defended side by side, enjoying the respect of the chivalrous Turk with whom we had fought shoulder to shoulder in his life and death struggle.

Our last troops were withdrawn from Bulgaria also. They were followed by the gratitude and honourable recognition of many, feelings which found their most vivid expression in a letter which the former Commander-in-Chief of the Bulgarian Army wrote to me about this time. I could not resist the impression that the lines expressed something which I had thought I detected so often in the words of this honourable officer: 'Had I been politically free, my military actions would have been different.' The revelation had come too late in his case, as in many others.

The political structure of Austria-Hungary went to pieces at the same time as her military organisation. She not only abandoned her own frontiers, but deserted ours as well. In Hungary rose the spectre of Revolution, inspired by hatred of the Germans. Can that be considered surprising? Was not this hatred an ingredient of Magyar pride? During the war the Hungarian had certainly had other sentiments when the Russian was knocking at his frontier. Mighty knocks and many of them! With what joy were the German troops greeted; with what devotion were they looked after, nay pampered, when it was a question of helping to overthrow Serbia! On the other hand in Rumania we often met with open expressions of gratitude. The Rumanian appreciated that without the destruction of Russia the free development of his country could never have been realised.

By the end of October the collapse was complete at all points. It was only on the Western Front that we still thought we could avert it. The enemy pressure there was weaker, but weaker was our resistance also. Ever smaller became the number of German troops, ever greater the gaps in our lines of defence. We had only a few fresh German divisions, but great deeds could still have been done. Empty wishes, vain hopes. We were sinking, for the homeland was sinking. It could breathe no new life into us for its strength was exhausted!

On November 1 General Gröner went to the front. Our immediate concern was the withdrawal of our line of defence to the Antwerp–Meuse position. It was easy to decide but difficult to carry out the decision. Precious war material was within reach of the enemy in this line, but it was less important to save it than to get away the 80,000 wounded who were in our advance or field hospitals. Thus the execution of our decision was delayed by the feelings of gratitude which we owed to our bleeding comrades. It was plain that this situation could not last. Our armies were too weak and too tired. Moreover, the pressure which the fresh American masses were putting upon our most sensitive point in the region of the Meuse was too strong. Yet the experiences of these masses will have taught the United States for the future that the business of war cannot be learnt in a few months, and that in a crisis lack of this experience costs streams of blood.

The German battle line was then still connected with the lines of communication, the life-nerve which kept it in touch with the homeland. Gloomy pictures were certainly revealed here and there, but generally speaking the situation was still stable. Yet this could not last for long. The strain had become almost intolerable. Convulsions anywhere, whether at home or in the Army, would make collapse inevitable.

Our fears of such convulsions began to be realised. There was a mighty upheaval in the homeland. The Revolution was beginning. As early as November 5 General Gröner hastened to the capital, foreseeing what must happen if a halt were not called, even at the eleventh hour. He made his way to his Emperor's presence and described the consequences if the Army were deprived of its head. In vain! The Revolution was now in full career, and it was purely by chance that the general escaped the clutches of the revolutionaries on his way back to Headquarters. This was on the evening of November 6.

The whole national organism now began to shake with fever. Calm consideration was a thing of the past. No one thought any longer about the consequences to the whole body politic, but only of the satisfaction of his own passions. These passions in turn began to foster the craziest plans. For could there be anything more crazy than the idea of making life impossible for the Army? Has a greater crime ever had its origin in human thought and human hatred? The body was now powerless; it could still deal a few blows, but it was dying. Was it surprising that the enemy could do what he liked with such an organism, or that he made his conditions even harder than those he had published?

The visible sign of the victory of the new powers was the overthrow of the Throne. The abdication of the Emperor and King was announced even before he had made his decision. In these days and hours much was done in the dark which will not always evade the fierce light of history.

The suggestion was made that we should use the troops from the front to restore order at home. Yet many of our officers and men, worthy of the highest confidence and capable of long views, declared that our men would unhesitatingly hold the front against the enemy, but would never take the field against the nation.

I was at the side of my All Highest War Lord during these fateful hours. He entrusted me with the task of bringing the Army back home. When I left my Emperor in the afternoon of November 9, I was never to see him again! He went, to spare his Fatherland further sacrifices and enable it to secure more favourable terms of peace.

In the midst of this mighty military and political upheaval, the German Army lost its internal cohesion. To hundreds and thousands of loyal officers and men it meant that the very foundations of their thoughts and feelings were tottering. They were faced with the hardest of all inward struggles. I thought that I could help many of the best of them to come to the right decision in that conflict by continuing in the path to which the wish of my Emperor, my love for my Fatherland and Army and my sense of duty pointed me. I remained at my post.

Index

Also available from Frontline Books

THE CONFUSION OF COMMAND
The Memoirs of Lieutenant-General Sir Thomas D'Oyly 'Snowball' Snow 1914–1918
Mark Pottle, Dan Snow
ISBN 978-1-84832-575-3

THE GERMAN ARMY HANDBOOK OF 1918
David Nash
ISBN 978-1-84415-711-2

THE MARCH ON PARIS
The Memoirs of Alexander von Kluck, 1914–1918
ISBN 978-1-84832-639-2

THE MEMOIRS OF KARL DOENITZ
Ten Years and Twenty Days
Karl Doenitz
ISBN 978-1-84832-644-6

INFANTRY ATTACKS
Erwin Rommel
ISBN 978-1-84832-652-1

AT HITLER'S SIDE
The Memoirs of Hitler's Luftwaffe Adjutant
Nicolaus von Below
ISBN 978-1-84832-585-2

For more information on our books, please visit
www.frontline-books.com, email info@frontline-books.com
or write to us at 47 Church Street, Barnsley, S.Yorkshire, S70 2AS.